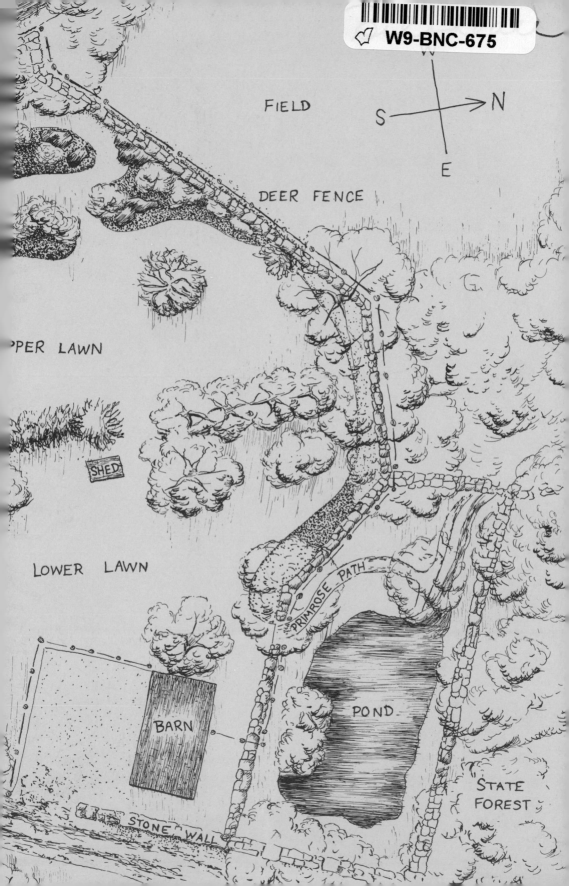

A Patchwork Garden

A PATCHWORK GARDEN

*Unexpected Pleasures
from a
Country Garden*

SYDNEY EDDISON

1817

HARPER & ROW, PUBLISHERS, New York
Grand Rapids, Philadelphia, San Francisco, St. Louis
London, Singapore, Sydney, Tokyo, Toronto

Grateful thanks to Gregory Piotrowski of the New York Botanical Garden for checking plant terminology.

Designed by Cassandra J. Pappas

FIRST EDITION

Library of Congress Cataloging-in-Publication Data

Eddison, Sydney, 1932–
    A patchwork garden : unexpected pleasures from a country garden / Sydney Eddison.
    p. cm.
  ISBN 0-06-016093-4
  1. Eddison Garden (Newtown, Conn.) 2. Gardening—Connecticut—
  Newtown. I. Title.
  SB466.U7E334 1990   89-45648
  635.9'09746'9—dc20

90 91 92 93 94 CC/HC 10 9 8 7 6 5 4 3 2 1

Contents

Introduction:
In the Beginning

ON A RECENT TRIP TO THE UNITED STATES, THE WELL-known English garden authority Penelope Hobhouse was gratified to find that "a fiercely determined breed of really good American gardeners is springing up. They actually read everything and try it out." I know this to be true because I have friends who belong to that breed. But my own affiliations—and sympathies—lie with the intuitive gropers who dig first and read later.

I came late to gardening books and courses in horticulture. And helpful as these sources of information have been, hands-on experience has been infinitely more so. Experience builds confidence; confidence is the foundation of independence; and independence is the name of the game. Making your own garden can be a very liberating activity. There are, of course, principles that apply to gardening and to garden design and the more you know, the better equipped you are to be independent. But in the long run, gardens aren't made according to theories. They evolve as their creators wrestle with a particular piece of earth and a specific microclimate and come to terms with their own personalities and prejudices.

Making my own garden has been the one activity in my life that I have pursued without ever looking over my shoulder or making comparisons; without worrying about whether I was doing the right thing or wondering if other people would like the result. And although it gives me great joy to have visitors come to see the garden, it gives me even more joy to spend the day alone shuffling rocks, pulling weeds, and seeing in my mind's eye that impossible vision that lures every gardener on.

To me, gardens are for pleasure. And, as every individual defines pleasure in a different way, every garden is—or should be—unique. Gardeners are in the enviable position of having to please no one except themselves and the plants they grow. This very freedom of choice intimidates some novice gardeners and drives them to books for verification of their own tastes and inclinations. But the best gardens are spun like the silk threads of a spider's web out of the gardener's being.

The patron saint of my garden is the sour-tempered little girl who found a missing key and discovered *The Secret Garden.* Mary Lennox was created by an Englishwoman who, like my mother, spent her entire adult life in the United States but could never quite reconcile herself to her adopted country. Frances Hodgson Burnett emigrated with her family from Lancashire to Tennessee while she was still in her teens. My mother was in her twenties when she left her father's vicarage to accompany my American father to her new home—sight unseen—in what was then rural Connecticut. I am not sure that she ever fully recovered from the culture shock.

I do know that she was very homesick. When I was young she used to talk to me by the hour, until the vicarage garden surrounded by high brick walls became as real to me as the farmer's hayfield next door. I could see my mother as a girl, her long skirt hitched up at the waist, pushing her blindfolded younger sisters around in a wheelbarrow. A born storyteller, she transformed the paths and flower beds into imaginary pleasure domes for the benefit of her siblings. In the same way, she made England and the gardens of her youth come vividly to life for me.

She used to describe a garden hidden away in the middle of a beech wood where huge gray-barked trees rose up from a carpet of bluebells and laced their branches overhead. In a clearing stood the circular hedge of yews with arches cut through into the garden. I no longer remember her description of what was inside. My memories are confused with the sight that greeted Mary Lennox—overgrown roses scrambling up trees and moss-covered stone seats beneath a swaying net of rose canes. Before I could read, Mother used to pour her considerable dramatic talents into reading aloud from *The Secret Garden.* The images stayed with me and later mingled with memories of real English gardens.

First and foremost, there was my aunt's garden. She lived with my grandmother in Norwich and I spent the summer with them when I was seventeen. I think of it as my aunt's garden because she did everything from cutting the lawn to pruning the roses—of which there were a great many. The garden was small—about the size and shape of a tennis court and enclosed on three sides by massive walls. The back of my grandmother's house formed a fourth wall. The freestanding walls, like the house, had been built in the seventeenth century from local flints embedded in mortar. They provided a textured gray background for climbing roses and borders filled with old-fashioned shrub roses, delphiniums, lavender, phlox, lilies, irises, and campanulas. Clove pinks lined the narrow gravel paths, and in one corner of the garden an old oak growing in the garden next door cast its shadow over a tiny round pool. The pool's mossy rim was half hidden by primulas. The lean-to shed where my aunt kept tools and a little reel mower sagged beneath a tangle of pale pink roses—

threaded through with purple clematis. The roses reached higher than the
clematis and ran along the tile coping at the top of the wall. Above it all, the
cathedral spire soared into the often overcast sky of East Anglia.

All three of my mother's sisters were wonderful gardeners. The
youngest—now in her eighties—gardens still. The next youngest died a year
ago, but during World War II she kept a "cottage garden" going in the middle
of London. Her husband practiced medicine in a seamy area near the docks,
which were virtually demolished by German bombs. Air raids drove many
Londoners into the country for the duration. But my aunt stayed on, tending
her chickens and growing a cheerful hodgepodge of annuals, vegetables, and
perennials in a little triangle of backyard. I visited her just after the war and
remember the red and orange and yellow nasturtiums spilling onto the pavement and scarlet runner beans climbing up the side of the henhouse.

The seeds of my garden were sown that summer. Wherever I
went, there were gardens. From the train windows, I could see the backyards
of city slums—every plot chock-a-block with shrubs and flowers and climbing
plants. In the villages, no house was without a garden or, at the very least,
overflowing window boxes and potted plants set out on the pavement. As for
country gardens, I had never seen anything like them. I was taken to one where
we walked through shadowy caverns under rhododendrons fifteen feet high.
Emerging on a hilltop, we could see rhododendrons below and around us—
acres of them covering the landscape with clouds of pink and red and white
bloom—while overhead the skittish sun passed in and out among real clouds
in the summer sky. At the end of three months, I knew that someday I wanted
a romantic garden wreathed in mists and mysteries.

So when I embarked on the adventure of transforming our cow
pasture, I came to the enterprise determined to impose an English garden full
of civilized plants on countryside that had brought tough-minded farmers to
their knees. But it didn't take long to discover that Newtown wasn't Norwich.
The average minimum temperature here is between zero and minus ten degrees Fahrenheit; there, the temperature rarely goes below freezing. The east
coast of England receives twenty-two inches of rain annually, delivered almost
daily in gentle doses. Connecticut rejoices in twice that amount. It comes in
bucketfuls between droughts—which are exacerbated in the summer by extreme heat. In East Anglia, temperatures remain moderate year round and
changes occur gradually.

Outside my aunt's garden walls lie pastoral scenes straight from
the brushes of Constable—open, barely undulating meadows that unfold to
meet the sea. Inside, the garden was level and furnished with a nine-by-twelve-
foot rectangle of emerald green grass as flat as a rug and finer than a dog's coat.
After nineteenth century farmers gave up our property in Connecticut as a bad
job, forest took over the fields. We are now surrounded by woodland criss-
crossed by dilapidated stone walls. Our lawn consists of two uneven acres of
coarse field grasses—which we mow. The underlying topsoil is sparse and
rocky. My aunt's flower beds were filled with eighteen inches of sandy loam
from which the last little knobs of flint had been removed perhaps a century

ago. This fall, I unearthed a five-hundred-pound field stone from a section of the perennial border that has been under cultivation for twenty-five years. So much for an English garden in a New England farmyard.

Letting go of a cherished dream isn't easy, but as I gradually became reconciled to a different kind of garden, the pieces began to fall into place. The garden reminds me of the patchwork quilt I inherited. It was made by an English actress friend of my parents who used to spend her backstage time sewing. The quilt is made up of hundreds of small hexagonal pieces in a rainbow of colors. There are bits from old costumes: gold brocade from a Restoration comedy and plum velvet from the repertory production of *Hamlet;* chintz in different patterns—pink and green flowers from her drawing-room slipcovers, red tulips on a white background from the bedroom curtains; and silks and satins from long-forgotten dinner dresses. The individual pieces— each one having a story of its own—contribute to the overall pattern. Like the quilt, the garden contains bits and pieces from many other lives and other gardens—each with a history.

Many of the bulbs and perennials that we found here on the property are still somewhere in the garden. In the spring, there are masses of daffodils planted by the former owners. When I see them in bloom, I remember the excitement of our first spring here—and the kindness of Mr. and Mrs. Knox. At the time we moved into the house, our furniture consisted of a love seat, a couple of chairs, an heirloom oak highboy, a bed, and an electric table saw. The Knoxes left us all sorts of serviceable items still in daily use.

There are no longer flower beds on either side of the front walk— we removed them when the new driveway changed our habits and our traffic patterns—but the peonies Mrs. Knox left behind bloom faithfully at the back of the perennial border. After the cabbage-sized heads of the newer peonies have shed their laundry baskets full of petals, it is a relief to see these old-fashioned rose-red flowers splitting open their round buds. Fragrant and small-flowered, they make an unpretentious contribution to the perennial border at a time when little else is in bloom, and when their petals fall, it doesn't take half a day to clean up the debris.

Mrs. Knox would be pleased to see divisions of her *Iris pallida* used throughout the border and to know that many others have been passed on to deserving friends. A wild species found originally in Dalmatia, *Iris pallida* appears somewhere in the family tree of most modern cultivars but it has none of their faults. Its gray-green swords of foliage are rarely damaged by borers and the three-foot stems bearing numerous modest-sized violet-blue flowers demand no support other than their own sturdy constitutions. I prefer this lovely, deliciously scented hand-me-down to all other tall bearded irises.

Not long ago, a van appeared in our driveway. It was driven by the Knoxes' adopted son, whom we had never met but who had grown up in our house. I had found his high school class ring twenty years earlier when I was digging a new flower bed and I sent it to his mother. He told us that day she had just died and that he was here in the Northeast for her funeral. It was a curious experience, meeting this man who had spent his childhood in our house and garden. It gave me a jolt because I realized suddenly that we are rapidly approaching the age his parents must have been when we first met them.

For years after we bought the house, we exchanged Christmas cards and were sad to learn, at some point, about a divorce. Awhile after that, we were startled to receive a surprise visit from Mr. Knox with a new wife. But it was the first Mrs. Knox with whom we had maintained the closest contact and now she was gone. Her son said that he wanted to see the old place again because he had been happy here. We said that we had, too. He walked around the garden, looked at the house, and pronounced himself satisfied. As the van was pulling out of the driveway—a driveway that had not been there in his youth—I remembered about the clivia and ran after him, but it was too late.

Like the peonies and the irises, the clivia came with the house. At the time, I didn't know a clivia from an aspidistra. I just didn't like its gloomy-looking dark green leaves that emerged in pairs and spread open like an enormous daylily fan. Their exposed surfaces were thick with dust. The plant was so potbound that the spaghettilike roots lay exposed in coils. I thought I'd never seen anything so ugly—even the wooden planter was ugly, a Grand Rapids barrel on the last of its three legs. The whole thing has to go, I told my husband. But his humane nature and an aversion to discarding things would not permit him to accept this solution. "I will have it in my office," he said rather grandly.

A few years later, he became bored with it and stuck it out in the hall. It hadn't grown an inch but hadn't died either. Still he wouldn't let me throw it out. However, we agreed on a compromise: We would put it outside for the summer, and if it still didn't do anything, we would leave it there and let nature take its course. But it did something—something spectacular. Woken like Sleeping Beauty by the kiss of rain, it burst into extravagant bloom! Bud clusters hidden between its leaves gradually emerged and opened into trusses of golden-throated orange flowers.

In addition to exposing my ignorance, the clivia story tells you something about this book. It involves personal experience, which unavoidably is conveyed either by using the personal pronoun "I" or the impersonal "one." There is this to recommend the latter: If *one* is describing *one's* mistakes, it establishes a comforting illusion of distance between the error and the perpetrator. This, however, will be an "I," or rather, a "we" book. I take in vain the names, characters, and gardens of my nearest and dearest. Willy-nilly, you will get to know Martin, my shy, long-suffering English husband—unsung hero of the garden he made possible. You will meet our neighbors and friends—even our cats and dogs—because these are such stuff as gardens are made on. Every garden is a record of the life and times not only of its creator but of a host of "significant others" who have contributed to it—with ideas and suggestions; with plants, seeds, and cuttings; with appreciation or generous admiration; with know-how or labor. I think with love and gratitude about the people who are responsible for the garden that has given me so much pleasure. This book is for and about them.

Early On

MY MOTHER DID NOT GARDEN. NEITHER DID SHE COOK, shop for groceries, or drive the family car. My father did it all. I was embarrassed by this state of affairs when I was growing up. There are people who to this day think that my mother was very spoiled. As an adult, I have a rather different view of the situation, believing instead that my father did her a great disservice by usurping all her prerogatives. He was—though my two brothers would doubtless disagree—an enchanting, thoroughly autocratic male chauvinist of the first order.

A gregarious man himself, he succeeded in keeping his wife figuratively—and his children literally—barefoot and down on the farm while he sallied forth to practice medicine fifteen miles away. His patients adored him. In the days before penicillin and the sulfa drugs, positive thinking wrought more cures than the feeble arsenal of drugs available and this was my father's strong suit. He simply refused to let patients remain sick. As for dying, it was out of the question. Fortunately, he specialized in diseases of the ear, nose, and throat and was generally spared catastrophic illness.

While he spread his special blend of medical expertise and bossy good cheer among his patients, my mother languished in the country. Our house was in the middle of a hayfield. There were hayfields to the right of us and hayfields to the left. These belonged to two different farmers. Both maintained small dairy herds and used to take their milk into the village for collection by the distributor. One farmer had a son my age with whom my younger brother and I were friendly. Our big excitement was to ride downtown with the milk cans in the back of his father's pickup truck. For my mother and a bookish older brother seven years my senior there were neither friends nor social life. It's small wonder that Mother dreamed of home! As for my older brother, he escaped as soon as he could while my younger brother and I embraced country life with enthusiasm.

We wholeheartedly subscribed to Luther Burbank's curriculum for a child's education: brooks to wade in, trees to climb, and an abundance of native flora and fauna to pluck, capture, and inspect. Children have a natural affinity for wildlife and wildflowers—I suppose because they are very nearly wild themselves. Their senses and emotions haven't yet been cordoned off from their intellects. They experience everything in three dimensions and glorious Technicolor. In addition, they are sharp-eyed, close to the ground, and inquisitive. It wouldn't occur to sensible adults to browse and sniff their way around the countryside and it wouldn't occur to children not to. How else would you find out that the twigs of black birch taste like wintergreen; that if you crush the little dull white flowers of catsfoot, they smell like autumn leaves and lemon juice; or that if you inhale the powerful scent of mountain mint, it makes the back of your throat feel ice-cold?

When we were very young, our favorite plants were the ones that *did* things: the snapdragon flowers of butter-and-eggs that offered up tiny jaws to be pinched open; the seed pods of jewel weed only waiting for the least touch to fly apart, hurling their seeds into the air; the papery green capsules of bladdernut crying out to be popped; and daisies that cheerfully sacrificed their white rays to resolve questions of the heart. When we outgrew the pinching and popping phase, we moved on to picking and eating—huckleberries (woody, tasteless blueberry relations); blueberries, blackberries, and black caps; and wild strawberries and wild grapes. After that, my brother lost interest but I advanced to the stage of nonparticipatory appreciation.

My mother claimed there were no American wildflowers. What she meant was that there were no primroses or cowslips. To her and to homesick Britons all over the world, no wildflower holds as much meaning as the common primrose *(Primula vulgaris)*. Only six inches high with flat, pale yellow blossoms that appear to rest on nests of crinkled oval leaves, this plant wields a power out of all proportion to its diminutive stature, evoking poignant memories of childhood. One nineteenth century Briton wrote: "The Primerose, Primrose or First Rose of Spring, the Cowslip, the Oxlip, the Auricula or Powdered Beau are so associated with our earliest recollections as children that we never, to the last hour of our existence, entirely cease to look upon them with pleasure."

In England, primroses were admired by courtiers and commoners, poets and prime ministers. They were the favorite flower of Benjamin Disraeli and also of his queen who, at his death, sent a wreath of them—hand-picked from her estate on the Isle of Wight. They were eulogized by the Romantic poets, mentioned often by Shakespeare, and included by his contemporary, Edmund Spenser, in a poetic garland composed for Elizabeth I. Country people ate them, concocted medicines from them, and loved them for the sweet scent and haunting beauty of their flowers. To all expatriot Britons, they mean home. And years later, when I first saw them growing wild, I fell upon them with a gasp of recognition. They are everything my mother said. They are the quintessential wildflowers—pure, luminous, fragile, and yet sturdy. Although I used to resent the spell they cast over my mother, blinding her to the beauty of American wildflowers, I understand it now. Primroses kept her memories of England fresh and alive—just as they keep her memory fresh and alive for me.

Cowslips *(Primula veris)* were close runners-up in Mother's affections. Instead of single flowers on thin, fuzzy stems, these untidy little cousins of the common primrose have loose umbels of very small, bright yellow flowers on sturdy eight- to ten-inch stalks. Each flower is dominated by a puffy calyx which gives the clusters what H. Lincoln Foster called "a certain untamed charm." Children of my mother's generation used to collect this wildflower to make Cowslip Balls—large bunches tied together with ribbon just below the flower cluster to form a nosegay.

The common name "cowslip" was familiar to me too, and with all the confidence of youth I assured my mother that our own brook was full of them. To prove it, I brought her a great fistful still dripping with water. She shook her head sadly. The yellow flowers with lacquered petals surrounding a brush of stamens weren't cowslips, she informed me, but kingcups. Kingcups, cowslips, marsh marigolds, or to be correct, *Caltha palustris,* I thought they were beautiful and was deeply offended that she didn't appear to agree. Nor could I interest her in the delicate lavender hepaticas *(Hepatica americana)* that grew in the woods or in the evanescent charms of bloodroot *(Sanguinaria canadensis),* with perfect sheet-white petals and stems that oozed an interesting-looking orange sap.

I produced violets—"too common"; bluets *(Hedyotis caerulea)*—"so tiny"; dogtooth violets *(Erythronium americanum)*—"they don't last in the house"; and trillium *(Trillium erectum)*—"What a horrid smell!" The petals of the fragile windflowers *(Anemonella thalictroides)* had fallen off by the time I got home but Mother did concede that trailing arbutus *(Epigaea repens)* had a "ravishing scent." Children being what they are, it may have been my mother's indifference to American wildflowers that made them the more appealing and desirable to me. But I wouldn't have known what most of them were—had it not been for Rob Clark.

Rob Clark was a farmer, but no ordinary farmer. In my day, ordinary farmers had wives who wore bib aprons and produced midday meals of meat and potatoes. In the winter, they rose at five—I could see the lights from my bedroom window—to make hot breakfasts for their families, and spent their days endlessly cooking, cleaning, and putting mustard plasters on sick children. In the summer, they tended huge vegetable gardens and for pleasure grew hollyhocks, tiger lilies, and magenta phlox. They canned great quantities of tomatoes and beans—of which my mother was deathly afraid because of botulism and which we were warned *never* to eat; and once a year, they made dandelion wine.

Ordinary farmhouses were trim and cozy. Although farming was always a struggle in hilly, rock-ridden Connecticut and our neighbors, sadly enough, were the last generation to keep up old family farms, their houses were well maintained. They had electricity, modern plumbing, and oil furnaces and their kitchens were equipped with gas stoves. The Fraziers even had a much-envied player piano in the parlor. On rare occasions, my younger brother and I and our friend Buster, the Fraziers' son, were allowed to put in the paper rolls and to pump out plinkety-plink melodies. As for ordinary farm buildings with which my brother and I were intimate, they were spotless. You could—and we did—eat the cow molasses from an immaculate cement well where it was stored.

I knew nothing about the private lives of these farmers and their families. Children are singularly incurious about the lives of adults. As nine-year-olds, the only discussion Buster and I ever had about our parents revolved around property. We figured that upon our marriage—an unromantic prospect but at the time a foregone conclusion—we would combine the holdings of our respective fathers and have quite a nice little piece of land. We both knew that a farmer had to get married.

Farming demanded the total participation of husband, wife, and offspring. Buster had chores and did them as a matter of course. If he dragged his heels or didn't "mind," his father meted out punishment with a shingle. I once discovered—to my cost—that the same went for disobedient visitors. As I had never been spanked at home, my parents were annoyed about the shingle incident. However, they refrained from saying anything. They were on friendly but rather distant terms with their neighbors—with the exception of Rob Clark.

In every way, "Dr. Clark" was exceptional. Why my parents called him "doctor" remains a mystery. As far as I know, he had no degrees of any kind. Nevertheless, he was treated with a measure of deference that was absent from their exchanges with other local farmers. He was a tall, angular man with a bushy mustache and a craggy New England face. He spoke with slow deliberation and his voice was very distinctive. I can hear it still. It was a voice creaky with disuse. He and his spinster sister shared the family homestead and neither of them were big talkers. He was unmarried and about ten years older than my parents. An artist friend of theirs found the combination irresistible. When I was in my teens, she took him for her lover. Her manner with him was coy and at the same time condescending, but I believe she was genuinely devoted to him—and he to her. She called him "Old Boy" and made no secret of their relationship, which was—by her own colorful accounts—more than satisfactory. On the strength of her reports, it seems safe to conclude that Rob Clark was a better lover than he was a farmer.

His farm really was a shambles. The barns were in deplorable condition. The roofs had shingles missing, their ridge poles sagged, and the floors were rotten. The troughs in the cow barn were often full to overflowing and the cows caked with dung. A pack of black and tan coon dogs quarreled incessantly over access to an open barrel of kibble that made up their regular diet. They were undernourished and had a variety of skin diseases but that didn't stop them breeding. There were always hordes of rickety pups that crawled out from under the wood pile.

The house was presided over by Miss Clark, a Latin teacher at the high school. Her hair was snow white and neatly marcelled. She wore white blouses with navy blue skirts and, because she walked two miles back and forth to school every day, flat shoes. Her domain was as clean and orderly as her brother's was the reverse and her kitchen smelled deliciously of oilcloth and wood fires. There was, however, no running water—the shallow sink was filled by drawing water by hand from a pump mounted on the drainboard. The heady aroma of wood fires emanated from the stove on which she did all the cooking. The rest of the house was heated by fireplaces. And in the backyard, there was a privy.

To me, the farm was a wonderful place and Dr. Clark could do no wrong. He was endlessly kind and patient with children and I adored him. So did his animals, despite his shortcomings as a provider. I have an old sepia-toned snapshot of myself at the age of four or five stuffed into a hooded snowsuit and perched on his horse-drawn sledge. Dr. Clark stands behind me with the reins in his hand and beside him is one of the ubiquitous hounds—a dog I still remember by name, Rosemarie. I am sitting on a stack of old blankets and grinning from ear to ear. The occasion is one of umpteen winter rides up to the woodlot where I used to jump up and down to keep warm while he chopped down trees and cut them into logs the length of the sledge. Riding back on top of the load was both thrilling and terrifying. Sometimes, one of the wooden runners would mount a rock outcrop and the sledge would heel over like a sailboat.

When I was a little older and allowed to walk the mile or so through the woods to his farm, I would trail around after him asking nonstop questions—all of which he answered. I soon discovered that he knew a great deal about birds and everything there was to know about wildflowers. He even sent away for plants native to the northeastern United States but not found locally and established colonies of them in his woodlot. He had very good luck with the bird's-foot violet *(Viola pedata),* an exceptionally pretty lilac-blue wildflower with an open countenance and eye-catching stamens tipped with orange. The leaves are not the familiar hearts on stalks, they divide at the base into narrow, outspread segments resembling a bird's foot—hence the common name. He planted half a dozen on a south-facing bank at the foot of oak saplings and eventually had quite a stand of them.

He was equally successful with the exotic-looking yellow ladyslipper orchid *(Cypripedium Calceolus).* Native orchids were his particular interest and he used to travel to other states to study species not found in Connecticut. He had several big patches of *C. Calceolus* at the edge of the woods behind the house. In this species, each leafy stem bears a single poised flower set off by a hoodlike bract rising behind the "slipper." On either side, a spirally twisted brown petal segment sticks out like a spitcurl. The pouch-shaped slipper is smooth, shiny, and a lovely shade of lemon yellow. In the moccasin-flower *(C. acaule)* which was already abundant in the woodlot, the pouch is pink and heavily veined with a distinct cleft down the middle. The yellow ladyslipper orchids—which are easier to transplant than their temperamental pink relations—grew robustly, increasing in size and producing more and more flowering stalks every year. I admired them inordinately.

Quite recently, in our own woods, I came upon a single plant of another native orchid, the showy orchis *(Orchis spectabilis)*. Of course, I recognized it immediately—the pair of nearly round basal leaves clasping a single twelve-inch stalk with a spike of little lavender and white flowers at the top. I remembered the colored picture from a well-thumbed reference book that Dr. Clark always kept by his chair and I could hear his creaky voice reading the text. The showy orchis was his favorite of all the hardy orchids. We were never able to find one but he described it to me, and one day we looked it up. It has a curious habit of lying dormant for years, then suddenly appearing—only to disappear again for no apparent reason.

We looked up everything in that reference book—even plants that were familiar—and in greatly simplified terms, he explained about habitat. He told me where and when to look for different wildflowers. I soon knew better than to look for woodlanders in a sunny meadow or for water-lovers in a dry woodland. I knew that a semi-open bank among hemlocks was a likely place to find trailing arbutus and that I should look for the little clusters of pink-tinted white trumpets at the end of March—at about the time the first peepers tune up in the swamp. By the time I was eight or nine, I knew the names and preferences of most of our common wildflowers.

By this time also, Europe was at war and my parents had many worries. The Constable landscape of East Anglia where my grandmother and two of my mother's sisters lived lent itself to the construction of airfields. Airfields were a prime target for enemy bombs, and for months at a time, air raids were a nightly occurrence. Although Granny's anxiously awaited letters were as jaunty as ever, they were full of deletions made with razor blades by the censors, who removed any reference to times or places of raids. My mother poured all her pent-up energies into war work; she was later awarded a medal for her services to Britain. And when America entered the war, my father took over the patients of another doctor who was of military age—an age which my older brother was fast approaching.

Even if my parents had been able to foster my interest in wildflowers, they were by now too harried to do so. Rob Clark came to the rescue. He took the time and trouble to share his own love of plants with me, giving as much consideration to my questions as he would have to those of another adult. In short, he took my interest seriously. And any adult who takes a child's enthusiasms seriously is entitled to that child's undying gratitude.

My Father and the Work Ethic

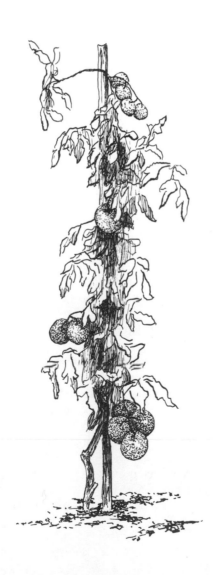

IT IS HARD TO IMAGINE TWO PEOPLE LESS ALIKE THAN my parents—with the possible exception of my husband and myself. It seems to work out all right—my parents were married for over fifty years and we had our twenty-fifth anniversary a while back—but my father and mother's marriage would certainly have confounded a computerized dating service. He was as positive and self-confident as she was tentative and insecure. My father exuded good cheer and optimism; from her own father, my mother inherited a melancholy streak. Dad had a short fuse and the scrappy temperament of a terrier; Mother had a sweet disposition and was submissive by nature. At home in England, she was always known as the amiable one. Her mother, on the other hand, was very much like my father—which may account for my parents' unlikely union. Granny handed Mother over to Dad with firm instructions to take good care of her, which—according to his lights—he did.

That was the trouble: He took care of everything. He was the most passionately domestic man I have ever known and an obsessive nest builder. He loved houses and furnishings in the way that I love the landscape and plants. He was deeply, possessively interested in making a house, its contents—animal, vegetable, and mineral—and its setting into a place of his own. If any man's house was ever his castle and fortress, my father's was. It was also his hobby and his mistress. He would buy an oriental rug for the house while my older brother slunk off to school in a secondhand sports jacket. Dad was hard up when we were young, but about the house he was like a gambler: Sometimes there was a bet he just couldn't resist.

He personally selected every stick of furniture and lovingly restored old pieces bought from one particular secondhand store where he was a regular. The proprietor, a middle-European with discriminating taste and a keen eye, would save anything good that came in "for the doctor." The only furniture my mother ever chose was a little oak tavern table and some chairs, which she got in England after World War II. My father couldn't afford two fares, and in 1947 Mother—who had not been home since before the war—made the trip alone. Dad was thrilled with the table and chairs. But he did not allow Mother's shopping spree to set a precedent, and for the rest of his long life he continued to buy everything from pots and pans to bedspreads.

Dad gardened for the sake of the house, adorning his beloved with annuals in bright, unequivocal colors. His idea of a really effective plant combination was yellow marigolds with purple ageratum—a combination which he repeated every year for as long as I can remember. He liked straight rows and straightforward flowers such as zinnias, snapdragons, and cosmos. His one concession to romance was the inclusion of old-fashioned nicotiana—the tall, rangy *Nicotiana alata* 'Grandiflora' with its sultry perfume and milk-white trumpets that open only in the evening. It wasn't that Dad's soul lacked poetry, it's just that he was incapable of expressing it in a garden—or, for that matter, verbally. But he did try to please Mother where the garden was concerned.

When she told him that she would like a secret garden, he obliged by planting a circle of Norway spruces. My father was fond of spruce trees. He also planted a row of them along the road as a screen—a use for which they are well suited. They are serviceable trees that make excellent screens and windbreaks but they are hardly an appropriate selection for the kind of garden my mother had in mind. In youth, a Norway spruce *(Picea abies)* looks like a Christmas tree, and indeed is a popular choice—as Dad was enraged to discover when a passerby topped one for that very purpose. The short, stiff, dark green needles and symmetrical outline lend themselves to holiday decoration but not to romance. As the tree ages and loses its military bearing, the silhouette becomes looser and more drooping. Today, this circle of gloomy old trees is still extant. I expect the present owners of the property think of it as a Druidical relic, like Stonehenge. But I can remember those trees when they were small enough for a child to jump over. My most vivid memory, however, is associated with lugging endless buckets of water to assuage their thirst.

When the circle of evergreens failed to arouse an enthusiastic response, my father tried again. This time he planted deciduous shrubs—forsythia, lilac, weigela, and flowering quince—around a square of lawn at the back of the house. The flowering shrubs met with greater success. He added some annuals and a few old-fashioned perennials, like baby's breath and bearded iris. It was the best he could do. Considering he was the gardener, in addition to his other functions, it was a very commendable effort. And when I was young, I felt that Mother was insufficiently appreciative.

I realize now, of course, that my mother was living in the past. The rough, rocky, half-wild acres of the Connecticut countryside with which she had been presented bore no resemblance to anything from her previous life. To her, a garden was a sheltered, refined place where children were allowed to roll hoops along the gravel paths, while their mother—in a large hat—snipped roses and gave orders to the gardener. World War II changed all that for my mother's sisters and they became their own gardeners. Overprotected by my father, Mother was trapped in an Edwardian time capsule from which she did not emerge until many years later. My father certainly didn't shackle his family intentionally. But the force of his personality was such that it inhibited my mother's growth and ours as well.

To my father, unrestrained growth was not desirable. In the garden, he favored flowering annuals and vegetables that are predictable and self-limiting. Of the two, he preferred the vegetables: tomatoes staked to attention; beans trained to climb up poles; undeviating rows of carrots, lettuce, beets and kohlrabi. The vegetable garden produced food and built character in the children who were obliged to weed it. Dad was a small, energetic man who believed that busyness was next to godliness and, as a corollary, that busy children were good children. The vegetable garden and the lawn—which we were supposed to mow—were proving grounds for his child-rearing theories. He espoused the work ethic with missionary zeal and managed to instill it in all three of his offspring. In my older brother, its physical side is muted. In my younger brother and myself, it manifests itself as an appetite for exertion which takes the form of competitive skiing in his case and gardening in mine.

Two as One

WHEN THE TEMPERATURE IN THE NORTH OF ENGLAND soars to 70 degrees Fahrenheit, Yorkshiremen begin to fan themselves. If the mist rolls back from the moors and the sun shines for three days in a row, there is talk of a heat wave. All summer, the great smooth hills and softly contoured valleys of the Yorkshire Dales are kept green by frequent, light rains. In the winter, "the tops"—a thousand feet higher and three degrees colder than the valleys—are dusted with snow. The valley floor remains snow-free for most of the season. Drainpipes are mounted on the exterior walls of Yorkshire homes in the comfortable knowledge that they won't freeze or, if they do, the cold spell won't last long enough to do permanent damage.

Made famous by James Herriot, the pen name of a local vet—a neighbor of my husband's sister—the high country is treeless, virtually uninhabited—except by sheep—and breathtakingly beautiful. The valleys follow the course of little rivers and are dotted with farms, stone villages graced by ancient churches, and a few larger towns where public markets are held. Darrowby, the town popularized by Herriot's many books, is a composite of Richmond, a lovely hilltop market-town in Swaledale, and three villages within a ten-mile radius of my husband's hometown.

My husband's father was a country doctor. And in his teens, Martin—more out of affection than enthusiasm—used to accompany him on his rounds. Once he had a license, he drove his father to outlying villages and to the scene of motor accidents on the main north-south artery road—now replaced by the M1. He secretly hoped that they would arrive at the scene to find the errand had been a false alarm. If it was not, Martin—to his infinite relief—would be dispatched to wake Mr. Parker, the chemist, for medical supplies, and with any luck by the time he returned the police ambulance would be there and the mess cleaned up.

At school—one of those character-building institutions where statesmen, professional men, and colonial administrators are wrought and wrung out of teenage boys—my noncompetitive, nonathletic husband chose rowing as a sport—"because," he told me recently, "the alternative was cricket, which meant all that running around." A reader and a dreamer of dreams, he was an atypical English schoolboy who thought about motors and wheels within wheels and longed to fly. Given the opportunity by World War II, he joined the Royal Navy Volunteer Reserve and as a pilot "slipped the surly bonds of earth," leaving behind the study of medicine. After the war, it came to pass that he did not resume his medical studies. Despite an earnest and commendable desire to please his father, Martin discovered that he preferred sick machines to sick people and became an engineer instead.

If you are beginning to wonder what this has to do with gardening, I will tell you. My husband does not like gardening. He doesn't even like the out-of-doors very much and he hates the Connecticut climate. At the first breath of "fantastic summer's heat," he's "thinking on the frosty Caucasus." But a wintry blast sends him scurrying for cover. He has been given by various friends and relations enough gloves and wool scarves to outfit an Arctic expedition. He claims that in New England there are approximately three perfect days a year when the temperature is in the neighborhood of 70 degrees, the sky is delphinium blue, and a light southwest wind caresses the countryside. He lives for these.

He hates bugs. There are few mosquitoes in Yorkshire and houses there don't need window screens. Where he comes from there aren't any Japanese beetles, gypsy moth caterpillars, gnats, no-see-'ums, horseflies, deerflies, or blackflies either. For Martin, the summer is purgatory. If I eat lunch outside on the terrace, he has his sandwich inside at the breakfast table and we communicate through the screen door. If it's chilly, he shuts the glass slider and we use sign language.

Martin dislikes snakes even more than insects. Last summer, he found an eighteen-inch milk snake coiled around a transformer in the cellar and I was summoned to evict it—something I was unable to accomplish. Now Martin doesn't go down in the cellar unless I go first. As for a walk in the woods, we proceed like Indians in reverse order: squaw leading the way; brave two steps behind. For my husband, the out-of-doors is fraught with dangers. There are seventeen species of snake indigenous to the Northeast and several of them appear regularly in the garden. The surrounding stone walls abound with yellow-and-brown-striped garter snakes. Little gold-banded ringneck snakes live in the walls of the stone-lined garden well—which Martin courageously hooks up in the spring and disconnects in the fall. Black snakes of impressive length occupy crevices in the foundation of our barn and one easily six feet long spends every summer in the crotch of the maple tree by the driveway.

At the time of our marriage in 1960, my tall, elegantly thin, and lightly built husband had spent the best part of four decades avoiding physical exertion. His entire working life—before our marriage and since—was devoted to dreaming up and creating machines to eliminate drudgery. Little did he know what lay ahead. My interpretation of the vows we had exchanged was rather literal. As far as I was concerned, we were one. For a nongardener to become one with a gardener is a misfortune so dire that an immediate annulment might be justified. In self-defense, I was unaware that I harbored the gardening virus. A seventeen-year-old's resolve to someday have a misty, marvelous English garden had been so long deferred that it was forgotten. But the second we became proud possessors of eight country acres, it sprang full-blown from the recesses of my memory.

Eight Acres in
Search of a Gardener

IT ALL BEGAN QUITE INNOCENTLY. I WAS NOT A GAR-
dener in search of eight acres. Martin and I were a pair of newly-
weds in search of employment and somewhere to live. Young
people these days seem so well organized. They think ahead, map out strategies, and pursue their goals with method and efficiency. We weren't that young
and had been living like gypsies. Our wedding was planned a week in advance—
we had to get a license and blood tests—and the arrangements took all of ten
minutes. I made two phone calls: one to a charming, broad-minded Congrega-
tional minister—Martin had been married before and the Episcopal church
would have none of us—the other to my mother and father. The minister said,
"How about Friday?" We said, "Fine." And my parents said, "Thank Heavens!"
The ceremony didn't take much longer than the planning and was attended by
the participants, my mother and father, one very dear friend, and the minister's
wife. Afterward, I made lunch for everybody at our friend's apartment. It was
the least I could do; we had been staying with her for nearly a month. It now
behooved us to find jobs and a place of our own as soon as possible.

All evidence to the contrary, Martin is not a city person. He hates
noise, dirt, and crowds and loves the countryside of his adopted New England.
He just likes to look at it from the windows of a snug, insect-free house or from
the air-conditioned comfort of his car. To us both, living anywhere else was
unthinkable. In this, at least, we were of a single mind. Fortuitously, an opportunity to design one-of-a-kind machines for an innovative outfit in southwestern
Connecticut suddenly presented itself. My one-of-a-kind husband seized it and
we began house hunting in Newtown—no doubt to the relief of our wonderfully
patient friend.

Selecting a real estate agent from the yellow pages of the phone book, we began our search. Unfortunately, Mr. Crowe turned out to be a stubborn old gentleman who insisted on showing us unsuitable properties. We explained exactly what we wanted: in order of importance, privacy, an old house, and a few acres of land. Despite our vigorous protests, he took us to spanking new "starter homes" in spanking new developments. After a few mutually frustrating days, we parted company, found a more tractable agent, and having convinced Mr. Crowe's successor that we were serious about privacy and an old house, began to make progress. Before long, we found a little eighteenth century Cape-style house on a country road. The elderly owner had died recently and her son who lived in New York was understandably anxious to get the property off his hands. He agreed to rent it to us—with an option to buy—and we moved in on the first of August 1960.

The house had its charms—not the least of which was the furniture that came with it, our own belongings being rather skimpy at the time. My father provided a dowry of six antique Hitchcock chairs. And one of his patients gave us their old dining room table. Martin had a few things in storage: his drafting table and an electric table saw; the heirloom oak highboy, a grandfather clock, and a golf cart. The golf cart was an artifact from his previous life. He had been obliged to play golf but found it a tedious, thwarting game and was delighted when he discovered that his clubs had been stolen from the storage container. Knowing that he would never have to play again, he envisioned a peaceful leisure of reading, listening to music, and gazing at the Connecticut landscape from the security of a screened porch.

He really should have known better. I was already beginning to exhibit telltale symptoms of the gardening virus. There had once been a little enclosed garden on one side of the house. The flower beds were overrun with grasses but their outlines were still visible and a few stalwart peonies thrust up clumps of dark foliage through the tangle. A tall hedge of arborvitae choked with honeysuckle formed two sides of the enclosure; the south wall of the house, the third. The remaining side was defined by a low retaining wall with steps leading up to a ragged lawn. Although it was too late to plant flowers for that year, I began to dig the grasses out of the old beds and generally to tidy up. I persuaded Martin to tackle the hedge—an experience which temporarily marred our marriage and permanently established honeysuckle in his mind as public enemy number one.

When diplomatic relations had been restored after the honeysuckle episode, we began to enjoy life in the little house. It was a blow, therefore, to learn a few weeks later that the hundred-acre farm next to us was for sale. Fearing one of Mr. Crowe's new developments, we reluctantly resumed house hunting. By this time, we were both working—I had found a teaching job—and we spent weekends looking at houses, this time with a sympathetic agent. She showed us a tiny old house in a woodland setting but the ceilings were too low. Martin couldn't stand up—except in one corner of the living room which had settled in a suspicious way. He suspected dry rot.

We were tempted by a colonial on four country acres but it was out of our price range and too big anyway. Besides, I'd grown fond of our little rented house and felt sad to leave it.

We were about to abandon the search when our agent told us about one more property she wanted us to see. She would meet us there but, due to some mix-up at the office, we would have to pick up the key from the owner of the agency—at her home. If it hadn't been for some clerical oversight, we would never have seen the Knoxes' house. It was way off the beaten track on a dead-end road that could have passed for a riverbed. You couldn't see the house until you were right on top of it. It was hidden by trees and there wasn't another building in sight—except the barn belonging to it. It had absolute privacy. It was old and it was surrounded by hardwood forest. There were maple trees everywhere shedding their yellow leaves all around the yellow farmhouse.

It was love at first sight. But "the course of true love never did run smooth." There was a problem. Mrs. Knox did not want to sell her house. We asked and she said no—kindly but firmly. She and her husband had no intention of selling now or in the immediate future. Sadly, we rejoined our agent and apologetically handed over the key we had collected from Mrs. Knox. We couldn't bear to look at another house. On the way home, we decided that we might as well sit tight. Maybe the land next to us wouldn't be developed for years. But the little rented house never seemed quite the same again.

From the start, my better half looked askance at the dirt floor in the cellar—which was reached through a trapdoor in the middle of the living room. He also had prophetic reservations about the roof and was not surprised when we awoke one morning early in December to the cheerful sound of rushing water. The source was the west end of the living room. It resembled a water feature in a city park. Ice which had backed up under the aged shingles was melting and water poured down the wall in a solid sheet. We decided then and there not to exercise our option rights. Anyway, we were still in love— sloppily, fatally, and irrevocably—with the yellow farmhouse in the woods.

I don't know what I believe in exactly: God in an abstract, ill-defined way; the power of love, certainly; and voodoo magic, maybe. In any case, two weeks after we made our decision and opened the trapdoor in the living room floor to let the flood waters find their own level, Mrs. Knox called. She had recently taken a bad spill on the terrace. Temporarily laid up, she had been thinking perhaps it was time to retire and move to Florida. She and her husband had discussed it. They were prepared to sell the house. Were we still interested, and if so, would we care to come over? After that, events moved swiftly.

It was just before Christmas but we dropped everything and went. An earlier blizzard had transformed the surrounding woodland from a mellow golden world softened by maple leaves into a monochromatic landscape dominated by rocks and endless ranks of straight dark tree trunks marching across the snow-covered hills. With the leaves gone, you could see craggy ridges to the west. Below and to the east, frozen, snowy Lake Lillinonah appeared through the bare branches like a pristine desert. In the bold black and white setting, the sunny yellow color of the house warmed the cockles of my heart.

The Knoxes' greeting—with the assistance of two black poodles—also radiated warmth. There was a log fire burning in the huge old fireplace and an orange cat curled up in a nearby chair. We were told almost immediately that the cat, Arthur by name, came with the house—did we mind? An elderly neighbor had died, leaving the cat homeless. Mrs. Knox didn't really like cats but she liked less the sight of Arthur sitting at the door of his empty house. And if we were able to come to an agreement about the property, perhaps we wouldn't mind feeding the outdoor cats—they were half wild and never came inside. We rashly didn't seem to mind them either.

So while Martin explored the cellar with Mr. Knox, the good Mrs. Knox showed me around upstairs. We reassembled in front of the fireplace. They named a figure. We went home to do some arithmetic. We couldn't swing it. With sinking heart, we made an offer. They accepted. Then, in a gesture of stunning magnanimity, they knocked a thousand dollars off the agreed price. The closing took place early in the new year. On January 26, 1961, we moved our scant belongings into our own house and settled down to await the willful, wonderful southern New England spring.

The First Spring

UNABLE TO APPRECIATE THE HALTING ARRIVAL OF spring in Connecticut, my mother was always homesick long before March. In England, flowers brighten even the darkest months. Snowdrops and cheery little winter aconites bloom in January; in February, hazelnut catkins scatter their bright yellow pollen to the wind and there are crocuses. By March, the flowers are too many to name. In gardens, there are daffodils and all sorts of small early flowering bulbs—scilla and squill and little purple *Iris reticulata;* and in the hedgerows, celandine and cinquefoil, periwinkle and primroses. The weather, though iffy and from a human standpoint quite raw and vile at this time of year, never turns bitter and an English spring seems to go on forever.

Here, spring comes once a week on alternate weeks beginning anytime from the end of February until late April. It may last one week or six. It may be followed by high summer or by a return of winter—complete with ice and snow. It is the least flamboyant season of the year. Summer is an interlude of warm colors against the pervasive greenery; fall is all shrill blue skies and blazing trees; even winter can be a dramatic, high-tech season of stark contrasts. But spring creeps up on Connecticut. One day, there is a sweetness in the air so piercing it is almost like pain. The peepers start sporadically. First one, then a tentative chorus, and finally the steady jingle, jingle, jingle of a thousand tiny sleighbells. The earliest wildflowers follow soon after. Small in size, fragile in substance, and pale in color, they are the fickle, ephemeral, and heart-rending essence of spring. Gardens don't come to life for another month.

Spring arrived late in 1961. The snow lasted until the middle of March. I don't know whether it was the length of the winter, the first potent whiff of wet earth, or a genetic quirk that in my father took the form of homemaking and in me manifested itself in garden-making, but at some moment in that month, an abecedarian gardener was born. As I descended on the unsuspecting landscape with brand-new rake, pruning saw, and loppers, my husband saw the writing on the wall and abandoned hope of peaceful Sunday afternoons with the crossword puzzle.

To date, the sum of my gardening experience had been futile efforts to rid the flower beds at our rented house of grass and, as a child, weeding in my father's vegetable garden. I hadn't the faintest idea where to begin or how best to employ my shiny new tools. But when the snow receded from a patch of lawn, I raked it. As it didn't seem right to have wild shrubs growing everywhere, I began hacking them down and felt it was a distinct improvement. While I might not know how to garden, I certainly knew what a garden was—and this wasn't a garden.

My conception of a garden was based on gardens I had visited in England in which the whole is greater than the sum of its related parts. What I meant by a garden was an outdoor environment with definite boundaries within which trees, shrubs, and flowers coalesce into satisfying pictures. As much of my garden visiting had taken place in East Anglia, smooth lawns and level flower beds also figured in my preconceived notion of what a garden should be. According to these criteria, there was nothing resembling a garden here. The land slipped and sloped every which way and any relation between its disparate features was pure coincidence.

There was a lawn of sorts, an arbitrary tract of mowed field grasses studded with rocks and an assortment of trees: a few large maples; some dogwoods; two young apple trees and a couple of old, ailing ones; and a pear tree so decrepit that a pileated woodpecker nearly gave it the coup de grace. The rock outcrops—which were prominent but unimpressive—had been camouflaged with roadside daylilies, creeping phlox, and sedum. *Sedum acre,* also known as wall pepper, has trailing stems that root at the drop of a hat. The small, fleshy leaves are abundant enough to provide protection for weed seedlings without being thick enough to shade them out. Given a few seasons of neglect and the nature of this obnoxious little plant, the abortive "rock gardens" had become weedy islands in a sea of unkempt grass.

The good news, as far as I was concerned, was that the lawn was fairly flat compared to the rest of the property—not that you could see the contours, which were concealed by a mantle of dense vegetation. The tangle of plants included brambles, barberry, bush honeysuckle, sumac, and hardwood seedlings—all roped together with sinews of wild grape. Somewhere underneath, there were tumbled-down nineteenth century stone walls. I remembered seeing them on the surveyor's map. Invisible to the naked eye beneath a shroud of poison ivy, they partially enclosed the original farmyard consisting of the house, barn, and surrounding two acres.

A wall running east and west separated the old farmyard from an abandoned pasture—now a jungle—rising steeply to the north. The house side, while only slightly less overgrown, was considerably less precipitous. The land tilted gently upward to the west. Its east-facing slope supported half a dozen mature maple trees and their struggling offspring. Beneath them, the weeds and woodbine concealed more rock outcrops, the crumbling field stone foundations of two small outbuildings, and an old dump filled with broken canning jars, bedsprings, and bits of rusting farm equipment.

Taking stock that first spring, I could see that *we* had our work cut out for us. Turning this old farmyard into an English garden was going to be a two-man job and uphill work. Ignorant and misguided—but enthusiastic—I set about it forthwith. Figuring that if we could see the stone walls they might establish boundaries and create the sense of enclosure that I missed, I began happily whacking away at the undergrowth. I had no inkling that there was a garden here already—not the garden made by Mrs. Knox or the ersatz English garden I proposed to inflict on the countryside, but a real garden, a garden like no other, a garden shaped by the land and the soil and the rocks of New England, by the macroclimate of southwestern Connecticut and the microclimate of a sheltered cul-de-sac in the middle of a hardwood forest, and by an American sensibility.

The garden was there waiting to be discovered, like the bear in a story Martin tells. The story concerns an old Maine carver who was well-known for his skill at whittling little wooden bears, which he used to sell to the summer tourists. Each figurine had such a personality of its own and was so lifelike that people asked him how he did it. "T'aint no secret," he replied. "I just look at the piece of wood 'til I see the bear. Then I cut away the rest." There is an elite group of gardeners who see the bear from the start. These fortunate few are capable of seeing through the surface features of the landscape to its essential form. They are blessed with a strong sense of design and a feel for spatial organization. They are unintimidated by the scale of the out-of-doors and know how to think big. Because they already see what they are driving at, everything they do contributes to the end result. And when all the pieces are in place, they are gratified but not surprised. I belong to the far larger group of gardeners—indeed, the vast majority—who are constantly surprised. We wrestle long and hard with our piece of property before tumbling to its unique ursine possibilities. But we get there in the end. And in this case, getting there really is half the fun.

Hunting for Bear

FINDING THE UNDERLYING BEAR IN OUR GARDEN wasn't going to be easy. So when it dawned on Martin that I seriously proposed clearing two acres of scrub armed with loppers, a wire rake, and a small Swedish saw, he resigned himself to the purchase of a Gravely tractor. You don't go after bear with a slingshot! A Gravely with a 7.5-horsepower gasoline engine means business—the state highway department makes extensive use of them to control rank vegetation along major roads. Self-propelled but ponderous to maneuver, they are built to take abuse. Equipped with heavy-duty rotary blades, they can chew their way through saplings three quarters of an inch thick. And so with Martin cautiously guiding the tractor and me ahead parting the undergrowth with the rake and keeping an eye out for rocks, woodchuck holes, and other obstacles, we forged into the wilderness.

Although we always proceeded in low gear with me tap-tapping in front like a blind person with a cane, we frequently hit rocks, and above the din of the motor dreadful noises would ring out as stone and metal made contact. Saplings too thick for the Gravely blades had to be sawed down and the stumps grubbed out with the mattock—another new acquisition. Related to a pick, a mattock has the same stout thirty-six-inch handle, but instead of pointed ends there is a wide blade fore and a dull axe blade aft. One good swing with the blunt end of this implement makes short work of roots and stumps. Progress, however, was slow. We were impeded by a network of low-growing blackberries whose thin, prickly stems had remarkable tensile strength. Seizing at our clothes and wrapping around our ankles, they threatened to trip us at every turn. Nevertheless, we succeeded in stripping back the vegetation a little at a time.

There is nothing to beat clearing land for instant gratification. In the susceptible, it even produces a dangerous euphoria. The more you clear, the more you want to clear. In early spring or late fall when the air is cold and damp and exhilarating, it drives you on and on. Your muscles and your back moan in protest—but you can't stop. Dragging the crushed yellow roots of barberry out of the ground and seeing an expanse of open space gives you a Godlike feeling—short-lived but oh, so sweet.

Although a clearing in New England is nothing but a forest waiting for you to turn your back, there is something immensely satisfying about ridding the landscape—however temporarily—of its weedy, woody burden. Mary Lennox in *The Secret Garden* experienced this same feeling when she freed the snowdrops from weeds and grass. She had the sense that suddenly they could breathe. And as the tractor churned through the jungle leaving behind a clean swath, I thought the countryside heaved a sigh of relief.

As the work of cutting down, pulling out, and carting off moved forward, more and more rocks became visible. There were all kinds: loose stones of different sizes and shapes, icebergs of rock with their sharp tops breaking through the ground, broad shoulders of gray bedrock rising slightly above the surface, and shelves of it jutting out of the hillside. A few huge boulders lay about on the slope like beached whales. I regarded them all with dismay. A Connecticut Yankee ought to have been reconciled to rocks but I was not. They had not been included in my plans for a smooth greensward, a civilized English perennial border, and the thirty-by-sixty-foot vegetable garden I intended to put in. The fact that many of the rocks were extremely beautiful escaped my notice. In fact, I took such a dim view of their ubiquitous presence that I began plotting against them.

Supported by my understandably dubious but loyal spouse, I declared war on the rocks and embarked immediately on an all-out military operation against them. Hostilities commenced with fierce hand-to-hand fighting. Armed with mattock and crowbar, my first objectives were the rocks that stuck up just enough to get in the way of the Gravely blades. These were the worst. From their above-ground appearance, there was no way of estimating their actual size. They might be glacial boulders of movable dimensions or they might be Mother Connecticut. If the former, my technical advisor would suggest the best technique for removing them; if the latter, he would advise orderly withdrawal. Either way, each rock had to be excavated before its nature could be determined. When it moved in response to a smart blow with the crowbar, by hook or by crook we got it out. Taking the rocks away required additional equipment—a hauling device optimistically called a Come-Along, a hand truck of the kind that porters use to move heavy baggage, and a sturdy wooden cart for the Gravely.

Sometimes it was possible to smash off the offending portion of a low-profile rock with the sledgehammer. But after one particularly long and arduous siege, I begged Martin to rent a jackhammer—which he did. With it, he managed to inflict a few scars but that was all. Subsequently he tried a blowtorch and water. Nothing worked. The rocks were here to stay. And like generations of farmers before me, I was obliged to acknowledge their prior claim. However, this did not mean admitting defeat. Sporadic fighting continued in the flower beds and in the lawn. But at the end of five years, the major campaign was over. Occasionally amid the Sturm und Drang of those years, I sensed that a garden was beginning to take shape—a garden that included rocks. Although the outline of the bear was far from clear yet, at least I sometimes felt its presence.

The Perennial Border: Phase I

THE THIRTY-BY-SIXTY-FOOT VEGETABLE GARDEN WENT in according to plan. We chose a recently cleared stretch at some distance from the house but within full view of the kitchen windows and of the terrace. The site was sunny, relatively level, and without obvious rocks. It seemed the logical place for a kitchen garden. Martin plowed it up with a new attachment for the Gravely—albeit with considerable difficulty because of the saxigenous enemy within. When he was finished, the ample rectangle of freshly turned earth made a strong, heartening statement in the landscape. As soon as I had removed most of the rocks and turf, broken up the clods, and raked the surface as smooth as possible, I put in tomato plants and sowed seed of a dozen other vegetables. I also sowed rows and rows of zinnias, tall bright orange tithonia, and sunflowers. By August, there really was something to look at from the windows and from the terrace.

The vegetable garden was in scale with the large, rough-and-tumble expanse we had reclaimed, and from the start it looked as if it belonged. The perennial border was another story altogether. It is one thing to fill a thirty-by-sixty-foot space with vegetables and annuals grown from seed at the cost—in those days—of a few dollars, and quite another to fill a comparable space with expensive perennials which arrive in your mailbox as depressingly small plants. On the other hand, a tidy little flower bed in the middle of a vast, untidy semi-wilderness is profoundly unsatisfactory—as I soon found out.

Most of my early gardening was characterized by a breezy, I-can-always-fix-it-later attitude, but the perennial border was to be the centerpiece of my English garden—the jewel in its crown—and I thought long and hard about the location. As far as I could see, there just wasn't any logical place for it. To me, a perennial border—by definition—had to be a long, narrow rectangular bed on a level site, preferably against a high wall or a hedge. Failing these requirements, a bed at the foot of the terrace retaining wall seemed the next best thing. That being decided, I marked off a thirty-by-five-foot section and set to with pick and shovel—making excellent progress until I hit an obstacle. The obstacle proved to be our septic tank, whose metal cover I had inadvertently prized up in my enthusiasm. Martin threw up his hands and I hastily abandoned this location in favor of the lawn.

Without even a retaining wall as a background, I had to settle for a reasonably flat area about a hundred feet from the terrace. I made the new bed much broader than the old one—about eight feet wide—but realized almost at once that even this was too small. Before the summer was over, I had scribbled the following note in an old school composition book: "The trouble with the perennial border is that it looks lost out there because the rest of the place is so big. And what it needs is big splashes of color, not little spots of it."

Color was one of my chief preoccupations in the early days. I filled composition books with notes such as, "Phlox 'Augusta,' is American Beauty red which is good with the blue delphinium but not a color to be played around with. Phlox 'Brigadier' turns out to be vivid salmon-red. Rather gorgeous but ghastly with 'Augusta.' 'Brigadier' might be good with pale pink." I ordered groups of daylilies in different shades of one color—pinks one year and yellows the next—just to see what they looked like and what they would go with.

I was concerned with finding different species that bloomed at the same time in order to combine colors. In the beginning there were never enough plants to create the effects I imagined but I made more notes: "Peonies, irises, painted daisies, and lupins all bloom together and would be lovely en masse—in shades of pink, red, white, and blue-purple." Years later, I used this combination of colors on a larger scale with a bolder group of plants—peonies instead of painted daisies—to provide the small-scale splashes of deep red against the voluminous trusses of pink rhododendron and the blue and purple shades supplied by Siberian irises, *Iris pallida,* and 'Allegiance,' the sole survivor of a brief infatuation with tall bearded irises.

My textbook was trial and error—lots of the latter. When you first embark on garden-making, you are dealing with all sorts of elements about which you know next to nothing. The growth of plants is not governed solely by their genetic makeup but by degrees of light and shade, the direction of the prevailing winds, the quality, quantity, and structure of the soil. If the soil is made up of minute, uniform particles, it retains water; if it is composed of irregular granules, the water quickly drains away. As each plant has its preferences with regard to soil, sun, shade, and shelter, its effectiveness in the garden depends on how well you interpret and meet these specific needs.

Plants that are not well grown react in a number of ways that spoil the garden picture and surprise the inexperienced gardener. They may not reach their optimum heights or flower properly. A lover of dry, sandy soil may rot in a damp location. Conversely, a moisture lover will almost certainly shrivel up in a dry situation. My astilbes are a perfect example. They started out life in the shade of a deep-rooted oak tree where they grew happily and their fluffy spires of pink, white, and red made a fine show at the end of June. One summer, the oak was struck by lightning and had to be cut down. I moved the astilbe a hundred feet away to the shade of a shallow-rooted maple. Here they barely clung to life because the maple robbed them of water.

Losing the oak was a sudden traumatic change but gardens are always in a state of flux. Changes occur throughout the day, throughout the season, and throughout the lifetime of each individual plant. Some changes occur gradually over a long period, others are brought about more rapidly: A horde of gypsy moth caterpillars can defoliate a huge maple in a few days; a single deer is capable of devastating an entire hosta planting in an evening. As the only constant in garden-making is change, even the simplest flower bed is a challenge. The variables are endless.

First, you have to take into consideration the cultural requirements of the individual plants and their hardiness with respect to the specific climate in your garden. Ours happens to lie in a pocket that holds both the heat and the cold. In the fall, our garden is the last in the neighborhood to have a frost and in the spring, the last to thaw. I know this from years of jotting down the date of the first frost, keeping track of winter precipitation, and making notes about signs of spring, such as the first snowdrop in the woods and the sound of the first peeper in the pond.

Once you've grasped the basic principles of growing plants, you are ready to think about the garden picture. Its effectiveness depends on combinations of color and form, what blooms with what and when, the position of your flower bed in the garden, the point of view from which it will be seen and against what background, and finally, how it relates to the whole big picture of the surrounding landscape. The trouble is that by the time you've mastered the basics and given thought to these other matters, you may not have the strength left to garden. It is with all seriousness that I say to beginners, *do* something first and think about it later. Otherwise, you may wind up like A. A. Milne's old sailor "Who had so many things which he wanted to do / That, whenever he thought it was time to begin, / He couldn't because of the state he was in."

You have to begin somewhere, so jump right in. Once you've made a start, you can move plants, move beds, move rocks, and even move mountains—if it is that important to you. In my first garden notebook, there are wistful observations about "the awful amount of time I spend moving things hither and yon every year!" However, I am not really sorry about the haphazard way I began. I was doing something, learning along the way, and on the whole, enjoying myself. Admittedly, I did move the perennial garden three times, but its final site was not in existence when I made the first bed. Anyway, I was young and strong at the time, and on each occasion the move was an improvement.

Because I blundered into gardening feet first, I learned about plants the hard way—but, perhaps, the best way. You don't *know* a plant until you grow it. And I don't mean for just one season or in just one place, either.

Any perennial worth growing is entitled to three years in your garden. It needs the first year just to recover its equilibrium. It has either been torn out of the field and potted up at a local nursery, or worse, it may have been transported under heaven knows what conditions by UPS. The gloomiest possibility is that the plant has traveled by parcel post, in which case, it should be placed in your garden's intensive care unit. A new acquisition needs the second year to get established and put on sufficient growth to prepare for its debut the following season. Only then should critics attend the performance. Even if that performance leaves something to be desired, there is still a chance that you, the gardener, are at fault, but at least you will have given the plant a fair trial. I observe this three-year rule—two years for the plant and one for me. If at the end of the third season I really don't like it or it steadfastly refuses to grow, out it goes.

In the early days, I tried a great many plants that for one reason or another I no longer grow. Some I miss very much. For a few years, I had wonderful delphiniums. I was so ignorant that it didn't occur to me to be intimidated by these beauties. I sowed seed of the Pacific hybrids in the vegetable garden at the same time that I planted the lettuce and radishes. By the middle of July, the delphinium seedlings were two inches high and I transplanted them. By the following year, they were spectacular plants with the sort of flower spikes you see in the more hospitable climate of coastal Maine. For two years, they graced the vegetable garden with their presence, but the year I moved them to the perennial border, they sickened and one by one died. I was never successful with them again and I don't know quite why. Too crowded in the border? Could be. They are susceptible to mildew if the air circulation isn't good.

Eventually I abandoned phlox, too. It was a sad parting because I really loved them—when they looked their best. There is no substitute for those baroque heads of bloom in white and luscious shades of pink and red. But when they look awful with their leaves fungus-spotted and turning yellow, they look more awful than almost anything else. Moreover, they require frequent division to maintain their vigor. I grew garden phlox *(Phlox paniculata)* over a period of ten years and tried a total of nine different cultivars. In time and in sorrow, I gave them up. The inescapable fact was that they proved more trouble than they were worth. Despite the drama of their huge flower heads, they didn't function well in a border where every plant must earn its keep— from the moment it emerges from the ground in the spring until it dies back down in the fall.

A well-functioning perennial border is like a repertory company in which featured players, supporting actors, and bit players are obliged at different seasons to serve in different capacities. In such a group, *Phlox paniculata* hybrids are out of place. If their frail health permits, they burst into the limelight for one glorious moment, then go into a decline for the rest of the season. Daylilies, on the other hand, pull their weight for the entire run. In the early spring, their upright tufts of light green foliage provide a background for daffodils and tulips. Later, their paired leaves fan out and cover up the dying foliage of the bulbs. In July, they take their rightful place at center stage where they hold forth for a month before withdrawing—with relatively good grace. Like all perennials, they have their leaden hour. For a couple of weeks after flowering, even daylilies look shabby and their hardworking outside leaves turn brown. But soon new leaves replace the old, and by autumn the plants are quite respectable again. Now, that's my idea of a good perennial.

Getting acquainted with a plant takes time and it isn't cheating to consult a good reference book, but pictures and descriptions have their limitations. Certain information has to be gathered firsthand if it is to be of any value. For instance, season and sequence of bloom can not be learned from a book. Every garden has its own microclimate. What blooms on June first in your best friend's garden three houses down the street may not come out in yours for several more days or you may have had it in bloom for a week already. I am convinced that the only way to determine when a plant blooms in your garden is by firsthand observation, and the only way to learn from your observations is to record them.

I learned a lot about garden-making simply by doing it and by keeping notes about what I had done. My first notebook was a Mead Composition book that once belonged to my younger brother. Entries were made in both ink and pencil. Occasionally I stuck in a plant label with glue. The first entry is dated April 4, 1962, and the last, June 2, 1973. None of these have that possibly-for-publication quality that—for a time—crept into my later journals. The descriptions are short and to the point. A plant that I like is either "good" or "attractive." Those I have no use for are "flops" or "disasters." The notes are often sketchy at best. One season, the last entry is dated July 22 and reads, "I quit! We are having a frightful drought which has wrecked great hunks of the lawn and everything is too depressing to write about!" During the mid-seventies, I ceased keeping a garden diary and instead filled the composition books with profound ruminations about "Life." When I returned to record keeping, the entries made livelier reading and were more useful.

In going through old garden jottings, I come across plants I don't remember growing and descriptions of flower beds that have been grassed over for years. There are even allusions I can't fathom. The garden has changed so much that I don't even recognize some of its former landmarks. But despite the mysteries and inadequacies, these notes are the nitty-gritty of my gardening experience. They represent what really happened—which is often quite different from what I *remember* having happened. In the course of keeping notes, I found out the exact height and spread of the plants I was growing and learned which ones actually bloomed simultaneously. I also amassed information about flower forms and colors and how they enhanced or diminished each other by association. Using the notebooks as a reference, I gradually acquired a vocabulary of plants with which to finally begin making the pictures I had in mind.

Studying my first attempt at a border in July 1964, I could see that there were "too many wild colors together in such a small space. On its own, *Phlox paniculata* 'Exquisite' is really quite an appealing bluish-pink but it doesn't go with *Phlox paniculata* 'Fairies Petticoat,' which is a delicate shell pink. Various white phlox are in bloom but they are new this year so it's hard to tell when they are supposed to bloom or how tall they will eventually be. *Lilium* 'Bright Star' is white with a golden blaze—lovely! I'd like more lilies. In fact, lilies would be good with the phlox and the light yellow 'Hyperion' daylilies."

I was enthusiastic about 'Hyperion' from the start—especially in combination with *Lythrum* 'Dropmore Purple': " 'Hyperion' is *very* good in front of the lythrum, which is really magnificent this year—it's as tall as I am and three plants make a huge clump as big around as the old peony clumps." On the other hand, I damned *Coreopsis grandiflora* with faint praise: "Coreopsis is pleasant but it sprawls all over the place. It would probably look better in the semi-wild than in a flower bed." Later that season, I decided it was "scraggly stuff, at best" and signed its death warrant: "not really a worthwhile border plant." I have since come to value the cultivar 'Sunray.' A relative newcomer, 'Sunray' forms a neat clump and produces double, egg-yolk-yellow blossoms that keep coming if you cut off the old stems and dead heads.

Sometimes I reversed harsh opinions. In the early sixties, I was fascinated with the idea of pink daylilies. At that time, hybridizers were working toward the clear, true pinks of today but most of the so-called pinks available then bore more than a trace of orange in their makeup. I was therefore disappointed when 'Pinafore'—which was described in the catalog as "deep rose"—turned out, according to my notes, to be "pink but tinged with orange and not particularly attractive." On its own the color isn't anything special but I discovered later that the soft, undemanding shade of muted coral was a wonderful blender and that it brought out the best in other colors—especially yellows. The plant itself is stalwart and, like most other daylilies, trouble-free.

A perennial border for all seasons is the goal of most gardeners but it isn't easy. In every border, large or small, space is finite and perennials—unlike spring bulbs, which die down and make room for other plants—occupy their positions in the bed for the entire season. If you think of the perennial bed as a checkerboard with a given number of squares, you'll see the problem. Allotting the squares so that a compatible group of plants will bloom together in every month of the growing season tests the powers of an experienced gardener. I've been at it for years and still haven't achieved an autumn display that satisfies me. I've finally arrived at plant combinations that provide three periods of peak bloom—spring, early summer, and mid- to late summer—and a little something for the rest of the season. But in the beginning, there were many gaps and barren stretches.

In my first perennial border, the end of May was a low ebb. Driving to and from work, I would look at other gardens and make notes of things I saw and would like to have—tulips, early irises, perennial candytuft, and *Phlox divaricata.* One spring, I came across a tiny garden in Danbury next to the parking lot of a new Grandway—of all unlikely places. There were painted daisies, big clumps of columbines in pastel colors, and the most incredible irises I had ever seen. They were planted in wonderful masses of yellow, light lavender, and flesh pink. The flower stalks must have been three feet tall and the heads were enormous. That was the beginning of a short but torrid affair with hybrid bearded irises. I was transfixed by the great size of these flowers, with their frills and flounces and their boudoir colors. I knew instantly that I had to have some of the exquisite things in my own garden. That summer I ordered eighteen plants, three each of six different cultivars from the Gilbert H. Wild and Son catalog.

Who could resist 'Broadway Star,' a cream and rose giant, or 'May Magic,' a frilly, feminine orchid-pink? Not me. I was also attracted to some of the more bizarre colors: bronze 'Inca Chief' and red 'Tall Chief.' 'Wintertime,' a snowy dazzler, and 'Allegiance,' forty inches tall with deep, navy blue flowers, rounded out my wish list. Of these, only 'Allegiance' remains in my garden. Every year, as I reinforce each one of its weak-willed stems with a bamboo stake, I mutter dark threats which—so far—I have been unable to carry out.

There is no flower form more beautiful than that of the iris. The kingdom of flowering plants abounds with daisy shapes, globes, trumpets, and spires, but there is only one fleur-de-lis. In the bearded iris hybrids, this pattern has been exploited and refined until the individual blossoms resemble ephemeral pieces of sculpture. But they belong in glass cases, not in a perennial border. Bewitching as the flowers are, they are so fragile that a handful of raindrops or one unseasonably hot day can ruin them. At best, they only last three or four days.

Bearded irises are also highly susceptible to iris borer. Invisible to the naked eye, the young borers work their way down through the leaves, which become slimy and ragged at the edges. Arriving at the leaf base, these revolting creatures settle comfortably into the rhizomes, where they get fatter and fatter until they hatch into moths. The moths lay eggs nearby and start the whole grim cycle over again. In my experience, borers are impossible to get rid of unless you spray with lethal substances. And the more irises you have, the more borers you have. A few clumps of disfigured foliage may be tolerable but a great many can ruin the appearance of an entire perennial border.

My experience with hybrid bearded irises made me the more appreciative of *Iris pallida,* the fragrant, old-fashioned lavender-blue which I inherited from the kindly Mrs. Knox. Among its other sterling qualities are a tenacious resistance to borers, stems strong enough to support the medium-sized blossoms, and superb gray-green foliage that is an asset in the garden instead of an eyesore. Siberian irises are equally borer-resistant and in their own modest way very beautiful. They have small, elegantly wrought flowers and rigid, self-supporting stems. A three-year-old clump produces countless flowers that appear to rest on the tips of the graceful, reedlike leaves—which form an attractive sheaf that remains dark green and relatively upright all season. Even the Siberian irises have the drawback of a short blooming season—but you can't have everything and I don't foresee a time when I could garden happily without them.

Finding homes for the best of my bearded irises to some extent assuaged my guilt. The rest I chucked over the stone wall into the woods. The same fate awaited pretty but floppy balloon flowers *(Platycodon grandiflorus)* and bee balm that spreads like wildfire. Asters were banished because they always developed mildew and dropped all their lower leaves, and I just gave up trying with lupines. I've forgotten some of the other rejects. In the course of discarding plants, I'm sure I must have thrown out some babies with the bath water. But when I finally relocated the peripatetic border for the third and last time, I had a dependable repertory of handsome, hard-working perennials ready and waiting in the wings.

The Pool

LONG BEFORE THE PERENNIAL BORDER FOUND A PER-
manent home, we did something so ill-conceived that I can only
shake my head at the folly of it. With about as much thought as
most people give to choosing a rental movie, we decided to put in a swimming
pool. Our small-scale tinkering with the property had done nothing so far to
substantially alter the contours of the land. Excavating for the pool did. In a few
hours, the landscape was transformed—with far-reaching consequences. For
better or for worse, the outlines of the garden as it is today were determined
by an eighteen-year-old at the controls of a backhoe.

At the time we put in the pool, the average family car cost about
as much per pound as a good cut of beef, roughly a dollar. By this reckoning,
the sixteen-by-thirty-two-foot in-ground pool with its fiberglass sides, poured
concrete bottom, and concrete edging came to less than the price of an automo-
bile. The pool was guaranteed for fifteen years—against what manner of imper-
fection history does not relate. It was immaterial anyway, because the owner
of the pool company and his guarantee skipped town three years later.

As it turned out, the pool did last as long as the worthless guarantee—which was far too long. One Sunday morning in its fifteenth year, I was
standing at the kitchen window admiring the garden under ten inches of new
snow. Martin had taken the Jeep to town to get the Sunday paper. Without
warning, a sonic boom rent the Sabbath stillness and before my eyes, a crater
opened up in the middle of the lawn. Unbeknownst to us, the pool's fiberglass
sides had cracked and the water had leaked out, leaving a sheet of ice. The loud
report had been the ice suddenly giving way beneath the weight of the snow.
It was one of the happiest moments in my life.

To be sure, the pool gave us a certain amount of pleasure but the decision to put it in was so half-baked that it makes me shudder to think of it. One day, out of what I recall as a clear, blue sky, Martin said, "Let's put in a swimming pool." To which I seem to have replied, "Why not?" Today, I could present a convincing case against it, but at the time I didn't know enough. Anyway, we were feeling reckless and the place was already torn up. That spring, having persuaded the town fathers to reopen a spur of town road approaching our house from the south, we built on an attached two-car garage and put in a driveway. In the wake of this activity, what was one more hole in the ground and another pile of fill?

With gay abandon, we flipped through the local paper and found a pool company promoting a novel construction method. Instead of lining the entire pool cavity with specially fabricated reinforcing material and spraying it with wet Gunite, the bottom would employ much cheaper poured concrete while the sides would be composed of preformed fiberglass panels. The savings were considerable and we fell for it hook, line, and sinker. Without more ado, we called the pool company. Upon learning that one of their prefab pools was being put in just down the road, we made a date with our neighbors to see it. Except for the objectionable cobalt blue of the fiberglass panels, it looked all right to us and we decided to go ahead. We did not know that the pool we were looking at was the second of its kind to be installed by the fledgling company; the first was on the property of the company's owner with whom we had an appointment.

The owner's Olympic-sized rectangular pool had a narrow concrete sidewalk around the edge with an extension at one end to accommodate a diving board. We thought it was ugly and asked as tactfully as possible if there was an alternative. When our host suggested a coat of aluminum paint to "dress it up," we knew that we were on different wavelengths. We dropped the subject and went ahead with choosing a pool from the brochure. There were two styles: rectangular and kidney-shaped. We chose the former. We had already agreed on the smallest model. A date was then set for the next meeting, which would be on our own property—to select the site.

Our site planning consisted of looking around the sloping farmyard—which we were still in the process of clearing—and deciding that we would like the pool handy to the terrace and on an axis with the long dimension of the house. Once it was in, I intended to straighten the sides of the vegetable garden to echo its rectangular shape. But we were worried about the grade. The change in elevation was considerable. However, when the owner of the pool company arrived, he dismissed our fears with a wave of his hand. "Naw," he said, "it's nothing but a cut-and-fill operation. Don't worry about a thing. You're gonna love this pool. It's gonna dress up your yard and make it into a showplace. In a month, you won't even recognize it." This last statement—if nothing else—proved to be true.

I think it is safe to say that the design of our garden was determined by a whim—indulged in by the ignorant and executed by the incompetent. The excavation and grading—which so profoundly changed the contours of the landscape—were done by a backhoe operator who was barely old enough to have a driver's license. On the first day, Martin and I stood by nervously as the owner of the pool company bellowed orders at the teenager and the machine gouged open what had been a lawn—of sorts. Almost immediately, the bucket of the backhoe gnashed its teeth on solid rock. When repeated swings of the mechanical arm produced the same result, the equipment was withdrawn and another hole was opened up. It was not a promising start, and thereafter, everything that could go wrong did.

The weather was extraordinary for July. Day after day of torrential rain brought work to a standstill. We watched gloomily from the kitchen windows as the crater in the lawn filled with water. The weather front eventually passed but not before three feet of mud had collected at the bottom of the hole. The backhoe and its youthful operator were recalled and the mud was removed. But no sooner had the last scoopful been dumped on the lawn than a new storm developed. Again we were deluged; the hole filled up and the backhoe was obliged to return. After each visit, we would peer anxiously into the pit. It might not be a very big pool, but it was certainly going to be deep.

After the second mudslide, the skies cleared and we were heartened by the arrival of the fiberglass panels. Once these were erected, the hole looked more like a swimming pool. We were feeling quite optimistic by the time the cement truck came to pour the bottom. When that operation, too, went off without a hitch, we were sure that the worst was over. Before long, the cement was dry enough to paint and a pair of teenagers appeared on the scene. Wearing painter's caps worn backward and armed with brushes, buckets, and a radio, they descended by ladder into the depths. At the bottom of the pool, they whiled away the hours—their backs comfortably propped against the steep sides, their heads back, and their eyes closed—smoking and listening to music. Occasionally, the boss would show up and roar at them. When he did, they would gaze up and, in slow motion, stub out their cigarettes—preserving the butts, which they placed carefully behind their ears—and resume languidly slapping paint on the cement.

In the fullness of time, the boys finished painting, the paint dried, and we were encouraged to start filling the pool. We did so from the shallow well, which was full to overflowing from the recent rains. Martin rigged up a pump and we ran lengths of hose from the well to the pool. Slowly, the water level in the pool began to rise. It was an exciting moment. Meanwhile, the boy with the backhoe was working on another pool and the trench surrounding the fiberglass shell remained open. On the evening when the water level in the pool had just reached the bottom of the fiberglass, thunderheads rolled in from the west, followed by a cloudburst that filled the trench. The pressure without became so great that in the absence of corresponding pressure within, two of the fiberglass panels cracked and muddy water poured into the pool.

To make a long story short, the water had to be siphoned off and the bottom repainted. This time, the owner of the pool company—overweight, out of condition, and in his undershirt, puffing and panting as he scrambled up and down the ladder—labored alongside his teenage helpers. When the pool was finally done six weeks later—there was a considerable delay before the replacement side panels arrived—we realized that the light was at the wrong end—anyone sitting on the terrace in the evening would be dazzled by the glare; that the diving board faced straight into the sun; and that there was no shallow end where children might safely disport themselves. The bottom was the shape of an inverted cone. Once, a friend visiting with two small daughters turned to say something to the little one and looked back to see the eldest partway down the precipitous slope, her round blond head several inches below the surface. Fortunately, the child was plucked from the water unharmed but her experience made us aware of the dangers.

There were other things wrong with the pool. It was too near one of the big maple trees. In the spring the tassels and later the winged seeds plugged the filter. In the fall and during the winter, leaves, twigs, and litter collected in the pool cover. One spring, thousands of luckless tadpoles hatched among the debris. Not long afterward, we were having a picnic for the cast of a school play and relays of humane students transported the tadpoles to an area behind the barn where runoff gathers in a hollow and forms a pond.

Never a thing of beauty, the pool aged gracelessly. The concrete edging cracked and the fiberglass sides faded, but when all is said and done, I might not have seen the possibilities in this piece of land had it not been for the pool. In the course of cutting and filling, we inadvertently transformed the sloping site into a terraced hillside. Construction of a bank to support the long side of the pool created a plateau of fairly level ground approximately fifty feet wide and over two hundred feet long stretching from the terrace to the stone wall that separates the farmyard from the field. The effect was striking. As a dam breaks the downward course of a river and gives rise to a body of calm water, so this unplanned earthwork interrupted the slope and established a restful plane. The long axis and uncluttered sweep drew the eye toward a distant, as yet undefined, point. Instinctively, I felt the need for a purpose—something to satisfy the impulse to look in that direction. There was nothing but the tangle of undergrowth in the field across the wall. But if we were to clear the field . . .

When we did, I saw the bear clearly for the first time.

Help!

SOMETIMES I FEEL LIKE CONSTANCE IN *THE MAD-woman of Chaillot,* with whom I have always felt a spiritual bond. In the musical version of the play, she is the one who hears friendly voices emanating from inanimate objects, such as her sewing machine and her vacuum cleaner. I hear voices all the time in the garden. Herb Achtmeyer's booming voice and matching laughter seem to issue from the vicinity of the front walk which he designed. Vincent's Polish-French and his only English word, "Stop!"—shouted out every time he saw the road sign—occasionally resound from the site of the old vegetable garden. There are dozens of others. But it was these two kind men who came to our rescue after the garage was built and the pool installed. Herb contributed ideas and Vincent, muscle power.

When the boy with the backhoe was gone, we were left to pick up the pieces. Confronting us was a daunting view to the north—the new pool surrounded by half an acre of rough-graded subsoil, a huge pile of topsoil studded with rocks and turf, and a raw, steep bank seventy feet long and three and a half feet above grade. Fill from the garage excavation formed another bank parallel to the pool but higher up on the hillside. Yet another escarpment rose abruptly from the pavement of the new driveway on the south side of the house.

I didn't know where to start, but in trying to sort out what to do first I realized that even if we managed to get a lawn established around the pool and something growing on the various banks, there was no relationship between these new features and the rest of the garden. The position of the perennial border in the lawn had been arbitrary from the start; now it made even less sense. It was below the pool and half out of sight. Only the askew vegetable garden seemed to have anything to do with the pool and terrace. I knew that a sense of order was needed to bring together the disparate elements. But first, we had to have help and I sent out an SOS.

Help came from an unexpected quarter—the plant where Martin worked. Before the F. W. French Tube Company was taken over by a large, humorless Canadian firm, it was a wonderful place—crazy, creative, and chaotic—as befits an outfit brought into being by happy accident. At his father's impeccably run tube mill, young Fred French was responsible for a machine whose function was to form copper tubing around a hardened steel rod called a mandrel. One day, a mandrel cracked and the soft copper was forced into the groove. On removing the tube, Fred noticed the ridge on the inside and thought to himself, "That's interesting." And in that instant, the idea of integral inner-fin tubing was born.

Fred was a dreamer and it takes one to know one. He sought out Martin, who also thought the idea of inner-fin tubing was interesting, and that's how we happened to come to Newtown in the first place. Martin joined Fred's company as an engineering consultant. In the early days, the atmosphere at the plant was upbeat and exciting and new ideas bounced off the walls. Fred, a metallurgist with a degree from M.I.T., had assembled around him a wonderful cast of characters with a variety of talents and temperaments. There were pillars of society like the widow, a former sergeant in the Polish army who still marches in the Labor Day parade with medals on her bosom, and rascals like the Saturday night cowboy who used to shoot out the traffic lights and indulge in a little modern-day cattle rustling.

Martin's tool maker was a former British merchant seaman with tattooed forearms and a passion for flowers. For years, Bernie filled the empty spaces in our garden with annuals and pansies that he raised from seed. His hobby was growing a particularly beautiful strain of Swiss pansies, which he sold locally. After he retired, he expanded his fields and grew them by the acre. A precise, fussy man with a trace of Cockney accent, he spent as much time at the plant keeping the tool room clean and tidy as he did making dies. At home, his tool shop had a carpet on the floor.

Herb was a nurseryman-turned-brass-worker. He learned the brass trade from his father-in-law and quit the nursery business. His responsibility at F. W. French Tube was overseeing production. He was also in charge of the annealing furnace and during the week thousands of pounds of copper tubing traveled through its heated chamber under his supervision. Sometimes on weekends, the great oven was pressed into service to cook rib roasts. However, it was Herb's old skills as a nurseryman that he generously put at our disposal.

Vincent was some relation of the Polish worker who ran the vertical saw. Like so many others, he was just passing through but he was a godsend to us. In the short time he was around, he managed to restore a modicum of order to the confusion in the garden. I used to pick him up at the plant after work. On the way home, we communicated in a medley of foreign words and universal gestures. He read out the stop signs and laughed a lot and we got along like a house on fire. He was a born gardener with a European love of pattern. The vegetable garden or "potager" was his special interest and once we had straightened the sides to line up with the swimming pool, he insisted that I make a path up the middle and plant yellow marigolds along each side.

He had the strength of ten and worked like a demon. He helped spread the topsoil around the pool and seed the lawn; he dug us a dry well and pried dozens of enormous rocks out of the vegetable garden and out of the established lawn—pebbles, he called them—"*cailloux.*" He prepared the entire seventy-foot-long bank below the pool and helped me plant it with rooted cuttings of vinca. Three years later, the small plants had formed a solid carpet of shiny green foliage—a tribute to his hard work. But the vinca proved as transient as its planter—it winter-killed a few years later. Even the vegetable garden is gone now. Nevertheless, for twenty years I went on making a path down the middle and planting yellow marigolds on either side of it.

Herb's contribution to the garden was longer-lived. He talked at first about making a landscape plan for the whole property, but it was too time-consuming a project for a busy man. He did, however, design walks and foundation plantings for the front of the house. I helped him take measurements. And not long afterward, he produced a very professional-looking scale drawing of curving beds and a fieldstone path leading to the front door. There was supposed to be an outside lamp and another fieldstone path to the kitchen door. We never executed this part of the plan but the shape of the front beds and the walk are just as he drew them.

Although Herb was no landscape architect and his planting scheme was typical of foundation plantings for new homes—many plants of many varieties in a confined space—what he did for us bolstered my confidence and courage. His plan gave us direction and something we could actually *do* to reassert our authority over the reigning disorder. And his design was infinitely better than anything I could have done at the time. Seeing that drawing rekindled my faith in the light at the end of the tunnel and kept me going. It was a couple of years before we could do anything to the front of the house, and in the absence of the plan I might have lost heart. But its very existence made it seem possible that one day we would succeed in gaining, if not control of the landscape, at least the upper hand.

When we finally did turn our attention to the front of the house, we made changes in Herb's planting scheme, especially when it came to the flowering shrubs. His list called for exuberant colors—fiercely scarlet azaleas (*Rhododendron obtusum* 'Hinodegiri') with shell-pink Royal azaleas *(R. schlippenbachii)* in dangerous proximity to pink flowering dogwoods. We simplified the list and stuck to white flowers: *Rhododendron* 'Boule de Neige,' white azaleas, and white dogwoods. But we used the pair of Japanese hollies (*Ilex crenata* 'Convexa') Herb recommended for either side of the front door and they stand sentinel there now—huge, handsome twiggy mounds covered with tiny lacquered evergreen leaves.

Herb lives alone in Florida. His wife, of whom we were also very fond, died quite a while ago. But when he was last in Connecticut visiting his daughter, they came for lunch. He looked well—he's a big, squarely built man—and his laugh was still hearty. His memory, however, wasn't what it used to be. I reminded him about his plan for the foundation planting and even went and got the drawing. He shook his head and laughed. He didn't remember doing it. But before they left, we went out to admire his handiwork. I still have the drawing and, although we haven't seen him again, his laugh continues to echo in the garden.

Some Thoughts
on Design

IN OUR WEAKENED CONDITION AFTER BUILDING THE garage and putting in the pool, we might have hired a landscape designer to bail us out—if we had thought of it (which we didn't) and if we had been able to afford one (which we couldn't). I am glad now that we didn't and couldn't, although I would have been sorely tempted at the time. I have very mixed feelings on the subject of hiring an outsider to make a garden for you. A lot depends, of course, on your definition of a garden, how you intend to enjoy the landscape, and how long you expect to remain on your property.

To many landscape designers, a garden can be described as a beautiful, orderly outdoor environment furnished with plants. In this kind of garden, the starring role is played by the works of man; nature is a bit player. But in the kind of garden that appeals the most to me, the reverse is true: Nature is the star; the works of man are not only subordinate but as unobtrusive as possible. No garden, of course, is "natural" any more than an actor's performance is real behavior, no matter how lifelike it may be. Gardens are to nature what theatrical performances are to life—creations of the human mind expressed in physical terms. And there are styles of garden design that parallel styles in theatrical presentation.

Alec Guinness is the sort of actor whose identification with a role is so complete that the man vanishes without trace into the characterization. The pleasure of watching his work lies in our fascination with this sleight of hand. Guinness is the quintessential actor. Laurence Olivier, on the other hand, was a great performer. Personal magnetism ran through his work like a high-voltage electric current. And the thrill of his performance derived from the powerful presence—in whatever guise—of the man himself. To me, he was like the landscape designer whose presence is implicit in a garden starring handsome stone work, ample spaces, and a gracious arrangement of plants—which might just as well be pieces of green sculpture.

Gardeners and designers will never, I fear, be in accord about plants. To designers, the function of a plant is not merely to give pleasure in its own good time and its own unique way. It is obliged to serve a purpose in the landscape: to frame or conceal a view; to soften hard, man-made edges with pliant foliage; to create boundaries; or to provide shade. Such a plant must have no bad habits such as shedding messy pieces of bark on the lawn or dropping fruit on parked cars or littering a terrace with unsightly seed pods. To gardeners, these "bad habits" come with the territory. A plant worth growing is entitled to its little ploys—especially those which perpetuate the species.

The pity of it is that gardeners and designers fail to realize how much they have to learn from one another. If gardeners could be persuaded to exercise a fraction of the designer's restraint in choosing plants, their gardens would have more order, purpose, and clarity. And if designers could be encouraged to make bolder choices, the suburban Northeast would not suffer from overexposure to azaleas, rhododendrons, and junipers.

There are, however, compelling reasons for the chasm that exists between gardeners and designers with respect to plants. Every perennial plant has an off-season—be it an herbaceous plant that dies down for the winter, a tree or shrub that loses its leaves annually, or even a broadleaf evergreen such as rhododendron, which molts a portion of its foliage each year. Gardeners accept this season with the same equanimity they display toward the fruiting season. The dormant period is another stage in the life cycle of the plant. But a landscape designer's client may be less sanguine about a plant that doesn't do its job for the full twelve months of the year. You can hear the client expressing doubt about hostas as a ground cover: "But they die in the winter, don't they? Then we'll have nothing except an ugly patch of dirt." Enter pachysandra or vinca or ivy. No gardener would object to the sight of bare ground for a few months and would, in any case, consider a bed of magnificent foliage worth the candle.

Designers feel constrained to use the few plants that look more or less the same all year, can be relied upon to stand up to the ministrations of inexperienced clients or indifferent garden help, and that change an absolute minimum during the course of their lives. For a designer responsible to unrealistic clients—who believe that their property is finished once "the garden" has been installed—change is the enemy. To gardeners, change is the coin of the realm. They are used to it and can even exploit it. Designers aim for permanence. By establishing structure and structures, they reduce change to a minimum. And they don't like surprises, while gardeners tolerate and often welcome them.

The flip side of change in the garden is that for designers—and for some gardeners as well—changes in nature may occur all too slowly. A nurseryman, like Herb, confronted with the owner of a brand-new home, hastily lays sod and jams foundation beds with young evergreens—which will all have to be moved in three years' time but which, for the moment, satisfy the new homeowner's desire for an instant garden. I once read a newspaper article written by a woman who was a designer herself but not a garden designer. She explained the rationale for instant gardens and the hiring of professionals. "In gardening, time proves to be money perhaps more obviously than in any other endeavor." The good lady arrived at this conclusion in the course of two summers. Displeased by the time she had wasted before recognizing the need to remove a group of shrubs in order to open up a view, she engaged a landscape designer. "At this pace," she explained, "it could have taken me twenty-five years to achieve what I wanted."

My argument with this way of thinking is that the garden you want today may not be the garden you want in ten or twenty years. Gardeners as well as gardens grow and change over the years. As a gardener, your priorities and your attitudes change. Beginning gardeners ask not what they can do for the plants but what the plants can do for the garden and the gardener. Beginners are wrapped up in their own concerns: flowers, first and foremost—their colors and forms and how well they complement each other. The habit of the plant, the form of its foliage, its aspect at different periods during the growing season—these come next. As interest in leaf shapes and plant structure waxes, so does a desire to compose more subtle combinations and garden pictures.

At about this time, most gardeners begin to develop an interest in gray and silver foliage and in less run-of-the-mill plants. And sooner or later, every gardener who stays the course begins to take a deeper interest in the plants themselves—in how they function, how they live and breathe, how they drink and absorb sustenance, how they are affected by heat and light and moisture. When this begins to happen, you are entering a new phase of your gardening career. You begin at this stage to care more about putting the right plant in the right place than about simply fulfilling some arbitrary scheme of your own. Moreover, the right plant in the right place grows better and looks better than one that doesn't enjoy its location. And so it goes on and the more you learn, the more you want to know.

Of course, not everyone wants to garden, but give yourself a chance to find out before hiring a professional. I believe that if you hire a landscape designer first, you may deny yourself the most wonderful voyage of discovery. Worse yet, a potential garden-maker may become a dropout. Besides, if you insist on having what you want right away, you may find that it's not what you wanted after all. If the result has been achieved at considerable cost, you will feel stuck with it. If, on the other hand, you do it yourself, you will find it easier to be flexible. And if, in the course of tinkering with your property, you find that you *like* gardening for the sheer, perverse pleasure of getting cold, wet, sore, and covered with mud, if you are willing to wait and to make mistakes, and if you conscientiously keep looking for the bear, you will eventually get a feel for the landscape. Its contours will become as familiar to you as the features of a well-loved face that you can trace from memory. Then you will begin to see what to do with this scrap of the earth's crust that belongs to you and the garden you make on it will be your own—as only the swirling patterns of your fingerprints are your own.

I realize with sadness that few people these days have the option of spending twenty-eight years on the same piece of property. To the would-be gardener in the unhappy position of having to move often, I can only say this: Every new garden that you make will be an improvement on the old one. You will learn as you go along. And one good thing about moving—you can turn your back on your mistakes. Each time as you begin again, you will be starting from a higher point on the evolutionary scale. And when you finally settle down for good, you will already have a vocabulary of plants and years of experience behind you. Because you know more, you will have to dig less—it is one of the compensations of being an older gardener. I used to pour time and energy into projects that were doomed from the start. Today, there are things I would approach in a very different way.

In what may seem a one-hundred-and-eighty-degree turnaround, I would never again undertake any project involving construction without enlisting the services of a landscape designer. There is no contradiction in my mind between subscribing to do-it-yourself garden-making and believing—as I do—that only a professional should undertake the design, siting, and supervision of pool construction; the installation of terraces, walks, and driveways; and the integration of buildings into their natural surroundings. A qualified landscape designer with a knowledge of proper grading and the drainage of surface water could have saved us untold headaches with our garage and driveway. As it was, neither was designed—they were merely allowed to happen.

We told the building contractor that we wanted a garage big enough for two cars. He presented us with a twenty-four-foot-square box with a pitched roof built into the hillside. One wall was four feet below grade. The lower half—a cement block retaining wall—caved in later because there was no drainage ditch behind it. On this occasion, the day was saved by an ingenious Italian stonemason who somehow tied the wooden portion of the wall—which was sagging perilously—to a nearby tree, while he and a powerful young helper excavated behind the collapsed cement blocks, filled the trench with crushed stone, and rebuilt the wall.

At the time the driveway was put in, I couldn't spare it a thought and it looks it. Unloved and unplanned, except by the man who put it in—on a sloping site and over the roots of a huge maple tree—it continues to reproach us with its ugliness and inefficiency. To save the tree roots, excavation was kept to a minimum, and for that reason the elevation of the driveway is considerably higher than that of the parking area-cum-turning-space. Surface water and detritus from above pour across the sloping blacktop and accumulate in the parking area. In fact, so much sand has collected there over the years that we've lost several feet of the driveway. The pavement is now covered with sod. Nor is the grass-covered parking area the worst of it.

The most offensive sight on our property is the bank by the garage. And it is the first thing you see as you drive in. The angle is extremely steep, which made planting it difficult. Try as I would, I was unable to get any kind of ground cover started successfully. And in the absence of competition, a kudzulike vine called *Akebia quinata* took immediate charge, consuming three large mountain laurels in the process. Through the nearly impenetrable mass of akebia and stinging nettles, long menacing brambles reach out for unsuspecting visitors. Although intrepid friends manage to overlook the approach to our house, it does not present a welcoming aspect.

A landscape designer would find a way to regrade the bank, perhaps employing a low retaining wall. It is comforting to know that in the hands of a professional there is always something that can be done to improve the shining hour. In the case of the driveway, our problems might still be solved by regrading the site of the parking area—providing a proper base for construction beyond the existing pavement—and finally spreading a layer of blacktop over the whole thing before rolling crushed stone into the surface. In short, if you want a driveway that looks like a courtyard instead of a seedy used car lot, get professional help. It will save you time, money, and maintenance.

It takes know-how and training to incorporate the functional necessities of a modern household into the landscape without diminishing the usefulness of the former and violating the integrity of the latter. To me, there is a deep and basic conflict between the residential works of man and the works of nature. And it is with profound respect that I bow to landscape artists, who through their insight and skill manage to reconcile the small geometry of man-made structures with the grand scale of the landscape's hidden geometry.

Some Thoughts on Design:
Betty

IN A VERY MINOR CAPACITY, I HAVE RECENTLY AS-sisted a landscape designer whose work I admire. It occurred to Betty Ajay, a friend of many years, that I might be able to suggest some background plantings and perennial combinations for two or three of her more plant-conscious clients. From my point of view, the idea was delightful. I had everything to gain: an opportunity to learn something about landscape design; the chance to experiment with arrangements I had no room to try in my own garden; the indulgence of buying plants without having to pay for them; and the luxury of expert help in planting them. With Betty as teacher, mentor, and troubleshooter, I agreed to this admirable arrangement; she would accept all the responsibility while I basked in the approval of her happy clients.

The best possible introduction to Betty's work is a visit to her own property. As an outdoor environment, it is beautiful because it is perfect—or as nearly perfect as a mutable entity can be. In both the readiest interpretation of the word, meaning flawless, and in the more precise sense of thoroughly done, complete, and exactly conforming to theory, the garden embodies her philosophy of landscape design. For Betty, a totally satisfying garden demands the rational arrangement of plants in relation to every other feature in the landscape. Achieving this coherence requires the utmost restraint—which she has exercised to stunning effect. Hers is a green garden. "The simplicity of a green garden," she says, "encourages strong design, upon which the ultimate beauty of the garden depends."

Betty began gardening in much the same way that I did and with very similar raw materials. She and her husband, artist Abe Ajay, moved out of New York City and found an old Connecticut farmhouse surrounded by eight neglected acres. The house is on a gentle south-facing slope with a hill behind it. By the time the Ajays bought the property, the hillside—which was once an apple orchard—had been overrun with the same woody aggressors that had taken over our field: sumac, red cedar, brambles, and poison ivy. Just as we did, the Ajays began beating back the wilderness. And soon Betty was digging flower beds and planting annuals and perennials. But there the similarities in our garden-making end.

Instead of keeping her eyes glued to the ground and becoming more and more enthralled with the plants themselves, Betty looked up and around her and concluded that beautiful plants did not necessarily make a beautiful garden. By the end of the first season, she realized that only by applying logic to the selection and grouping of the plants could she have the sort of garden she wanted. In pursuit of a unified garden, she began limiting the means and arrived over the course of the next few years at a sense of personal style which stamps her own garden and those she designs for other people.

Her definition of good garden design is "a discipline which brings order, coherence, and unity to diverse elements." The natural landscape brought into being by a seething disorder of molten rock and covered with a vegetative layer of exuberant, irrepressible woody growth presents a formidable challenge. And to harness and harmonize it for human purposes is no mean feat. The harnessing requires singleness of purpose, willpower, and control. The tension and drama of Betty's work derive from the exercise of this control. The creation of harmony results from her sensitivity to and understanding of the underlying volumes in the landscape.

I learned something about underlying volumes in a life drawing class. The instructor covered the model from head to toe with lengths of string arranged across her body parallel to each other and at one-inch intervals. When he had finished the elaborate ritual, he told us not to draw the model—but to draw the string. The results were quite remarkable. In faithfully reproducing the pattern of the string, we achieved far better definition of the body than we had in any outline drawings with shading. Instinctively, Betty sees what we had to have pointed out to us—the hidden geometry. Her eye cuts through the cluttered surface of the landscape to the underlying forms. Her success in relating man-made structures to their natural surroundings springs from a strong sense of form.

Her house and terrace are fitted so sensitively into the volumes of the hillside behind them that they seem part and parcel of the landscape. A curved retaining wall following the contours of the hill—just as the strings followed the contours of the model's body—creates the transition from rounded hill to the flat terrace, from which arises the cubic volume of the house. The curving wall subtly tracing the shape of the land makes a tremendously satisfying resolution to the change in grade and the change from natural to man-made structures.

The wall and the edge of the terrace follow the hillside in a wide arc which wraps around the swimming pool. Pool design is Betty's forte. "The shape of a pool," she says, "should be determined by the natural character of the land and the spirit of the garden. We built this pool soon after moving to the country. And it was a big undertaking, as we planned to do most of the work ourselves. But we felt that it had to be large—a small pool would have been dwarfed by the sweep of our hill—and we wanted the perimeter to curve gently with the contour of the land. We also thought that the pool should have sloping sides like a natural pond and that the color should blend in with the setting of trees and shrubs."

After staking out the shape they wanted, the Ajays hired a bull-dozer operator, a mason, and a team of helpers to do the excavation and pour the concrete. The rest they did themselves. It is a beautiful pool. Not round, though nearly so; not oval either, and certainly not "free-form" in the sense of being an irregular shape, it most closely resembles just what they had hoped—a natural pool filling a hollow at the foot of the hill. As the color of water depends on the color and depth of the container, they settled on a deep shade of green to enhance the impression of a natural pool. In the summer, the still, dark surface reflects the sky overhead. When the water freezes over in the winter, the sheet of ice matches the slate-colored flagstone of the terrace. Betty claims there are things wrong with the pool—youthful swimmers miss a diving board; their feeble elders have occasional difficulty negotiating the sloping sides—but even she concedes that it has aged gracefully while continuing to give pleasure. To me, it is one of the loveliest of many handsome pools which she has designed and a fitting centerpiece for this perfect, understated garden.

There are so many similarities between our property and the Ajays' that comparisons—while odious—are unavoidable, and in the long run instructive. Both old farms came with barns separated from the houses by a considerable distance and at angles that have no relationship to the dwellings. Our barn—set askew three hundred feet from the house—is cut off from the rest of the garden by an untidy spirea hedge that was planted long before we came. The barn was and still is painted "barn red"; the house was yellow and we have since stained it a more subdued shade called Desert Sand. The distinction between the two different colors is now less sharp and therefore less jarring than it was. It doesn't really bother us, as we seldom look at the two simultaneously, but it certainly does not make for unity.

In contrast, the Ajay house and barn, which are just as haphazardly placed in the landscape as ours, present a united front. Both buildings are stained a soft shade of gray. Furthermore, they are linked by a planting of pachysandra, which seems to draw them closer together. Thus, the relationship between them is reinforced visually by using the same color and physically by using the same ground cover. In addition, both buildings are joined in a purposeful way to each other and to the pool terrace by a system of fieldstone walks edged with pachysandra. As a binder, there is no substitute for this vigorous, reliably hardy ground cover that remains green all winter. Uniform in height and texture, it runs like a theme throughout the property, gathering in its embrace the disparate elements of a complex garden, and thereby creating harmony.

Within the calm green world of Betty's making, not a single plant is selected without thought. A few years ago, she was looking for exactly the right perennial to plant between low-growing blue junipers in raised beds on the terrace. Her requirements were for long-lasting white flowers in scale with the containers and foliage that would look attractive all year. Her present quest is for the perfect vine to embellish a new arbor. Preferably evergreen, its habit of growth must be restrained, its blossoms white, and its behavior impeccable. Wisteria is too rampant and clematis too untidy. The winter aspect of every plant receives as much consideration as its appearance in flower and during the growing season. And clematis doesn't measure up in the winter—especially those species which blossom on the previous year's wood and must not be pruned until after flowering.

As trees are the slowest growing and longest lived plants on any property, they have been chosen with particular care—and with a purpose. For the crescent of lawn above the swimming pool, canoe birches with straight single trunks were preferred to multistemmed clumps with trunks that lean this way and that. The vertical lines of the single trunks repeat the vertical lines of the nearby house, establishing yet another link between the natural and the man-made. Other trees used have been limited to a few species, for the most part North American natives.

Eastern white pines, Canadian hemlocks, and American arborvitae screen the periphery; one beautiful Chinese dogwood *(Cornus Kousa variety Chinensis)* occupies a prominent position on the lawn; and a row of perfectly matched flowering crabapple trees crowns the curved retaining wall above the terrace. Although a few native dogwoods remain on the property, many have succumbed to the diseases and climatic stresses that have plagued this tree in our region. The dogwoods notwithstanding, there are good reasons for Betty's reliance on native plant material. As she points out, "Plants selected on the basis of natural affinity grow well together because they share cultural preferences. Moreover, they look well together. A garden in which native plants have been used has a unity both within its boundaries and with the countryside beyond its confines."

The Cubist painter Georges Braque wrote, "It is often limited means that make the charm and the force of primary paintings. Extension, on the contrary, leads the arts to decadence. . . . I love the rule that corrects the emotion. . . . I love the emotion that corrects the rule." A green and white garden such as Betty's derives its charm and force from its limitations, and its beauty from austerity. Its atmosphere is one of repose rather than excitement. When I once told Betty that I wanted my garden to be exciting, she smiled and said, "I would rather have excitement in my life than in my garden. In a garden, I want serenity."

Possibilities

A PERFECT GREEN AND WHITE GARDEN IS SOMETHING I have never wanted—which is just as well. Possessing neither the discipline nor the inclination to limit the means to that extent, it is something I could never have. Many of the things I want in and from my garden—besides excitement—are the reverse of what Betty Ajay wants and expects from hers. I want plants that emphasize rather than diminish the impact of the changing seasons. In the fall, I want foliage that turns from green to morocco-red or bronze or clear, bright yellow; I want plants that set enough fruit to weigh down the boughs with clusters of scarlet or purple or blue. For winter, I want plants with eye-catching bark, like the lacebark pine *(Pinus bungeana)*, with an outer layer that peels off in irregular gray-green flakes, revealing lighter shades of gray, green, and white beneath.

I also want mystery, magic, and surprise. Some of the best effects in my garden have been the result of serendipity: The trumpets of a handful of pink daffodils stuck in the ground at the base of *Viburnum Carlesii* turn out to match the coral-colored flower buds of the shrub; I fail to cut off the gray chenille flower stalks of the lamb's-ears and they grow up through the dark red foliage of a threadleaf Japanese maple; a homeless daylily with cinnamon-orange flowers winds up next to a rhododendron whose leaves are lined with cinnamon-orange felt. *Serendipity,* by the way, is a word coined by eighteenth century writer Horace Walpole from the title of a fairy tale called "The Three Princes of Serendip," which was once the name for Sri Lanka. In the days of Serendip, this now-troubled island was a place where the three princes kept stumbling across good fortune. The same thing happens in the garden. I could never forfeit these happy accidents for a more orderly approach to garden-making.

66

I don't want a low-maintenance garden either—if that means a garden in which there is nothing to do. There is a difference between "maintenance" and gardening. Preparing the perennial border for winter is gardening. Raking leaves is maintenance. Both are repetitive, have to be done every year, and require time and effort. But while you are removing limp daylily foliage from the border and pulling the stray weed and cutting down the rigid stalks of lythrum and sunflowers, you are mumbling to yourself about the things you are going to do next year: divide this and move that; put in more of one thing and scrap another; and maybe even shoehorn in a new something else. Meanwhile, you feel thoroughly heartened to find tiny ice-blue rosettes at the foot of the old stalks of *Sedum* 'Autumn Joy' and red "eyes" at the base of the peonies—ready and waiting for spring. That's gardening. Shearing the hemlock hedge and employing the string trimmer—that's maintenance. Gardeners will readily grasp the distinction.

I want to work in the garden—weeding, pruning, and planting, and doing things that I enjoy. I want the room and the opportunity to experiment with many different kinds of perennials, ornamental grasses, shrubs—even trees. I want a spring garden that doesn't resemble the summer garden and a fall garden that is different from either. I am lured by the idea of water in the garden—the sound of it, the movement, the plants that would appreciate the additional moisture. The rub is that I would like all this—and more—without creating a monster by whom I am enslaved and without arriving at utter chaos.

Improbable as it may sound, my gardening life has been devoted to the search for form. The ideal form would be flexible enough to permit experiment without producing confusion and disciplined enough to satisfy a yearning for purpose and pattern without sacrificing variety. It is my belief that a beautiful piece of land should set the course and govern the form of the garden—based on geology, topography, and climate. This is the sort of garden I have been groping toward all these years. But it wasn't until we had the field cleared and the features of the landscape had been laid bare before me that I began to move in the right direction.

Clearing the field cleared my vision. After the pool went in but before we had even finished taming its surroundings, we decided to get someone in to cut down the brush in the field. It was a bigger job than we felt capable of tackling on our own. So we contacted the Agricultural Extension Service and were lucky enough to find a state forester who was willing to help us out in his spare time. Humorous, good-tempered, and deft with a chain saw, Dave Thompson arrived the following Saturday accompanied by a bearded helper. At the end of day, we had a view.

A tree person at heart, Dave was selective in his clearing. He spared the native red cedars *(Juniperus virginiana),* the dogwoods—of which there were at least a dozen and all about to bloom—and a single pin oak *(Quercus palustris),* which stands low down on the steep part of the slope. It's a big tree now and still handsome, despite recent storm damage. The trunk is straight and in the winter you can appreciate its distinctive skeleton—the topmost branches reaching upward; those in the middle spreading horizontally, while the bottom ones angle downward. Dave removed a few of the lowest limbs so that we could look up toward the dogwoods and cedars that stood out now against the shorn hillside.

Dave was wonderful and we were exultant. We had been starved for the sight of open countryside. The clearing was small—only about an acre and a half—but the prospect was gentle and charming. Although no bold outcrops or pinnacles of rock had been uncovered, just the sight of the land was beautiful to us. Rising quite steeply to the north and west, it reaches a broad plateau before rolling onward and upward to meet the edge of the state forest. Hidden by trees, the forest floor continues to rise, eventually reaching a height of about eight hundred fifty feet above sea level—Newtown's highest elevation. The farther north you go in Connecticut, the higher the elevation, until at last you reach the Berkshire mountain chain across the border in Massachusetts.

On May 19, 1965, I scribbled a note in one of the trusty composition books: "Dave finished clearing the field today and it looks like a park. The dogwoods are in full bloom—layers and layers of white. It's heavenly! I'd like to put in a few pink ones among the white and maybe a cluster of hemlocks at the top of the hill." Unfortunately, I gave in to the first whim—the pink dogwoods were a great mistake but short-lived in any case—and never followed through with the second, which would have added a welcome evergreen accent on the crest of the hill. But whatever the limitations of my vision in the first instance and energy in the second, clearing the field opened more than the view. It opened my eyes. I could suddenly see that the garden was part of a larger landscape. Little by little, I began to get a sense that the landscape of New England was *meant* to rise and fall and that to deny its essential character was not only a losing battle, it was wrongheaded.

The immediate effect of opening up the field was the strong north-south orientation it gave the whole property. Everything that we had done suddenly seemed to fall in place along this axis—the pool, the vegetable garden, the long, irregular panel of lawn. It was as if the garden was slowly taking its rightful position in the system of valleys and ridges that make up a great fold in the earth's crust running north to the Berkshires and south to the Appalachians. Although a feeling for the shape of the land and a growing awareness of the larger picture didn't tell me what to do next, it gave me a sense of the possibilities inherent in our small piece of the Connecticut landscape.

Clearing the field spurred us on. By the end of the summer, we had hacked down or grubbed out enough of the woody shrubs so that we could mow right up to the stone wall. In the process, we found substantial rock outcrops, upon which I was beginning to look more kindly. We also discovered a strange arrangement of large rocks twelve or fifteen feet from the foot of the wall and roughly parallel to it. It is hard to imagine their purpose but they formed a sort of raised bed sixty feet long. I didn't know what to do with it. It was impossible to mow, and I didn't want to make it into a flower bed. However, if something wasn't planted—quickly—nature would once again take its course. As the result of my first visit to the Oriental Stroll Garden at the

Hammond Museum, I had recently become aware of the natural affinity between rocks and evergreens and conifers. So I planted mugho pines, Japanese hollies, junipers, and ground-hugging cotoneaster. Over the long haul, the evergreen garden has proved to be the most permanent and successful of all my early plantings.

The Hammond Museum

WEARING A SMOCK OVER A PLAIN BLOUSE AND SKIRT with flat-heeled, sensible shoes, Natalie Hays Hammond looked more like a high-school science teacher than a multitalented artist of considerable repute. A distinguished miniaturist, a designer of theater costumes and jewelry and, later, of needlepoint canvases, her watercolors were praised by a Boston critic for "charm without vagueness," while the same reviewer found in her pencil drawings "a melancholy strength"—not surprising for an artist trained in the exacting discipline of the miniature. However, no artistic pigeonhole seems appropriate for this woman of boundless energy, enthusiasm, and intellectual curiosity, who used to welcome visitors to her museum and garden.

Best known for the Oriental Stroll Garden, the museum complex has suffered over the years but the Guild Hall continues to house exhibits of interest and there is a move afoot to restore the garden. In its prime during the sixties, the garden—designed, laid out, and planted by Ms. Hammond in 1958—attracted hordes of visitors. Even now it is a fascinating and evocative place. The site alone is worth a visit. Spread out across a three-acre hilltop in North Salem, New York, the museum and garden command a breathtaking view to the west. Far below, rolling farmland and wooded hills converge on the shores of the Titicus Reservoir, backed by low blue ridges in the distance. From the garden, every prospect pleases.

We were first taken there by Newtown neighbors who were loyal supporters of the museum. The occasion was an evening performance—of what I have forgotten but the garden was unforgettable. It was so different from anything I had ever seen. My ideas of what constituted a garden hadn't progressed much beyond the British convention of the perennial border and the American convention of foundation plantings. Heretofore, I conceived of using evergreens only in the most limited sense: in the obligatory plantings around a house, or as my father had used them—to screen out the road, and of course, in his one flight of fancy, the circle of spruce. But here was a garden made up primarily of evergreens combined with rocks and water. There were only a few floral accents—in the spring irises bloomed at the edge of a pond, and in August the extraordinary serpentine buds of lotuses and water lilies emerged from the water.

The stroll garden employed a great many pines, which shed their fine needles among the rocks in an attractive way. Another favored tree was the unfamiliar Japanese cedar *(Cryptomeria japonica)*. This tall, tapering evergreen resembles our native red cedar. The straight trunk is covered with stringy gray bark overlying reddish underbark; the crown is narrow and pointed but more irregular than the American *Juniperus virginiana.* Low-growing junipers were another favorite motif sweeping over and around the rocks. There were masses of azaleas and a terrace planted with red-leafed Japanese maples. But it was the use of evergreens that I found inspiring.

I was also very much impressed by the intricate organization of the garden enclosures; each garden is separate and yet part of the complex whole—linked together by paths and courtyards surfaced with gravel. On entering through the covered Garden House, there is a little waterfall constructed of local stone and descending in shallow pools to a miniature stream lined with pebbles. Following the Japanese tradition, the water flows from east to west and trickles into the pond that is the focus of the garden. Stepping stones lead to the perimeter path that passes through or gives onto the individual gardens—each with a purpose. A courtyard set in a little grove of pines is dedicated to Buddha's disciples. At the foot of an artificial hill covered with native red cedars, sixteen upright stones are set in pine bark to represent the followers who forfeited Nirvana and remained behind to uphold Buddhist law on earth. The thought of a garden based on ideas or a philosophy intrigued me.

The oriental appreciation of rocks was perhaps the most striking feature of the whole garden—the symbolism of the rocks, their precise and careful choice. I very much doubt that a Japanese gardener would find much authentic about the Hammond Museum stroll garden but that isn't the point; the garden is intended to convey the spirit of an Eastern garden. In an introduction to the unique three-acre world of her devising, Ms. Hammond described it as a translation or adaptation of the stroll garden—a form originating in seventeenth century Japan. The symbolic use of plants and rocks derives from several sources: the religion of Buddha, the philosophy of Confucius, and Shinto myths centering on the presence of a *Kami,* literally translated "above" or "superior" but meaning "godlike" and found in everything from an elemental force such as thunder to animals, a handsome tree, or a beautiful view. The desired effect of the garden—which is to recreate the tranquillity of its oriental model—is achieved with haunting beauty. Ms. Hammond wrote that "its calming flowing pattern offers no surprise, but special points of interest symbolic of outer and inner windows—from which to view the broader landscape or review one's own thoughts."

I couldn't at the time have said what affected me most about the garden. But on returning after a hiatus of many years, I knew that it was the atmosphere of profound tranquillity that had made such a lasting impression. The recent visit was on a warm November afternoon. The garden was officially closed for the season. I was given permission to walk around by the elderly caretaker, who soon took himself off, followed by a decrepit black dog to whom he crooned a steady stream of obscenities. When his voice had faded, the garden was perfectly silent. I sat for a while in the Zen Garden. It was distressing to see everything so run-down. Maintenance must always have been a nightmare—it was a garden which required so much hand weeding and the kind of expert pruning that doesn't come cheaply. Now, piles of huge dry leaves from the plane trees outside the garden had gathered in a corner of the symbolic rectangle of sand. I could remember when the surface had been meticulously raked into the Cloud Pattern drawing precise lines around each rock. Instead, the sand was dimpled by a recent rain. Even the rocks representing man and earth in relation to heaven appeared awry. Nevertheless, the peace here was palpable. When I came in through the covered entrance, I had picked up a copy of Ms. Hammond's garden manifesto. There was only one left on the reception desk—weighted down with a smooth stone. I planned to return it on the way out. Glancing at it now, I read:

> We allot time for business, domestic duties, for study and recreation, but how much do we grant for the refreshment of the spirit? Must every thought be measured by its attainment; must every phase of life be walled by a conclusion, or may we not think to the exquisite borderline of wonder, wherein we realize that we are infinitely small within the scheme of things, and find our immortality through appreciation of the light and shadow of a single hour, through the iridescence of a spider's web.

The intention of the garden's creator transcends the neglect. She has succeeded admirably in providing a place and an atmosphere which fosters contemplation and refreshes the spirit.

It is probably a function of age that today I find peace to be the garden's most compelling "take-home message"—a Madison Avenue phrase of which Ms. Hammond would not approve. In the sixties, I had less use for peace and took home instead two additions to my gardening vocabulary—evergreens and evocation. The latter, I regret to say, assumed the form of a token Buddhist disciple among the mugo pines and Japanese hollies. After scouring the property, I found an irregular obelisk of local stone. Embedded in an upright position in front of the mugos and in the midst of the dwarf hollies, it added an exotic—if inappropriate—touch. I have since heard such arbitrary use of rock denounced by my rock gardening friends. Rocks that are not integrated into the landscape in a naturalistic way are scathingly referred to as "pet cemeteries." Fortunately, my symbolic rock seems to have escaped the notice of critical visitors. One winter, the rock was heaved forward by the frost and thereafter has been allowed to remain prone among the shrubs.

Instead of borrowing a Buddhist disciple from the Hammond Museum Oriental Stroll Garden, I would have been better advised to borrow the concept of adaptation. As a student of oriental religions and culture, Ms. Hammond had absorbed the lessons of the East without losing sight of her own heritage. Furthermore, she made no attempt to impose a literal translation on her hilltop; rather, she synthesized ideas from Japan—a country that once eagerly imported Chinese arts and learning—with other Eastern influences, and as an artist filtered them through her own consciousness. Therefore, the garden works on an intellectual and artistic level. It is a creation, not a copy.

Daylilies

HAVING TRIED TO COPY AN ENGLISH PERENNIAL BORder without success, I was obliged to fumble along until I hit upon a way of gardening that fit the domestic landscape. It would please me more to think that one day I had suddenly come to my senses and said, "See here, you've got to stop trying to make an English garden and start thinking in terms of a garden that will suit this particular terrain and climate." But the revelation never took place, at least not just like that. What did happen was that in desperation—and because I didn't know what else to do with them—I planted twelve daylilies in the bank of fill that had been excavated for the garage. As soon as the first clump went into the ground, I knew I was on the right track.

A garden along the bank solved everything. East-facing and blending into the natural slope above the pool, it provided an almost perfect site for growing perennials—plenty of sun, good drainage, and with the woods rising behind and to the west, protection from the prevailing winds. It was also in full view of the terrace. The soil was terrible but there were things that could be done about that. I had finally found a permanent home for the perennial border—thanks to a dozen daylilies.

I owe a lot to daylilies in one way or another. I love them because they are tough and easy to grow. They are survivors—and the most forgiving of perennials. Like most garden plants, they grow best in fertile soil that holds moisture—moisture is the vehicle for soluble nutrients; they prefer soil that isn't soggy either—if the air spaces in the soil are full of water, the roots can't absorb the oxygen the plants require. But they will grow in almost anything. Mine grew in fill—with the rather casual addition of some peat moss. For beginning gardeners, daylilies are ideal plants. Increasing in size and in the production of flowering stalks relatively quickly, they can soon be divided and spread around the garden. On the other hand, they will go on blooming prolifically for years without division; I am embarrassed to admit there are twenty-year-old clumps in my garden that have never been divided.

The flowers may only last a day but the plants are long-lived. Daylilies are often found around old houses and abandoned farm buildings. And roadside daylilies are the descendants of plants imported by the early settlers. In my own garden, there are masses of twenty-eight-year-old daylilies whose offspring are growing in gardens all over the neighborhood. I love some of the good old-fashioned cultivars, like 'Marionette' for their stamina, and expect them to be around when I'm long since dead and gone. It is a singularly comforting thought.

Most of all, of course, I love daylilies for their incredibly beautiful and abundant flowers. Their botanical name *Hemerocallis* comes from two Greek words—*hemera,* meaning "day" and *kallos,* "beauty." How could perfection be expected to last longer than a day? And their poignant underlying message of *Now! Do it now, enjoy it now, take it now!* is not lost on even the most literal-minded grower of this lovely plant. There is something to be said for having no past to regret or future to fear and for pouring everything into the moment.

I love the fact that daylilies are so easy to hybridize that far too many people get into the act and introduce far too many new cultivars. In 1987, there were 29,960 registered cultivars. I can't help feeling great affection for all these dear, crazy people of all ages and persuasions who become so enamored of these flowers that they can't stop breeding more and more of them. I applaud their wild dreams of a blue daylily—which I would personally hate— and a pure white—which I might like but feel, on the whole, I prefer the iridescent off-whites that glitter and gleam with hints of pink and mauve and peach. I particularly love these indescribable colors and the catalog descriptions of the indescribable. In one catalog, the cultivar 'Jim's Pick' has a base color in the morning hours of gold, which by afternoon is "smooth deep cream on which is blended the rose tones," which in turn blend into a "tangerine heart." To top it all off, "the raised ribs on each segment are orchid-pink and the edges of the petals burgundy or dusty rose." Whew!

Even in daylilies of a single color—a flower in which all the segments are one hue is called a "self"—the range is enormous. Wild daylilies display a range confined to shades of yellow and orange with timid excursions into the reddish tones. From this limited pallet, hybridizers have developed a spectrum that includes every ramification of yellow; reds and pinks—from the darkest to the palest; and royal purple and white, or so nearly white as makes no difference. Then there are the patterns: the shadings, bands, and watermarks around the eyezone; the edgings and even, perish the thought, polka dots. And the blends—two colors combined in a single flower. There is no end to the subtlety of the blends. And finally, back to the indescribable polychromes, such as 'Jim's Pick.'

Bless the hybridizers for their unrestrained creativity! Where once there was a single clarion form, there are now dozens of different shapes. Each flower is composed of an inner whorl of three petals and an outer trio of sepals—to be botanically correct, all six segments are called tepals. In wild daylilies, these segments are similar in design, relatively narrow and slightly flared—which gives the flower its classic trumpet shape. But modern cultivars come in all patterns and configurations. A side view can be described as flat, flaring, or recurved. From the front, the blossoms can look as round as buttons with wide overlapping segments or they can be star-shaped with narrower, outspread segments. So-called "spiders" have the narrowest and most widely spaced segments of all. And there are orchidlike shapes and tailored forms that are nearly triangular. The edges of the segments can be unadorned or blowsily ruffled, finely crimped or widely fluted. There are doubles with extra segments in all sorts of arrangements—from knots at the center of the flower to graduated hose-in-hose patterns in which sets of tepals are tucked one inside the other. It's hard to imagine where the ingenuity of the hybridizers will lead them next. But that's part of the charm of daylilies—and of their admirers. Nothing new under the sun? In the world of daylilies, there's *always* something new.

Daylilies were the first perennials I ever bought and it was love at first sight. My early composition books are filled with guilty admissions: "Have gone daylily-mad this year. I can't resist that half-price sale." Another year, "I've ordered a whole collection of pink daylilies. And I don't even know where to put them!" So it went over the years. And in time, an affair—at first, headlong and adolescent—matured into an abiding love. The great range of flower sizes and heights alone make daylilies the most versatile of garden plants. These two elements give you so much to play with.

The flower sizes fall into three categories, which are of importance chiefly to breeders and to people interested in exhibiting at shows. According to the American Hemerocallis Society handbook, the flowers of a "miniature" must be under three inches in diameter. In fact, most miniatures nowadays are considerably smaller, which has been the aim of many breeders— the smaller, the better. The next size up is "small flowered" with blossoms from three to four and a half inches, and anything over four and a half inches is considered "large flowered"—which can mean anything up to nine inches in diameter. To a gardener, however, these categories haven't much meaning. An inch one way or another doesn't matter. It all depends on where and how you want to use the plants.

I must confess, I love all sizes—the great and the tiny and those in the middle. The huge ones—I have one called 'Yellow Pinwheel' with blossoms at least eight inches across—make a big, bold splash of color. Admittedly, the flower stalks—"scapes" to the cognoscente—are clumsy-looking and should be hidden by bushy, floriferous plants in the foreground. But at a distance, those magnificent flowers are a wonderful sight. In a large, informal country garden you *need* big plants. This was one of the things I discovered fairly early in my gardening career. A small plant surrounded by a great deal of space has very limited impact in the landscape—except en masse. However, in a more confined and civilized garden, smaller daylilies would be preferable. They have other advantages over the whopping big ones—the spent heads of miniatures and small flowered cultivars are much less noticeable and don't have to be slavishly removed, unless you are a perfectionist.

I love some of the immensely tall daylilies with small flowers. The scapes are so long and slender that they disappear against a green background and the flowers appear to float in space. Off in distant corners of the garden, I have clumps of a six-footer called 'Autumn Minaret' which holds aloft clusters of starry yellow flowers. They are like a grace note in the landscape—just a touch of color, a small, welcome surprise. The tall ones are useful in a deep perennial border, too. Many plants that provide height also take up a substantial amount of lateral space but the tall daylilies require only a modest area. Flower scapes range from six-footers, like those of 'Autumn Minaret' down to wiry little stems only a few inches high. "Dwarf," a term which appears in daylily catalogs, applies to daylilies with scapes under twelve inches. The flower of a dwarf may be any size.

I don't think I have ever gotten rid of a perennial because its flowers were a disappointment. But any number of plants have left my garden via the back door because their foliage didn't pass muster. To be worthy of a permanent position in the garden, a perennial must have—at the very least— serviceable foliage which never goes through such an unattractive stage that it draws attention to itself. On a scale of one to ten, daylily foliage is below the very top—with hosta awarded a perfect ten—but well above the middle. Emerging from the ground as fresh yellow-green tufts in the spring, the long, folded leaves rise from the crown in pairs and arch over as they mature. Some have more upright foliage than others. The habit of growth and width of the leaves varies depending on the cultivar. Some of the miniatures have grassy leaves, while some of the strapping giants have great sheaves of upright foliage. The majority of the daylilies in my garden produce graceful fountains of leaves rising to different heights—again, depending on the cultivar.

For most of the season, daylily foliage adds to the attractiveness of the garden, supplying a pleasant green background for the flowers of earlier blooming plants, and those long, swishy leaves are a wonderful cover-up for the yellowing foliage of spring bulbs. For a brief spell immediately after flowering the outer leaves of a daylily clump go through their leaden hour—many of them turn partially brown. At this stage, they can be cut off without harming the plant. I sometimes cut down the worst offenders, but in a few weeks new leaves will appear anyway, and by fall the plants are perfectly respectable again.

It is worth mentioning here that daylilies have three types of foliage habit—deciduous or dormant, evergreen, and semi-evergreen. Under-standing what these distinctions mean is far more important to gardeners than knowing that a miniature has a three-inch flower. Deciduous daylilies—as might be supposed—lose their leaves at the onset of winter and produce new ones in the spring. Evergreens—also, as one might imagine—retain their green leaves but—and here is the rub—in a cold climate, these can turn to mush and rot. The leaves of semi-evergreens behave in a manner halfway between the two—the part of the leaf closest to the crown stays green and the rest dies back.

Although foliage type cannot be used as a totally reliable guide to hardiness, as a rule of thumb, northern gardeners do best with dormant or deciduous daylilies and southerners do best with the evergreens. Semi-evergreens seem to have a very wide range of hardiness. And if you cover your daylily plants with six to eight inches of salt hay or shredded leaves in the fall, the chances are you can get away with growing all three types. I have been conservative in my choice of cultivars. I have only one evergreen about which I am quite passionate—'Dwarf King,' a mini that has shocking-apricot flowers banded with a red eyezone. But this much loved and much admired plant is less vigorous than most of my other daylilies. The evergreen leaves die back to the crown in the winter and the plant doesn't increase in size as it should because half the clump rots every year. Not using a winter mulch—the garden is too big for that kind of extra care—I have usually stuck to dormant daylilies.

I can hardly bring myself to say a negative word about one of my all-time favorite plants but there is an observation I feel duty-bound to make. All daylilies are not created equal. Some hybridizers have concentrated so hard on flower forms and colors that they have neglected to put enough emphasis on the behavior of the plant—the appearance of the foliage, the strength of the stems, and the number of buds per stem. A daylily with only a few flower buds will be in bloom only a few days, whereas 'Sparks,' a wonderful militantly red-orange cultivar with small flowers, boasts as many as fifty buds to a stem and goes on blooming for weeks. 'Sunrise Serenade,' a cultivar with irresistible polychrome flowers of vast size and the most delectable hues—pink, lavender, and cream—cannot hold its own head up if two buds happen to open on the same stem on the same day. Naturally, catalogs neglect to mention these drawbacks.

In buying daylilies by mail, the beginner can't go too far wrong in ordering cultivars singled out to receive the Stout Medal. Awarded by the American Hemerocallis Society and named for Dr. Arlow Burdette Stout, the medal is reserved for the crème de la crème. Gardeners have Dr. Stout to thank for the breakthrough that dramatically increased the color range in hybrid daylilies and led to the development of the luscious reds and pinks we now take for granted. Purveyors of daylilies are not shy about calling attention to cultivars that have received the coveted Stout Medal. Another way to select good cultivars is to be guided by the popularity poll conducted each year among members of the American Hemerocallis Society. Catalogs regularly list award winners.

In addition to information about awards and each cultivar's bloom size, color, height, and type of foliage, calalogs also identify tetraploid daylilies by the abbreviation "Tet." Most daylilies are diploids with twenty-two chromosomes per cell. Tetraploids have double that number—44 chromosomes per cell—and as a result are larger and have more intensely colored flowers, stronger stalks, and lusher foliage. However, there is often a price to pay in loss of grace and elegance. This genetic manipulation is accomplished by the use of colchicine, an alkaloid derived from the autumn crocus *(Colchicum autumnale),* and the increase in chromosomes expands the horizons for breeders—which hardly seems necessary to me. Nevertheless, I have succumbed joyfully to tetraploid temptations such as the polychrome 'My Hope' and golden yellow 'Mary Todd.'

Daylily catalogs have always been my downfall. It takes a stronger character than mine to resist a notice like this: "May we help? We have put together several lists of daylilies that you may be looking for. We grow many TETS, DIPS, MINIS, DOUBLES and SPIDERS which we can't fit into our usual catalog each year. They range from the old and commonplace to the very new. Please let us know what interests you and send a self-addressed stamped business sized envelope." Well, of course, I will. I adore daylily lists and catalogs. I even love the fulsome, foolish, funny names. How about 'Blushing Angel' and 'Cherry Cheeks'; 'Gentle Sunbeam' and 'Heavenly Hope'; 'Eenie Weenie,' 'Cutie Pie,' 'Little You,' and 'Little Me Too.'

At breakfast, I pore over the names and descriptions and always find something that I can't live without. That is the problem with daylilies. After a while, your garden is full of them; the ones you already have are on the increase. You really haven't room for more but you can't help yourself, so you go ahead and order more. The new additions haven't a proper home, which leaves you three choices: discard something that you have had for years (heaven forfend!); cram the new ones into the overcrowded perennial border; or dig up more of the lawn and make another bed. I do a little of each. The design of the garden suffers but my thirst for daylilies is temporarily slaked.

In a big, rambling country garden there is nothing more right than masses of daylilies. Look at them along the roadside. What could possibly look more at home than a great bank of graceful, flowing leaves with hundreds and hundreds of slim, wiry stems—all leaning in the same direction and offering up a host of orange trumpet-shaped blossoms? Daylilies and a slope are made for each other, especially an east-facing slope like mine. Inclining gently toward the morning sun, each flower reveals the glowing color at the base of the corolla. The minute I saw the first scapes of 'Marionette' bending slightly toward the terrace and the pool and exposing the handsome dark red eyezone at the heart of the golden trumpets, I knew what to do next . . . if I added to the daylilies and extended the bed . . . if I brought up the other perennials from below and started working along the slope toward the evergreen garden at the far end . . . And that's just one more reason why I love daylilies.

Daylily People

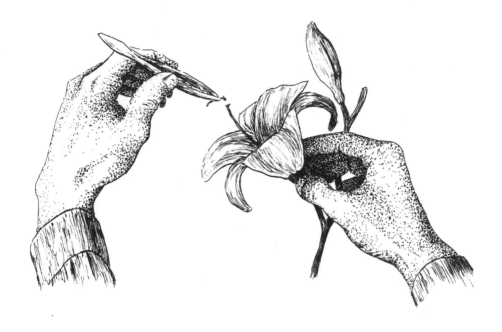

Ray

 THERE ARE GARDENERS, AND THEN THERE ARE DAYLILY People. What must be understood from the start is that daylilies are addictive. Let the case history of my friend Ray be a lesson. His is a classic example of daylily addiction and its far-reaching consequences. Until eight years ago, Raymond J. Doyle, Jr., led a perfectly normal life. He had a job, as an assistant state attorney; a happy marriage of thirty years; and hobbies—he played a little golf and enjoyed swimming. Both he and his wife, Jeanne, are certified in scuba diving. "We used to be beach people," she says. "We were both brought up on the water, and until Ray went hog-wild with the daylilies, we used to do a lot of boating and swimming and shelling." There is an outside chance that they may once again become beach people, as they have moved from Newtown to Florida. But a recent letter from Jeanne announced that three days after their arrival in Naples, Ray had made friends with another daylily hybridizer and had finished constructing a raised-bed garden large enough for the thirty cultivars he had brought with him.

A little while ago, when I asked Ray what he used to do before daylilies, he remembered mowing the lawn, lounging around the swimming pool, and helping Jeanne with her garden. But since, he hasn't touched a golf club or spent more than three hours in their old pool and Jeanne has become the garden gofer. "In the old days," Ray says with a chuckle, "I used to dig up whatever the wife wanted me to dig up and I'd help her with the watering and things like that. Now the shoe is on the other foot." His spouse cheerfully agrees. "Our roles are reversed. When it's time to mulch, I mulch with him. When it's time to do anything with the daylilies, I do it with him."

Ironically, it was she who first introduced daylilies into their New-town garden. She had been raising flowers and vegetables for years and was one of the founding members of the Town and Country Garden Club. After hearing a lecture on the subject of daylilies by the late Connecticut hybridizer May McCabe, Jeanne visited the McCabe garden in Branford and brought back a few plants. She put them in along the driveway. "But I never gave them a second glance," her husband admits. However, a short time later, the couple took a run up to Lee Bristol's daylily nursery in Sherman, Connecticut. For Ray, it was a fateful trip.

Having visited the nursery myself in mid-July, I can easily under-stand how it happened. The daylily fields bask in the sun surrounded by a picturesque landscape of hayfields, sheep pastures, and low, wooded hills. Approached via a long driveway hedged with wildflowers and native shrubs— sweet pepperbush and black alder—the flat, open nursery fields burst upon you with unfair suddenness. Sandy, rock-free loam amended with manure from the sheep pens and from local farms provides an ideal environment and the daylilies respond with enthusiasm. At the height of the season, a billowing sheet of cream, yellow, gold, copper, orange, pink, red, and wine—with touches of purple—lies in wait for the unwary visitor.

Ray was bowled over. Without prior warning or any telltale symp-toms of a genetic weakness for hemerocallis, he was smitten with the daylily bug. "I started wandering through the fields and I said, 'These flowers are just beautiful,' and I came home with nine of them." He preserves the sales slip as if it is a love letter—which, in fact, it is. He wouldn't even allow Jeanne's purchases to be totaled on his bill. Secretive and possessive, he clasped the new daylilies to his bosom—all the way home planning where he would put them. He liked the idea of the slope above the swimming pool. There was a little birch tree halfway up the hill which rises steeply to the southwest. He imagined looking up at the flowers from the poolside—his own garden; his first. The next day, he dug a four-by-eight-foot plot around the little birch, but before he had even finished the bed, he knew that he wanted more daylilies.

By the second year, he had increased the size of the bed to twenty by fifty feet and joined the American Hemerocallis Society—a support group for addicts. Founded in 1946 by Helen Field Fischer, a Midwest garden-lover whose radio program *Garden Club of the Air* did much to popularize daylilies, the society now has a vast membership. Succeeding beyond reasonable expec-tation in its avowed purpose of promoting the development and improvement of the genus and encouraging "public interest therein," the group has divisions all over the country. For anyone who gets caught up in hybridizing, membership is mandatory. But ensuring sympathetic understanding and providing a social outlet for the addicted is another important function of the organization.

It was through a fellow member that Ray heard about Charles Trommer's Tranquil Lake Nursery in Rehoboth, Massachusetts. After a sum-mer visit to the nursery, he was hooked on hybridizing. He recalls the occasion with obvious relish. "There was nobody around, so we just walked up and down the rows, but pretty soon Trommer himself showed up. We started talking and he wanted to know if I did any hybridizing. I said, 'No. How do you do it?' 'Easy,' he said, and he showed me." Then Ray showed me—taking the pollen-producing anther from one flower and brushing it against the pistil of another. "Morning is the best time," he explained, "the earlier the better—in order to beat the bees. At that time of day, the pollen is at its freshest. As the day goes on, it dries up and becomes hard."

After the trip to Massachusetts, Ray started getting up earlier and earlier, and for a couple of hours each day before going to work he could be found among his daylilies making new crosses. I have a seedling from one of his most successful crosses in a place of honor in the garden. The plant is small of stature and the three-inch flower is almost white with a beautiful clean form—six well-spaced segments devoid of frills and ruffles. In 1988, a thousand of Ray's own seedlings bloomed in nursery beds at the top of the hill. By this time, the Doyles' lawn of earlier years had given way to terraced beds devoted to an ever-growing collection of nationally registered cultivars. I have photographs of the hillside in full bloom—thousands of individual flowers of more than four hundred cultivars leaning into the morning sun. Dead-heading used to take the Doyles four man-hours a day. In half that time, the wheelbarrow would be full to overflowing with a faded rainbow of spent blossoms. To support his habit and make room for new acquisitions, Ray was having to sell the surplus to friends and acquaintances.

Already the Doyles had a five-year plan. They had friends with a young son who had worked with Ray in the garden. When the boy, too, fell under the spell of the daylilies and thought he might like to try his hand at growing and propagating them, Ray became his teacher and mentor. A plan evolved in the process. It was decided that the two would work together tending the collection, selling the surplus, and sharing the profits, and eventually the younger man would take over the stock and move the operation to land his family owned. But when Ray had the opportunity to retire early, the five-year plan was squeezed into a single season. All through the blistering hot summer of 1988, the two worked side by side.

At the end of the season, Ray and Jeanne moved to their Florida home, taking with them only the thirty evergreens which would adapt to the subtropical climate. For the new owners of their house, they left behind a representative collection of beautiful daylilies, all fertilized, weeded, and mulched with wood chips. The young couple had seen the daylilies in bloom and were thrilled. "Greenhorns," Ray told me with a sly smile. "But you know, I think the young man is getting interested in gardening. . . ." I haven't met the new owners but it wouldn't surprise me in the least to learn that another daylily addict has joined the ranks.

Before leaving Newtown, Ray filled my garden with treasures: the tiny 'Cricket' with yellow thimbles for flowers; two luscious off-whites, 'Ivory Platter' and 'Shepherd's Light'; a scintillating neon-yellow called 'Green Fringe'; and neat little 'Butter-pat.' Knock-your-socks-off 'Decatur Bullseye' is a very tall one for the back of the border; it has huge, creamy orange flowers with a striking red eyezone. I always had a craving for a little pink number called

'Siloam Toddler'; he gave me that, too. And 'Little Joy,' a gorgeous red velvet miniature, and many others. However, it is the small near-white of his own breeding that will always mean the most to me.

Jane

Jane Conningham is another kind of Daylily Person. An unconventional loner, she is as solitary and introspective as the Doyles are gregarious and outgoing, but she shares with Ray the hybridizer's singleness of purpose. By her own admission, she has never had any urge to make a garden, but for the joy of the individual flowers, she labors endlessly, carrying dirt and rocks up a hillside that would defeat a mountain goat. "Actually," she says, "it annoys me when flowering plants get too close to the house. Architecturally, I really like a sort of barn-style relationship between buildings and the land—a building sitting in a field—without a muffler of green stuff around the bottom. I've always felt you should take a chain saw to most foundation planting.

"I don't want to have to justify an arrangement of plants. Out here on the hillside you can have orange next to pink next to purple. It's a tunnel-vision garden. I look at the plant, and then I look at the next one, and if they have something to do with one another, that's neat; and if they don't, that's okay, too. It isn't really gardening, it's growing things—healthy flowers. If they cut nicely for the house, that's great, but if they're too beautiful, then I can't cut them because they won't make seeds."

Nevertheless, cut flowers were the route by which Jane became a hybridizer of irises and daylilies. Having had the country dweller's obligatory fling with vegetable gardening, she found that she didn't particularly enjoy it. Sooner and more honestly than most, she came to the conclusion that there were things she would rather be doing for the summer than slogging down a fifty-foot row of green beans picking vegetables she would have to freeze, give away, or live on for the foreseeable future. "Pretty soon, I decided that I just didn't want the damn things," she says candidly. "What I really wanted was cut flowers—which is basically what started me off. I would put in the flowers I wanted for the house—not in any order or with any real thought. One just gets lured into growing for the sake of the flowers. And then, if you have a certain turn of mind, you wind up specializing. I have a turn of mind that makes me prefer to work with a couple of things and to know all about them—which, of course, you can't, but it's sort of the way I attack things."

What this turn of mind ultimately led to was the discovery of irises—Japanese irises, Siberians, and the species irises with their smaller, more delicately wrought flowers. She began growing and studying them with a kind of single-minded fascination that led her on and on. She tried crossing different individuals and species—just for the fun of it and to see what would happen. "What really intrigued me," she recalls, "was this concept of making your own seed; planting it out and growing it on ["growing on" refers to the period before a seedling reaches maturity] until you had this line of plants in bloom. There would be a couple of beauties and a handful of cripples—but even the cripples gave you a special kind of delight. You knew you had to trash them but you also knew that this flower had never existed before."

The only trouble with Iris as a genus is that by the end of June most have finished flowering, and that's where daylilies came in. The easy-to-grow plants weren't a challenge—"a three-year-old can grow daylilies, but, again, how do you resist hunting down some of the rarer species?" From Jane, I learned about species like the late-blooming *Hemerocallis multiflora* with foliage less than half an inch wide and thin, arching scapes that produce several wiry branches and masses of small, starry yellow flowers. This graceful native of China is the ancestor of many small-flowered, autumn-blooming cultivars such as 'Wee Willie Winkie' and 'Autumn Daffodil.'

I've rushed over to her hillside to catch a final glimpse of the night-blooming *H. citrina* before the extremely fragrant flowers closed at mid-day. The pale yellow blossoms have the classic trumpet shape, but in this species it is very much attenuated and refined. *H. Dumortierii* from Japan is a wonderful garden plant. I now have clumps of this early-blooming species throughout the border. Starting to bloom around Memorial Day, a medium-sized clump will send up a dozen scapes bearing bunches of golden-yellow flowers in a bouquet at the top. The backs of the buds are streaked with cinnamon-brown.

With her artist's eye, Jane—in real life a free-lance graphic artist who designs books and other publications—was quick to appreciate the subtle charms of these wild daylilies, and through her I came to know and love them and to delight in their understated elegance. Last year a newcomer to my garden appeared on the doorstep in a plastic bag accompanied by the following note:

> Hi—The scuzzy-looking plant you might want to stick in some out-of-the-way corner for appraisal. I think you'll like it: *H. Fulva* 'Rosalind'—a stolo-niferous species similar to the one you showed me but smaller—and of course, quite rosy.

Once committed to daylilies, Jane naturally turned to hybridizing. I have a stunning, large flowered plum-purple hybrid of her breeding. To her this plant is known as G10-1. On the label, the name appearing at the top indicates the pod parent—'Chicago Thistle'—and the one below, the pollen parent—'Olive Bailey Langdon.' Sixty to eighty days after the transfer of pollen from the anther of the pollen parent to the stigma of the pod parent, the seed-bearing capsule turns brown and begins to crack open. The ten to twenty shiny black seeds are then gathered and put in the refrigerator.

Jane leaves her seeds in the refrigerator over the winter and plants in the spring, while Ray only used to give his a five-week chilling period before sowing them outside in a cold frame. Either way, dormancy is broken by the cold treatment and the seeds germinate in the spring. The first year, they produce small, grassy leaves; during the second, a good-sized plant develops; and by the third season, the first eagerly awaited blossoms appear. This is the moment of truth. Both Jane and Ray expect many of the new plants to be what she calls "ho-hums" but they keep on studying family trees and experimenting with new crosses. Nor is that the end of it. Even if a new flower shows promise, it must be tested for several more years in the garden before a decision can be made whether or not to give it a name and go through the registration process.

It isn't everyone who has the stamina for hybridizing—especially on an exposed hillside in Connecticut where deer are frequent and destructive visitors. Jane and her plants live an embattled life. If it isn't the deer, it's voles, rabbits, and woodchucks. But the worst invasion was by a herd of cows that escaped from the farm above and streamed down the precipitous slope. Back and forth through the garden they stumbled and scrambled, reducing the precariously terraced beds to a slippery mess: "You know what a cow crossing looks like—well, that's how it was. Cows don't climb hills in loamy soil very well." They pulverized what they didn't browse on, and in so doing destroyed every scrap of a pink Japanese iris introduction that had once turned the Iris Society inside out with excitement. "I still get letters requesting even a shred of 'Miss Tomopink' but it's all gone now.

"Sometimes I think I'm running out of steam. For years I've been swallowing hard and bouncing back from attacks of one sort or another but the stuff I do takes years. You've got to make the seeds and grow on the seedlings; you have to increase the stock; and finally, when you've got a chunk of it, somebody gets it—the deer come by and wipe out the whole thing. It's almost overwhelming. And yet, gardening is the only thing I never tire of doing."

Greg

The youngest of my daylily friends—and the only professional horticulturist among them—Gregory Piotrowski was finally able to explain the form and function of the daylily's mysterious underground stem. Not long out of his twenties but possessed of Joblike patience, this modest, knowledgeable young man has always been pleased to share his expertise, and when it comes to the genus hemerocallis he is a gold mine of information. From him, I finally came to understand the process by which daylilies increase in size, and therefore why they must be divided. Gardening books are long on the how and when of horticulture but short on the why—which is a pity, because once you know the why, how and when become either self-evident or of limited importance.

Daylilies, as all the books will tell you, are made up of roots, a crown, foliage, and flowers. You are expected to know that the roots anchor the plant in the earth and take up nutrients, while the leaves manufacture food by means of photosynthesis and the flowers are involved with reproduction. But the work of the crown or "underground stem" is left up to your imagination. When Greg undertook his explanation, I knew only that the crown is the point at which the leaves and the roots meet. How the juncture could be considered a stem escaped me.

"Look at this," said my tutor, offering me a twig from a cherry tree at the New York Botanical Garden, where he is on the staff. "Here you have leaves and, at the base of each leaf, a node or point of attachment. If you pull off a leaf, there is a bud which will develop into next year's stem. Then, between the nodes, you have spaces called internodes. Taken all together—nodes, internodes, and axillary buds—these make up this six-inch twig or stem.

"Well, all these parts are present in the daylily's underground stem or 'crown'—only they have been squeezed together like the folds of an accordion, so you have practically no internodes. If you look closely the next time you're dividing a daylily, you'll see thin rings—which are the leaf scars—circling the stem. And above each leaf scar is an axillary bud that could develop into a new daylily plant. That's how daylilies increase in size. As the plants get bigger, the stems often fuse and have to be cut apart when you are dividing the clump."

Greg went on to explain that as more and more new stems develop above the old crowns, the young plants are hoisted up above the soil level in a sort of hummock—which has happened to many of the oldest clumps in my garden. At this point, the clumps need dividing because the newer crowns have limited access to the surrounding soil and therefore are being deprived of water and nutrients. But, since the rate of increase differs considerably from cultivar to cultivar and species to species, it is a waste of time to slavishly divide all daylilies every three years—which is the recommendation of every book I've ever consulted. According to Greg, some clump-forming daylilies grow so slowly that they almost never need dividing, while others require frequent division in order to maintain the proper planting depth and an adequate supply of water and nutrients.

So how did this young man get so smart? It all began in Dearborn, Michigan, with a gardening family: a mother who gardened, a father who gardened, and a grandmother down the road who grew more than thirty different roses. "I used to go over and help her take care of them," says her grandson. "Then I started planting more roses at my parents' house, but what really gave me a big shove toward horticulture was joining the Rose Society. You start gardening and you get a lot of pleasure by yourself and in your own garden. But when you can share that enthusiasm with a group, it makes you even more enthusiastic. And if you're a new member and young, the plant societies are so happy to see you that they just take you in and treat you terrifically. You not only make a lot of good friends, you learn a tremendous amount. At least, it was a big learning step for me."

Joining one plant society led to joining others, among them the American Hemerocallis Society. Even before he came east a few years ago, Greg had done some hybridizing with daylilies. He had also completed the Master Gardener program offered by the cooperative extension service and worked for three years at a local nursery—after a brief detour into the automotive industry. "You know, being near Detroit, everything was auto-oriented so I did my bit as a machinist in a machine shop but didn't like it all that much." The nursery job he liked very much. "That's kind of how my career in horticulture began—working for the nursery." While there, he saw an ad for the New

York Botanical Garden School of Horticulture. As there was nothing comparable in the Midwest, he arranged for an interview and was accepted. Graduating
two years later, he joined the staff.

Fortuitously, another plant-minded Midwesterner had gravitated
to New York from neighboring Wisconsin seventy years earlier. As a boy,
Arlow Burdette Stout's scientific curiosity was aroused by the roadside daylily
(Hemerocallis fulva) and its failure to produce seed. Attracted to a career in
botany, this observant young man found his niche at the New York Botanical
Garden, where he remained for the next thirty-seven years, serving as director
of laboratories. Although his research extended to other genera, he is best
known for his work with hemerocallis. Daylily species from all over the world
were sent to Stout for evaluation and inclusion in his breeding program. In
addition to producing the first true reds and pinks, he was responsible for
introducing ruffles and semi-double blossoms. He also worked tirelessly to
improve the plants themselves and to increase the number of flowers to a
scape. Although Stout considered hybridizing daylilies secondary to his other
scientific research, it is for this contribution to ornamental horticulture that he
will be remembered.

It was a bit of luck for Greg to find himself at the School of
Horticulture at just the moment plans were being made to resurrect Stout's
daylily display garden. Later, Greg threw himself into the project with his usual
enthusiasm. "It suited everybody because I was already interested in daylilies
and really happy to do it. It was up to me to try to find the plants to put in the
garden; to decide what, how many, and how to arrange them in a way that would
be pleasing and at the same time educational." To date, he has succeeded
splendidly, rounding up all the known Stout hybrids on the grounds, ferreting
out others from commercial sources and private individuals, placing ads in the
Journal of the American Hemerocallis Society, and making endless phone calls.
With the patience and persistence of a tracking dog, he has accumulated a
representative collection of Stout cultivars.

On the site of its predecessor, the garden was formally reopened
July 25, 1987. A semi-circle of lawn divided into beds is backed by the surviving
hornbeam hedge *(Carpinus betulus)*—now a magnificent backdrop twelve feet
high. On the perimeter of the semi-circle, a matching pair of beds follows the
curve of the hedge. One is planted with tall Stout cultivars; the other is devoted
to Stout Medal winners. A smaller bed in the center of the garden contains
species daylilies, such as Jane's night-blooming *Hemerocallis citrina* and the
good old roadside *H. fulva;* my *H. Dumortierii;* and old-fashioned, scented *H.
lilioasphodelus,* the lemon lily. In another pair of beds, the fair *H. fulva* 'Rosa-
lind' disports with my 'Autumn Minaret,' and across the road from the display
garden, a great sweep of a lovely rose-red cultivar not of Stout's breeding—
'Enchained Heart'—draws the visitor's eye.

After a personally conducted tour of the Stout Daylily Garden, I
was awed no less by my companion's modesty than by his knowledge and
dedication. "I'm just a gardener," he said. "I don't pretend to be anything else.
But studying horticulture at a botanical garden is a good way to be educated.

You are taught to look at things in a different way because one of the priorities of an institution like this is scientific investigation. When people talk about horticulture as the marriage between science and art, it's really brought home to you here. On the one hand, you want to please the public and have an attractive display, but on the other hand, you want it to have some kind of educational value, too."

For my money, the Stout Garden fulfills its educational and its aesthetic role. As for Greg, he has given me food for thought and valuable information about the history, culture, and morphology of daylilies. We have exchanged plants and visits, and we have shared enthusiasms: He loves "spiders" and I love six-footers; we both love the minis and the late bloomers. One of the best things about gardening is the garden friendships that cross lines of age and other prejudicial barriers. Much of my pleasure, I owe to daylilies—and to my daylily friends of all ages.

The Key:
Relationships

THE KEY TO MY GARDEN LAY HIDDEN AMONG THE rocks on the quarter-acre hillside above the pool. Naturally, I hit upon it quite by accident. It sounds too grand to describe the sketchy operation that preceded moving the perennials from the lawn to the hillside as "site preparation," but while I was thus engaged, the light dawned. There were, of course, rocks everywhere. Those that could be gouged out with a crowbar came out. But what to do with them? The answer seems obvious now—build a low retaining wall to support the slope, thereby saving the labor of hauling the rocks away and at the same time reducing the steep angle of the flower bed. So I began arranging them at the foot of the slope. The retaining wall proved successful beyond my expectations.

Although its lines and location bore very little relation to the straight lines and boxlike presence of the garage—its point of origin—a pleasing outline began to emerge as the wall traced the edge of the slope. Hugging the foot of the hillside, it looked as if it belonged there. In fact, I was so well pleased with the effect that, in a burst of enthusiasm, I completed a thirty-foot section during the first summer. A mason would blanch to hear the row of earthy boulders referred to as a wall. Arranged in one or two courses along the edge of the garden and reaching less than two feet at its highest point, it was more serviceable than beautiful. But it definitely did kill two birds with one stone, if you'll pardon the pun, and its appearance improved with age. As I became more skillful, I rebuilt the worst sections.

Another important consequence of my wall-building was a growing entente cordiale with the rocks themselves. I was already resigned to the exposed outcrops. In the days before string trimmers, they were a curse to clip around by hand but I was beginning to actually admire the more impressive slabs jutting boldly out of the lawn. However, in the perennial border when the tines of the fork rang out against the backbone of Connecticut, my heart still sank.

It took a visiting Scot to reconcile me to the inevitable. A keen gardener herself and not loath to point out my failings, this good lady demanded to know why on earth I kept battling the bedrock. Instead, why didn't I put another rock on top of the submerged ledge and be done with it? That way I wouldn't forget its whereabouts and make the mistake of trying to plant over it. Import a rock? Actually *add* one to the garden that I'd spent the entire summer trying to render rock-free? I was aghast at the idea. But my Scottish visitor was adamant. "This one will do." She selected a large specimen shaped like a miniature cliff and we shoved it into place. "There," she said briskly, brushing the dirt from her hands. "That's better." And of course, it was.

Accepting the presence of one visible rock in the flower bed led to incorporating others. Instead of changing the lines of the border to avoid an outcrop, I included it in the scheme of things by swinging the bed around it. Thus, I tumbled to at least one way to create order: reducing the number of unrelated elements in the landscape. Instead of two or three isolated rock outcrops and a flower bed, there was now a single unit—the flower bed—which could embrace as many rocks as necessary. Similar treatment is a way of achieving unity. The rocks—no longer self-governing entities—were under control within the clearly defined limits of the border. A flower bed complete with plants and rocks makes one harmonious statement—instead of a dissonant chorus of vegetable and mineral voices.

Later, I would apply this simple method of organizing the landscape to the entire east-facing slope. As we gradually tore away the mantle of brush, revealing the outcrops, uncovering the foundations of the two little outbuildings, and clearing around the base of the maples, I began making small isolated beds around each thing—foundation, tree, or rock—knowing that in due course I would link them together in a system of long, narrow, interconnecting beds. The technique I employed was to clear a little and immediately plant what had been opened up. Clear and plant; clear and plant. I planted rhododendrons because I had fallen in love with them in England. The dry slope wasn't the best place for them and there was more shade than they like but we took down one maple and removed the lower limbs of the others. I added a lot of peat moss to the planting holes and mulched heavily with wood chips. The chips served a dual purpose—they conserved moisture in the soil and kept down the weeds while forming a uniform ground cover.

I also planted a lot of hosta and native ferns with and among the rhododendrons, around the rocks, and under the maples. Repeating the same species in each tier of planting proved another method of unifying the disparate elements. To be sure, it didn't always work. The top tier of planting did not thrive. The situation was too dry for the ferns and hosta, which had to be rescued. Instead, a wreath of euonymous now gathers in the rock outcrops at the base of two maples in the uppermost corner of the garden.

As time and energy would allow, I joined the individual beds into long continuous strips that took in outcrops, trees, rhododendrons, and ground-covering plants—with a heavy emphasis on hostas, ferns, and epimediums. The lines of these parallel beds were arrived at by letting the slope have its way and following its dictates. Where the incline was steep, I made low retaining walls similar to the one supporting the perennial border—which increased in length every passing year. The repetition of low walls helped to establish continuity, relating the upper and lower layers of planting to the perennial border. In treating the whole slope as a single unit—made up of ribbons of plants among the rocks and trees separated by ribbons of grass path—a sense of rhythm and order gradually replaced the chaotic wilderness.

The hillside has been under development for twenty years and is still a work-in-progress. There still are abrupt changes in grade that cry out for stone work; I continue to tinker with the lines of the beds and paths, trying to make them more fluid in their movement back and forth across the slope. Meanwhile, the rhododendrons have become huge shrubs—partially concealing one tier of planting from another—inadvertently adding excitement to glimpses of the garden and the perennial border below as one traverses the paths. I've thrown in a few deciduous shrubs: yellow-flowering witch hazels *(Hamamelis mollis)* for their spidery flowers that unfurl before the snow has melted; a silverbell tree *(Halesia carolina)* in the uppermost tier so that you can walk under it and look up into the campanulate blossoms; clumps of daylilies here and there, because I can't resist them; and masses of foxgloves and columbine, which self-sow everywhere and are welcome wherever they turn up.

Our property still has all sorts of ragged, unfinished corners; there are dead ends and a few downright eyesores, like the none-too-well-hidden compost piles. But the east-facing slope is a success. Without heavy equipment or outside help and without incurring the national debt, we eventually transformed a quarter of an acre of confusion into shady walks punctuated by splashes of color and views of a perennial border that blooms a good part of the growing season. I am sure now that the key to a pleasing landscape lies in relationships—in finding ways of connecting one thing with another. And it is my belief that each garden possesses its own key—a key that unlocks the secret of that particular piece of land.

In a really flowing, beautifully designed garden—as I was soon to discover from exposure to the Gills' garden—relationships between all the elements seem easy and inevitable. In their garden, the plantings incorporated trees, shrubs, and a richly varied collection of herbaceous plants. These were linked by lawns and paths—all of which fit gracefully within the boundaries of the property. Every path led somewhere or served to connect different parts of the garden in a smooth, continuous pattern. There weren't any dead ends; transitions seemed to glide easily one into another; even the storage area was incorporated in such a way that it was a decorative part of the whole. From the Gills' garden, I began to learn something about design. And from the Gills themselves, I learned a great deal of what I know about gardening.

The Gills

WHEN HELEN GILL DIED A FEW YEARS AGO AT THE AGE
of ninety-three, there was a brief obituary in the local paper. The
only survivors mentioned were a brother and two nieces. But
survivors from her garden must number in the thousands. She left a legacy of
plants in gardens up and down the East Coast of the United States and as far
away as Greece and France. In my own garden, there isn't a square foot that
doesn't remind me of Helen. She was the single most influential person in my
gardening life and the garden that she made with her husband, Johnny, is the
benchmark against which I measure all other gardens.

My admiration would come as a complete surprise to Helen—not
because I failed to express it while she was alive but because she never believed
compliments, expressed or implied. She didn't even believe Johnny the first
time he proposed to her. "I thought he was joking," she said, smiling that
strange little archaic smile behind which she always hid her real feelings. "He
had to start all over again," she added with some satisfaction. When I told her
not long before she died that I would like to write about her and the garden,
her reaction was typical. "Me? I can't think what you want to write about me
for."

She had a down-East, down-to-earth, deadpan style of delivery
that tickled her friends, but it masked a deeply felt insecurity. Her sister-in-law,
who knew her for fifty years—and better than most people—said that marrying
into the volatile, gregarious Gill family had not been altogether easy for her.
"No one ever gave her an opportunity to talk about herself and it was only by
asking questions and expressing an interest in her that I ever gained her
confidence. She was the shy, silent type. She left the making of friends to John."

John Gill was as bouncy and ebullient as Helen was diffident and reserved. North Carolina born, he was a southern gentleman of the old school and loaded with charm. When we knew him, he was already suffering from a slight physical disability which resulted in a permanent crick in his neck. But instead of suggesting infirmity, the cocked head and lively dark eyes gave him the air of a very bright, interested bird. In some ways, he reminded me of my father, though he was considerably shorter than Dad. They were both jaunty, self-confident little men who favored snappy sports jackets and took pride in their appearance.

Helen was small, too—barely five feet tall. She always made me think of a little wooden figure of Mrs. Noah—quite solid from the waist down and attached to a round flat disc. Instead of bending her knees when she gardened, she seemed to fold in half as if she was hinged in the middle. Her uniform was an absolutely plain dress of a solid color in either linen or wool—depending on the season—with a jewel neckline and short sleeves. She had a yellow one in which she resembled an Easter egg and a turquoise one that made her eyes look as blue as chips of sapphire. Her cheeks were bright pink and her hair was white and extremely fine. It is hard to imagine that her mother could possibly have thought her an ugly child but apparently she did—and told her so.

As different as they were in temperament, the Gills agreed on most things and a telephone call—with Helen on the upstairs phone and Johnny on the library extension—was exactly like talking to one person. They finished each other's sentences without missing a beat or interrupting the flow of conversation. And in the garden, they complemented each other perfectly. In the Nicholson–Sackville-West tradition, he was the planner and she was the planter.

While the gardening team of Harold Nicholson and his wife, writer Vita Sackville-West, was transforming derelict Sissinghurst castle into one of the most famous gardens in England, Helen—soon to be joined by Johnny—was hard at work on an equally neglected property in New England.

In 1930, Helen's father—a wealthy shoe manufacturer from Lynn, Massachusetts, and a recent widower—bought the seventy-three acres in New-town complete with a fine old eighteenth century house for $10,000. Of course, the house had no electricity, running water, or heat. It had been occupied by Hungarian farmers who were still slaughtering cattle in the room that we knew as a formal dining room with white wainscoting and pale yellow wallpaper, antique furniture and wall-to-wall Canton china. Although the condition of the house was primitive at the time of the sale, the surrounding fields were still under cultivation and had not, therefore, reverted to forest. As soon as the house was livable, Helen, her father, and her unmarried brother moved in and she began to garden.

The site was relatively level and enclosed on three sides by stone walls. Helen did the obvious thing. She dug beds along the walls—borders eight to ten feet wide with straight lines and no nonsense. At the back of the beds, she began planting all sorts of trees and shrubs. She used to tell a story about a large order of woody plants that had been scheduled to arrive midweek. As

she was still working in New York and could only be in Connecticut on weekends, she had arranged to have a neighboring farmer pick up the order with his
truck. Imagining substantial plants with large root balls, she had already prepared enormous planting holes. But when she arrived on Friday night, she was
chagrined to find instead a bundle of twigs displaying a note from the farmer:
"Here are your trees!"

Helen—then Davis—met her future husband through Margaret
Merwin, her friend and business partner in the firm of Merwin-Davis, Statistical
Analysts. Margaret had a sister with a country home in Connecticut. Johnny was
a frequent visitor, and introductions were duly effected between the weekend
neighbors. After that he used to spend a lot of time working in the garden at
the Davis house. According to his sister-in-law, it was a family joke that John
married Helen because "he just couldn't bear for anyone else to get the credit
for all that yard work!" The wedding took place at the Episcopal church in
Newtown on an unseasonably warm day in May 1939. At the reception that
followed, the roving photographer broke Helen's most treasured Staffordshire
figurine, her brother came down with appendicitis, and the refrigerator failed.
The strawberry ice cream intended for the wedding feast melted. But the
marriage endured for more than forty years and resulted in the creation of a
memorable garden.

An architect by profession, Johnny brought to their joint enterprise a sense of form, structure, and balance. He laid out the deep, curving
borders that were the garden's crowning glory. Helen filled them with a cornu-
copia of shrubs, herbaceous perennials, and bulbs—mingling the rare with the
common, the new with the old-fashioned, the native with the exotic. In its
prime, it was the most original and most beautiful garden I have ever seen—a
Yankee Sissinghurst with a southern accent.

Although Helen has only been dead for three years, the garden has
virtually disappeared. On a recent midwinter day, I drove over to the house to
have a last look before the new owners took up residence. A garage and a
chain-link dog run occupied one of the great side borders. Old age and three
years of neglect had taken their toll of the trees and many had already been
cut down; most of the huge deciduous shrubs were also beyond repair and
would soon, no doubt, meet a similar fate. The winter sun had had its way with
the English boxwoods—or what was left of them. In the flower beds, dried
morning glory vines encased the few remaining perennials in brittle nets. But
the lines of the old garden—half hidden under long grasses—bore witness still
to Johnny's talent as a designer.

I had forgotten how large the garden was. Toward the end of
Helen's life, it had become so overgrown that one lost a proper sense of scale
and I don't remember ever walking around it in the winter. For the first time,
I was able to appreciate its full extent—two or three acres under intense
cultivation—and the complexity and subtlety of the design. In the old days, a
reach of lawn stretched from wall to wall across the breadth of the garden with
openings marked by sentinel shrubs—columns of trimmed box and yew. From

a central opening, fieldstone steps led up to a broad path cutting through an apple orchard and stretching uphill to the edge of the woods. Helen told me that years ago, she and Johnny had been friendly with their neighbors at the top and the path had continued on through the woods to their house.

Within the garden, a matched pair of curving borders thirty feet wide and more than a hundred feet long flanked the entrance into the orchard. At opposite ends of the main lawn, a rock outcrop planted with evergreens faced a deep semi-circular bed of shrubs and perennials—the physical bulk of the informal rock garden balanced by the stature of the shrubs and the generous size of the crescent-shaped bed. The rest of the garden was organized into pleasing open spaces and hidden surprises: an enclosed round garden edged with silver lamb's ears and devoted entirely to plants with white flowers; a tiny flagstone terrace with a white balustrade overlooking the round garden. An opening between two huge yews at one end of the round garden led to an allée of lilacs. The collection of lilacs—mostly gone now or in poor repair—included what were once the latest cultivars, with massive flower trusses in shades of purple, lavender, white, and pink.

It is twenty years since my first visit to the Gills' garden, and in today's climate of greater horticultural sophistication, many of the perennials that were new to me then would not be unfamiliar to an enthusiastic gardener now. *Amsonia tabernaemontana* with its attractive willowy foliage and powder-blue flower heads has become readily available. *Iris tectorum* straight from the brushes of a Japanese artist—pale lavender falls streaked and stippled in deep maroon—is listed in several catalogs. Airy thalictrums of which Helen was very fond are better known now than they used to be and species of snakeroot other than the native *Cimicifuga racemosa* are making their appearance in the more adventurous lists. But Helen had been growing a variety of snakeroots for years. She had fall-flowering *C. simplex* and an unusual European species with large broad leaves rather like maple leaves. It flowers later than *C. racemosa* and has stiffer, more upright wands of seed-pearl buds that open into narrow white flower spikes. She grew the native white veronica *(Veronica virginica, also called Veronicastrum virginicum),* Carolina Lupin *(Thermopsis caroliniana),* False Indigo *(Baptisia australis),* Golden Star *(Chrysogonum virginianum),* and other native American plants long before the rush to include wildflowers in the perennial garden. And if anything had a white form, it was in her garden.

The sheer number and variety of perennials that she grew was staggering, but in addition there were the flowering trees and shrubs. Beginning in mid-May, the parade of bloom was nonstop for a month: first, the early flowering *Viburnum Carlesii* with clusters of deep pink buds that open into perfumed snowballs of bloom; then, sheets of dogwood underplanted with white-flowering *Kerria japonica* and white azaleas; followed by the fringe tree's *(Chionanthus virginicus)* trembling masses of shredded white flowers that smell of honey; giant beauty bushes *(Kolkwitzia amabilis)* covered with dainty pale pink flowers; white *Deutzia gracilis;* a bower of Carolina silverbell *(Halesia carolina);* and my personal favorite of all flowering shrubs, *Exochorda x macrantha* 'The Bride,' which I have still not seen in any garden except Helen's—and my own.

One fall, Helen—then in her seventies—got carried away and ordered a thousand white lily-flowered tulips. Somehow, she managed to get them planted. I can see her now—pink in the face with the exertion of having to fold her solid little wooden body in half a thousand times. The next spring, she and Johnny gave a party in May. The garden was a sight. White flowers everywhere—overhead and all around us. And for once the rodents must have spared every tulip, because the vast sweeping borders were full of them—uniform stands of elegant white vase-shaped blossoms among drifts of wood hyacinths and early-flowering perennials.

The Gills were a presence in our lives until they died. And plants from their garden poured into ours. After the first visit, I came home laden with flats and pots and cardboard boxes. Helen always did the digging. At the slightest excuse, she would stump off to the tool shed for a trowel—or worse still, a shovel. One of her earliest contributions to our garden was a huge shovelful of *Chrysogonum virginianum,* which quickly became—and still is—one of my favorite small plants. It has a fabulously long blooming season in the spring, more five-petaled golden daisies appear on and off all summer, and finally, in a last winter-defying gesture, it throws a few more flowers in November. Years later, Helen lost her chrysogonum during a drought. Fortunately, I was able to replace the missing plants with divisions of those she had given me. But I was always afraid to admire anything in her garden for fear it would send her trundling out to the shed to fetch her digging implements.

Another time, she gave me clumps of giant, early-blooming snowdrops *(Galanthus elwesii)* with flowers three times the size of the common snowdrop *(G. nivalis).* The buds are like tiny perfect snow-white eggs. And when they open, the three large outer segments spread apart, revealing a little underskirt patterned with a green hourglass. I have an interesting and unusual clematis *(Clematis integrifolia)* from Helen. It grows into a floppy bush two feet high covered with small dark-blue bells that are produced over a long period of time. And my garden is edged with her lamb's ears *(Stachys byzantina)*—so are gardens all up and down the road. Our neighbors took their lamb's ears with them when they moved to Long Island, where no doubt they will eventually pass divisions on to neighbors there. I have Memorial daisies all along the perennial border. Helen got the original plants from an aunt who lived in Maine. No one seems to know the species but I am especially attached to them. The flowers are like oversized field daisies with laundered white rays surrounding large flat yellow discs. The list is endless: white sidalcea and blue geraniums, nepetas and foxgloves—she only grew white ones—columbines, amsonia, and several species of iris.

The plant I treasure most is *Iris lactea.* It was known to Helen as *I. ensata,* a name now assigned to those luscious beauties from Japan—formerly *I. kaempferi*—with the huge flat flowers perched on tall stems. *I. lactea* has the most unusual and attractive foliage and habit of growth. Because the narrow steel-blue leaves are held stiffly away from the center, a clump looks more like an ornamental grass than an iris. The small, refined flowers—lavender-blue and lightly penciled in a darker shade—appear among the leaves. The flower stems are only half the height of the leaves but the plant's open habit permits a good view of the blossoms, which seem to dart in and out among the thin spears of foliage.

When I met the Gills, I had been gardening for nearly ten years in a sort of horticultural vacuum. I wasn't familiar with botanical nomenclature, and if I needed information, I consulted *The New Illustrated Encyclopedia of Gardening.* I didn't read much about gardening or even talk much about it because I didn't know any other gardeners, and nongardeners soon begin to look glazed if you go on and on about plants. The Gills changed all that. What a pleasure to find, not just like-minded friends, but friends who knew so much and were eager to share *everything*—their plants, their expertise, and their books—I had never heard of Sissinghurst and Vita Sackville-West or Gertrude Jekyll or even home-grown gardeners such as Louise Beebe Wilder and Elizabeth Lawrence. I was soon treating the Gills' bookshelves like the public library.

They shared their gardening friends as well, and we were invited to tea with Ruth Stout—matriarch of mulch—whose garden was her compost pile. Helen would have no truck with garbage in *her* garden. She held out against using mulch of any sort—she liked the look of the open soil—but she and Ms. Stout had been friends for years and had much in common. At the time we met her, Ms. Stout was in her nineties and still spreading the word to receptive audiences all over the state. Her book *How to Have a Green Thumb without an Aching Back* has been through umpteen printings and is still making converts—of whom I am one.

During the early years of our friendship with Helen and Johnny, it was a source of frustration to me that there was nothing in our garden that they didn't already have, so there was never anything we could give them. It was therefore with great delight that I came across a book which I was sure they would enjoy. A teaching colleague had given me a copy of *The Country Garden* by Josephine Nuese soon after it was published in 1970. To this day, it is my favorite garden book. It's a useful, intelligent, generous book—unpretentious, down-to-earth, and appealing. It makes you want to go straight outside and grab a spade. In the book, she talks about plants and plant people, garden books and garden design. Her advice is clear, smart, and eminently worth following because she is funny, thoughtful, wise, and honest. In writing about her own garden, she tells about her successes, which appear to surprise her, and about her failures, which don't—but which amuse her. She is a gardener whom you want to know—and whom I was fortunate enough to meet.

I gave the Gills a copy of *The Country Garden.* It set in motion a correspondence with the author and led to an instant, deeply satisfying mutual friendship that ended a tragically short time later with the death of Josephine Nuese from leukemia. Naturally, it was the convivial, outgoing Johnny who wrote the first letter. I have the reply and three others carefully preserved in the Gills' copy of *The Country Garden*—the one I gave them so many years ago. When Helen died, her sister-in-law was kind enough to let me have the book and the correspondence. Helen had numbered and dated the letters.

In the first letter—after thanking Johnny for his enthusiastic response to her book—Mrs. Nuese wrote:

> I should indeed love to see your garden which is "at moments quite nice"
> (!)—I appreciate the understatement (the mark of a true gardener) and can
> imagine how lovely the "quite nice" must be as, being an architect, your
> first consideration would have been line and form and proportion—so much
> more important than flowers. I only wish I had realized this 40 years ago.

On the strength of a meeting and a visit to the Gills' garden, they were on first-name terms. "Dear Helen and Johnny," she wrote afterward:

> I fell in love with you both—your gentleness and kindness (to me the most
> important qualities in any human being), your enormous knowledge of gar-
> dening and your modesty about same. I feel that you should have written
> *The Country Garden,* not me, because you have done so much more with
> your property than I have with mine—and with so much more subtlety and
> originality. Yours is a garden to long remember.

She ended the letter with my own sentiments about Helen and Johnny—and about herself. "Thank you so much, my dears. . . . I feel the richer for having met the Gills and seen their garden."

Tim

DURING THE EARLY SEVENTIES, I WASN'T THE ONLY one removing truckloads of plants from the Gills' garden. Helen and Johnny made frequent reference to Jim's visits. "Jim was over here dividing hostas the other day," they would say. Or Johnny would tell Helen to "wait until Jim comes to dig up that big clump of Siberian iris." As we knew a friend of theirs whose name was Jim, I assumed that he was the digger and the divider, though I was rather surprised. It struck me that his wife was the gardener of the family. In any case, I thought no more about it until we met Jim York at a party.

It has always been my contention that parties are not the place to meet people and that very few friendships ever result from encounters at such gatherings. Parties tend to be artificial environments in which the guests are trying too hard either to be polite or to be entertaining or simply to hear what the other person is saying. But I was wrong about the party at which we met Jim and Michael. At first it seemed no different from other similar occasions. There were quite a few people, as I recall, and by the time Martin and I arrived, the revels were in full swing. Our hostess took us under her wing because we didn't know many of the other guests.

It was therefore with considerable astonishment—and some alarm—that I found myself an object of hilarity and mirth to a perfectly strange man. About my own age, over six feet tall, and weighing in the neighborhood of two hundred pounds, the stranger threw back his head and guffawed when he heard my name. He laughed so long and so hard that he wheezed and wept. He produced a colored bandanna from his pocket and mopped his streaming eyes. "Helen's told me about you," he said when he had recovered enough to get out a few words, "and from what she said, I thought you were a funny little old lady in sneakers!" "Well, that's all right," I replied, "because I thought you were somebody else, too!" We both laughed. Then this giant bent down, placed a noisy kiss on my cheek, and enveloped me in a bear hug. Needless to say, I thought I had never met anyone so warm and affectionate. Moments later, we were joined by Michael, a cherubic figure with a flushed countenence who wanted to know how Martin got "that phony English accent." Whereupon my spouse delivered one of those understated British one-liners. And we all became friends.

Johnny Gill had designed a house for Jim—at least, he had been allowed to *assist* Jim in the design of a compact, elegant contemporary perched on the crest of a rocky hill. Simple and boxlike on the outside, it has an inside wall of glass that overlooks distant blue hills to the west, and below, a remarkable garden. It was a wonderful house for entertaining, and for years people came in droves to admire the garden and to savor the exquisite food provided by this generous pair. At that time, Jim and Michael were both working in New York and only came to the country on weekends. Jim was the gardener. Michael did the cooking—and what cooking! A stockbroker by trade but a chef at heart, he spent every waking moment in the kitchen. Dressed in old slacks and a red sweatshirt that proclaimed him a Boy Wonder, he padded across the tiled floor in his socks, from refrigerator to counter to stove, turning out pies as beautiful as Della Robbia ware and the most delicious desserts I've ever tasted.

Meanwhile, Jim single-handedly turned a rugged, untamed hillside into a unique rock garden. Neither an attempt to simulate a mountainous environment nor a naturalistic treatment of the existing landscape, the garden is a composition of natural elements handled in a stylized manner: a native gray birch tree pruned to create a desired pattern; local stone rearranged to expedite traffic through the garden or to enhance a certain shrub; evergreens purposefully clipped and groomed to add line or bulk to an abstract design. The effect is formal because no shape or volume or outline has been left to chance but informal because the underlying structure of the landscape has been respected.

Jim is one of those rare gardeners with a built-in sense of design. Before he lifted a rock, he had a picture in his mind. The hillside fans out below the house. On one side, a little stream descends rapidly between huge boulders to a rustic bridge made of two enormous flat stones. A level cow path skirting the foot of the hill has been widened into a broad band of lawn which describes the contours of the steep slope. Between it and the house lies the rock garden spread out athwart the hillside. I remember it as a wilderness of weeds and rocks and scrubby trees and Jim—filthy, dripping with sweat, and clad in earth-covered shorts and an undershirt—laboring weekend after weekend. Even as I watched the garden develop, I couldn't believe my eyes. But he saw it all along—the design, the forms of pruned shrubs, the arrangement of the rocks.

He called it "a visual"—this preconceived picture. "I knew how I wanted the whole thing to be," he said. "I saw this wonderful staircase that ran down from the house to meet the cow path. I felt it was important to maintain that path and follow it down to the brook and the stone bridge. Then, the whole central area between the staircase and the brook became this enormous natural rock garden—the rocks were there. It was just a matter of working with them—clearing out among them. After that, the garden just kept evolving. I began seeing paths in it—out of necessity. Otherwise, you had to climb all through it. Then, one path led to another. In the end, it all fell into place very naturally. The design was there all the time—you just had to see it." Jim grinned and added, "Like the bear, don't you know"—referring to the story of the Maine woodcarver who saw the bear and chiseled away the rest of the wood.

Before he had a garden of his own, Jim gardened at the homes of friends on weekends. He was so good at it that one grateful hostess gave him a pair of handsome stained-glass windows as a thank-you present for cutting back her ancient and overgrown old mock orange. But the garden-making instinct was there long before the opportunity. In a Bronx, New York, backyard his father had made a garden "so jammed with stuff, you couldn't walk through it." When I asked Jim about his father's garden, he couldn't remember the plants—just that they grew in great numbers. "I suppose my interest in gardening was bred in but it was exposure to the Gills' garden that gave me something to strive for."

How Jim and I managed to miss each other at the Gills' I can't imagine! I was there frequently, filling my car with plants. So was he. Helen told him that he could have half of anything he could dig up, provided he replanted the rest. Jim—who could divide a blade of grass if he had to—wanted half of a great many things. But Helen didn't mind. It saved her a lot of strenuous work. Besides, she had a theory that every garden comes from other gardens. Established gardeners pass on plants and know-how to beginning gardeners, who in time become established themselves and carry on the tradition. The aunt in Maine—source of the Memorial daisies which still bloom in my garden—had been her mentor. Jim told me recently that "Helen used to drive up north and come back with the car loaded with stuff, so when I came along and needed plants, she felt that she was repaying her aunt—in a roundabout way."

In addition to the untold numbers of plants that she gave Jim and me, Helen offered us her own three-part formula for amending the soil—equal parts decomposed cow manure, homemade compost, and superphosphate. Neither of us know how she arrived at this combination but I have since read that soils in the Northeast tend to be deficient in phosphorus—one of the essential nutrients that affect plant health and growth. The function of phosphorus in the soil is to encourage root development and the formation of flowers, fruit, and seed. It is also thought to increase resistance to disease. Helen is the only gardener I've ever known to make much use of superphosphate.

Although we failed to coincide at the Gills' garden, Jim and I knew of each other's visits. "I remember one of Helen's lines with regard to you," he told me the other day. "I heard that you'd been up there so I asked how it had gone, and Helen said, 'Fine, except she wants to know the name of everything, including the weeds!' After that I wanted to meet you." Once we did get together, we became great buddies. It was fun having a partner in crime and we used to go off on plant-buying sprees together—each egging the other on. We also exchanged presents—partly to justify further self-indulgence. We never missed the White Flower Farm sale. Jim reminded me of a prostrate form of blue spruce we bought there years ago. "I was out in the garden recently," he recalled, "looking around at these huge shrubs and thinking how some of them ought to be moved—just to give the others room—and I got to thinking about that blue spruce. It's magnificent now and just gigantic. How could you be without it for $8.25? But do you remember how outrageous we thought that was—for a little twig?"

Jim admired my evergreen garden and so I took him to the Hammond Museum. He was as impressed as I had been. "It was one of the first formal rock gardens I'd ever seen," he said later. While we were there, he fell in love with katsura trees *(Cercidiphyllum japonicum)* and was delighted not long afterward when he received a small specimen as a membership gift from the Brooklyn Botanic Garden. He picked up another locally. That was years ago. Both are now magnificent trees. His garden is full of unusual woody plants. "I think the thing about my garden is," he said, "that there is one of everything I ever saw that was different. If it was different or new or I didn't know it, I bought it. Of course, I've had a lot of failures that way." But he's had far more successes—such as an envy-provoking specimen of the coral bark maple (*Acer palmatum* 'Senkaki'), which has stunning red twigs for a spot of winter color and leaves that turn bright yellow in the fall. We each have the curious Japanese fan-tail willow (*Salix sachalinensis* 'Sekka') with branches that end in flattened corkscrews and shepherd's crooks—a flower arranger's dream.

Jim's fan-tail willow and mine are so unalike in appearance it seems as if they might belong to different species. The reason is that his is pruned regularly and relentlessly; mine is not. I am no better at pruning than I was at seeing the bear, while Jim has a marvelous eye and is a wizard with a pair of clippers. However, he is also a headstrong pruner who yields no quarter. In his garden, plants had better shape up—or else. One day, I had occasion to be there when he was not at home. I hadn't seen the garden lately and was horrified to find that the beautiful weeping willows had obviously suffered irreparable storm damage. They had been reduced to stumps—but such tall stumps. Why hadn't they been cut to the ground? I wondered. The answer came the next day when the demon pruner called to find out how I liked his handiwork!

Years ago, Jim gave me an exquisite thread-leaf Japanese maple (*Acer palmatum* 'Crimson Queen'), which he used to insist upon "trimming" for me. In the spring, he would appear with his tools—like my father making a house call with his little black bag. Dr. Jim would walk around the poor tree, studying it through narrowed eyes and from every angle. Then he would spring at it, clippers in hand, and snip away—snip, snip, snip—until there was nothing left. My cries of anguish were in vain. Of course, I rue the day I denied him access to my tree because today his own Japanese thread-leaf maples are gorgeous and undoubtedly worth a fortune. The bare trunks zig and zag in beautiful patterns; every secondary branch contributes to the overall design—

even the tiniest twig has a purpose in the greater scheme of things. Each tree is a masterpiece. Mine, alas, looks like the nest of some large, sloppy bird.

In 1981, generous, affectionate, food-loving, life-loving Michael died of a heart attack at the age of fifty-three. Afterward, Jim lost interest in the garden. There were no more gala parties, wonderful desserts, table settings that looked like magazine covers, people milling around, and Jim conducting tours of the garden. Even now, he says, "I look at it and admire it and I'm glad I did it. But nobody sees it anymore. People don't go down into the garden. They stand up at the top. They look down and say it's beautiful. And it is. But I only maintain it now. Except the new section." My ears pricked up at that. "I've started something over by the tool shed. . . ." Nothing will convince me that Jim can hold out against his garden forever.

Patches

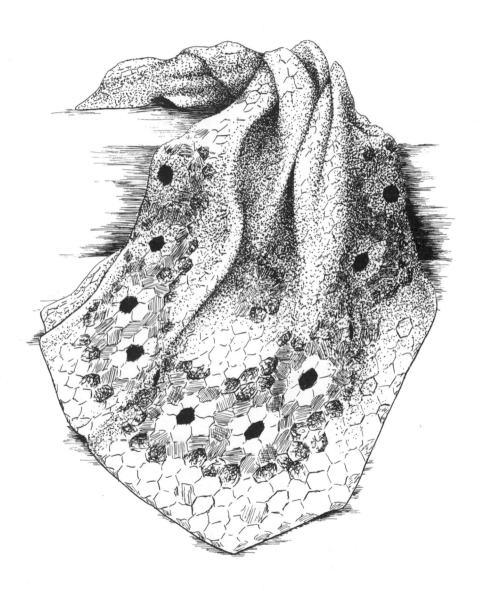

UNDOUBTEDLY, I WOULD HAVE RUN INTO JIM AT THE Gills' in due course, but what fascinates me about all our patchwork lives and gardens is the way in which the pieces come together. Until a long-ago party, the Gills touched Jim's life and our lives—but separately. When we met Jim and Michael, a new pattern emerged. What had simply been adjacent "patches" formed a new bond and extended the pattern in another direction. I took Jim to the stroll garden of the Hammond Museum, where he fell in love with katsuras. Another piece of the quilt in place—Natalie Hays Hammond's garden touching Jim's garden and touching mine. I gave the Gills *The Country Garden* but would never have met Josephine Nuese had it not been for the extroverted Johnny. Now, pussy-toes *(Antennaria rosea)* from Mrs. Nuese remind me of her—and of Helen and Johnny and contribute a pinkish furry scrap to the pattern of my quilt.

The Gills and their garden are like a sunburst in the center of the quilt; the radiating design results in many different connections. Almost all my gardening friends are linked by threads that can be traced to this central figure in the pattern. There are, of course, other independent pieces that add color and spark to the overall effect, individual plants that remind me of people who have given a fillip to our lives. Martin's entertaining, companionable sister Elisabeth—whose face is a scaled down, feminine version of his own—is represented by a little shrub—a species of genista. I've long since forgotten what species, but every spring for eighteen years it has covered its short, arching gray-green branches with small bright yellow flowers. Planted against the shoulder of a rock outcrop in the lawn, the little broom dropped seeds in a crevice. Now, an offspring of the original plant trails over the face of the rock. Elisabeth, a keen gardener herself, met the Gills and visited their garden. And after her return to England, she continued to ask about them whenever she wrote.

My pretty, talented neighbor Lori, another avid gardener, gave me the most beautiful peony in the garden—an early-blooming hybrid called 'Burma Ruby.' Living up to its exotic name, the great round buds—a single one to a stem—split open at the end of May and release incredible silken petals of an incandescent red. From the same source came *Hamamelis mollis,* the Chinese witch hazel. It has become a small, multitrunked tree which blooms as early as February during a warm spell. The strange little blossoms emerge from small clusters of knobby brown calyxes. Consisting of four thin streamers of yellow, the petals literally unroll—like party favors. The scent is as refreshing as cologne—flowery and bracing—unlike the scent of warm-weather flowers, which always seems to have the velvety heaviness of perfume. Lori and her husband were friends of the Gills, too. Although she has since moved away, lamb's ears from Helen went with Lori to a new garden and her many contributions to mine keep her close to my heart.

Plants of *Geranium sanguineum var. striatum,* a low-growing crane's bill with pale pink flowers delicately veined in red, were the gift of a strange, intense woman whom I knew briefly and not well. She had a passion for gardening and both she and her contractor husband were frustrated artists. Their home was called Spice Hill. Around the contemporary house sheathed in barnsiding, she had made a charming, quirky cottage garden. I took Jim there once. Most of Marie Luise's plants were grown for their fragrance: masses of dianthus for the tingling scent of cloves; rugosa roses for their warm, gentle summery smell; and a huge fringe tree—like Helen's—which produced a shimmering, honey-scented cloud of blossom in early June. Through Marie Luise, I was introduced to the original, opinionated Carl Deame, then the superintendent of Mrs. Bruce Crane's Sugar Hill Nursery in Dalton, Massachusetts.

Deame really was an artist. He took weathered rocks, old tree trunks, and stumps from the Berkshire hills and planted them with a variety of sedums and sempervivums. In his mature creations, offsets of the sempervivums filled every crack and cranny—until there wasn't any more room, and then they began to mound up on one another. Finally, the receptacle together with its contents became a living sculpture. I had never seen anything like these small, intricate, and ever-changing three-dimensional works in stone, wood, and plant material. They caught light and trapped shadows in a way that changed their appearance from different angles. Deame pointed out that they also changed from season to season: light greens deepening; reds and purples—bright in the spring—turning somber in the winter. And from year to year new rosettes forming in, around, and among the sedums. I became entranced with the idea of growing sculpture—and with sempervivums. I still have many of the ones that came from Mrs. Crane's nursery twenty years ago and I fully expect they'll live forever—as their Latin name suggests: *semper* meaning always and *vivus,* alive.

Few plants in my garden have been admired as much as a tall sunflower with three-inch-wide chrome-yellow flowers that resemble starry, single dahlias. The plants—which spread by underground runners but not lethal ones—grow six feet in height. And the tall stems are clad in handsome, gray-green leaves that have a suedelike texture. The foliage is one of the plant's great charms. Another is that the flowers last well in water. I have not seen *Helianthus mollis* in any garden, except Lori's and mine. The donor is a mutual acquaintance—a weekend gardener from New York who tends his property meticulously, growing stands of these sunflowers around the rocks in his lawn. He has kindly added a green and yellow piece to my quilt.

A glorious patch of rose-pink came from a well-known hybridizer of rhododendrons in the sixties. As a very beginning gardener, I ordered ten rhododendrons from his nursery in New York state. When the plants arrived—large, bushy, and most beautifully packed in individual boxes—there were three more than I had paid for. I wrote immediately to report the error and received a charming note from the totally unknown Mr. Warren Baldsiefen. He said that he was in the process of moving his nursery and declined to "sharpen a point too fine" with respect to the additional plants. Rhododendron *Roseum Elegans* is now ten feet high and as much or more across. I still treasure one of Mr. Baldsiefen's old catalogs and think of him with gratitude.

When my mother died twelve years ago, a beloved friend said, "I want to give you a tree in memory of your mother." I chose and planted a lovely weeping Japanese cherry (*Prunus subhirtella* 'Pendula'). In May—if the winter has not been too severe—it turns into a shower of fragile pink blossoms. I think of my mother. I am also reminded of Nell, who gave it to me—and who died last fall at the age of ninety-five. She knew Helen and Johnny and had visited the Gills' garden many, many years ago as a friend of their neighbors—the people at the top of the hill. In the spring, I shall plant a tree in memory of Nell—a fragrant snowbell *(Styrax obassia),* which produces drooping clusters of sweetly scented white flowers, or perhaps Ben Franklin's tree, *Franklinia alatamaha,* that has exquisite white fall flowers with cupped petals. For Nell, it must be a rare, beautiful, long-lived tree.

My English cousin is part of my patchwork garden. He recently sent me *V. Sackville-West's Garden Book* with this note: "Huh! How far would V. Sackville-West have got if she'd had to dig out Connecticut rocks!" He labored long and hard in our garden when he was a droll, ginger-haired twenty-one-year-old. The youngest son of my mother's youngest sister, Neil came to America to teach. Fresh from Cambridge University himself and none too sanguine about the prospect, he found himself at a boys' boarding school in a remote corner of New York state. For transportation, he bought an old wreck of a car which he named "Wellington." In fairly short order and to the consternation of his employers, he managed to drive Wellington off a cliff. Unhurt but with his car—and his credibility—damaged beyond repair, he opted to stay with us for a while and undertake manual labor. I can't think what I would have done without him.

Patty

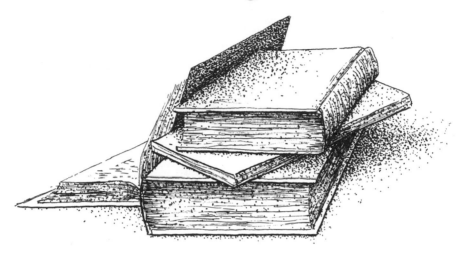

IT IS HARD TO KNOW WHETHER PATTY, HER MOTHER, and Granny B constitute a patch or a theme in my quilt. Plants, memories, and the sweat of Patty's brow are all part of my garden. Granny B, who had been a presence in my life during my childhood, became a presence in my garden in the early sixties. At that time, her house was on the market and Patty brought me a beautiful English boxwood, announcing matter-of-factly that I'd better have it because the garden would probably go to wrack and ruin anyway. Sheltered from the winter sun by the L of our house, the boxwood has prospered. Now four feet tall and five feet across, its tiny, dark green leaves form a dense globe—perfectly shaped. I shear it once a year and think of Granny B as I do so.

The boxwood is the only aristocratic, formal plant in my garden—a suitable reminder of Patty's grandmother. The word *aristocratic* comes from two Greek words—one of which means "best" and the other, "power." Granny B was "the best." And in our young lives, powerful. A tall, elegant woman with magnificent bone structure—high cheekbones and a strong jaw—she carried herself like a queen. I could feel my own spine stiffen and my chin come up the second she stepped into a room. Not that she was a frightening person; she was warm, wise, and tolerant. But she commanded respect and, from children, obedience. As children, Patty and I lived in each other's pockets, so I came to know and love her family.

She and her mother lived in an apartment above Granny B's garage. And in those days, my father used to drive Patty and me to school. On short school days, I came back to lunch with Patty, and on Fridays, we both went to dancing school. We were an awkward pair in our party dresses. I was short, round, and shy. Patty was tall for her age and already had Granny B's bony, well-constructed face—the kind that lasts for a lifetime but isn't appreciated by a twelve-year-old who wants a snub nose and freckles. Not that Patty had such frivolous aspirations. She was far too sensible. I have always felt that the attraction of opposites must account for our long friendship.

Until she had a garden of her own, not a year went by that Patty didn't work in ours. My old notebooks are full of references to her working visits: "Patty dug potatoes and froze beans." "Patty edged and weeded the perennial border today." "Patty and I raked leaves all afternoon." She even succeeded in organizing relays of luncheon guests to work in the garden: "Patty was here this weekend and we also had people to Sunday lunch. Afterward, at her instigation, we all excavated two huge rocks from the lower lawn." As for the plants that she has given me, I don't know where to begin.

From the Catskill Mountains where she and her husband had a fishing cottage came marsh marigolds *(Caltha palustris),* foam flower *(Tiarella cordifolia),* tall white meadow rue *(Thalictrum polygamum),* yellow perennial foxgloves *(Digitalis grandiflora)* and the exquisite little oak fern *(Gymnocarpium dryopteris)* with dark wiry stems about eight inches tall and delicate lacy triangular fronds. She also gave me wood sorrel *(Oxalis montana),* which has pretty shamrock foliage and pale pink flowers marked with red veins. I loved it but the feeling was not mutual—it wouldn't grow in our woods.

Many of the most unusual plants in the garden came to me either as generous gifts from Patty or from a fascinating and, alas, short-lived nursery which she discovered. The nursery, run by an elusive young woman called Virginia, proved a gold mine of hard-to-come-by English cultivars. "I'm sorry you didn't meet Virginia," Patty said after the demise of this precarious operation. "She was a very private person and never talked about herself, except little snippets here and there, but I know she spent time in England. And she would have been a very interesting lady for you to know." Although I never had the opportunity, I have wonderful plants from the now defunct nursery. One is the superlative *Artemisia* 'Powis Castle,' which in a single year became a symmetrical mound eighteen inches high and three feet across of soft, feathery gray foliage. Despite a summer of nonstop heat and humidity, this gorgeous plant looked pristine and perfect all season. Huge mops of *Nepeta* 'Six Hills Giant' also came from the mysterious Virginia. Catmints have always been a favorite in my garden and these new ones are three times the size and stature of the other forms.

Patty indulged my daylily habit with gifts from her own garden: pearly 'Tone Poem' and the almost white 'Astolat.' Both came with exhaustive notes about height, habit, and size of bloom, heritage and family history, the hybridizer responsible for their creation, and the date of their introduction. In addition, there were Patty's observations, such as "Astolat looks white at a distance—unlike the yellowish ones, which don't." A positive, thorough, dedicated, and determined gardener herself, she believes in knowing everything there is to know about a plant and would be shocked by the gaps in my horticultural education. Even as a child, she was a conscientious, able student with a well-developed sense of responsibility. And she used to bully me into doing my schoolwork.

Although Patty's garden-making postdates mine by more than a dozen years, her gardening career began at a tender age under Granny B's tutelage. She had a gardener "but Granny thought Fred didn't know the weeds from the flowers," Patty recalled recently. "She taught me to do the weeding and other things, too. I can remember being given specific tasks. She would say things like, 'Now, you are going to take every single dead flower off of this plant, one by one, and then you're going to move on to that one and you're going to cut it down just to here.' So little by little, I learned to deal with most of the plants that were in the garden." I had rather forgotten what the garden looked like, but as Patty described it, it all came back to me.

"Remember at the old house, there were those arbors covered with yellow and white and pink roses? There was one at each end of the garden and, in the middle, a sundial and birdbaths with things planted around them. Granny had quite nice, old-fashioned perennial borders on either side. She was very big on delphiniums, which she grew with copper sulfate all around and bordeau mixture—I don't dare use it anymore. Then, there were big patches of shasta daisies—heaven knows what they were—and blue and white campanulas and masses of yellow marguerites. She used to put in bulbs for the spring and annuals in the summer. She always planted zinnias and dahlias—she had wonderful dahlias—which I don't grow at all. She used petunias, too. I wouldn't have a petunia as a present! But Granny liked them. She used to mix her annuals and perennials with things that she saved from year to year—like the dahlias. It's interesting, though. There are some things she didn't grow at all—or only a few. Iris, for instance."

In the course of reminiscing with Patty, I was enchanted to discover that Granny B's mother had been a gardener, too. Her name was Isabelle but she was always known by her nickname, Belle. According to her great-granddaughter, Belle was "quite a snazzy lady," who divorced Granny B's father—which was bad enough—and remarried—which was worse. In those days, divorce under any circumstances was socially unacceptable and there was great dismay in the family. "Granny was not forthcoming about all of this," said Patty. "I practically did not know about Mr. Clinton—although it would appear he was married to her mother for at least thirty years. As we never actually discussed the divorce, one has to infer a good deal." What she has inferred is that Belle found her second husband more compatible. In any case, he indulged her passion for gardening and Patty has inherited some wonderful old gardening books inscribed "To Belle from Clintie—Christmas 1905."

For Patty—as for me—garden-making began with the purchase of an old house in the country. The house that she and her husband bought in 1973 had been rented for five years and the most recent tenants hadn't even cut the grass. An enormous privet hedge covered half the front yard and by the time the new owners managed to whack it back, the lawn underneath was dead. Apparently there had once been a flower bed at the top of a retaining wall behind the house. However, struggling phlox and iris had long since been overwhelmed by the stronger-growing weeds. That was the garden. Patty responded to the challenge with her usual determination. "When one goes to live in the country and one is presented with some acres that are in disrepair, I suppose you can choose to leave it alone but it never occurred to me that one had that choice. So I began digging."

This may sound familiar—but as gardeners, Patty and I follow the beat of different drummers. Not content to fumble along in ignorance and on her own, Patty began reading everything she could get her hands on and immediately set out to develop a network of gardening colleagues. "It helps to have friends," she says firmly. "They push you along and you push them. It's good for you because when you start out, you're very tentative about gardening." Patty did more than seek out like-minded gardeners. She created them. "Mary's definitely a creation of mine. She had this house with nothing growing around it and I couldn't stand it so I volunteered. I said, 'Now, you must do this and you must do that and by the way, what colors do you like?' When she said 'Red' I said 'Oh, dear! Red is not one of my colors.' And then I had to learn about red. Of course, I was only one step ahead of her all the way. If I learned it on Tuesday, I'd tell it to her on Wednesday. And I got away with it because I read such a lot." This story made me laugh. I guess you could call me one of Patty's creations, too.

With only a small rural community in New Hampshire to draw from, Patty has marshaled a group of gardeners as dedicated as herself and they study together. "There are about four of us who try to investigate one new genus—sedums one year, alliums the next. This year we're into scree gardening and alpines." They also work together on community gardening projects, place joint orders, and visit local nurseries together. Because New Ipswich is off the beaten track and the ladies have nongardening or, in some cases, older husbands, they don't have an opportunity to visit many other gardens. Patty's solution to the problem is reading about them. But realizing the limitations of literature with regard to garden design, she says, "I think if I went to look at more gardens, I would be better on the planning and designing. I would actually see how other people do it. As it is, I'm more interested in the plants and how to grow them. I want to see what each plant is going to look like—as it grows, flowers, dies down, and comes up again next year. After I've had it about three years, unless it is something I happen to become absolutely enamored of, I'd just as soon give it away. Then I can try some new plants. I find I have to do that because I have limited space.

"We're all into small-area gardening. Nobody has the help to do those Gertrude Jekyll borders. So one has to find some other method—on a smaller scale. Of course, what happens is that one has to move things around all the time—you have to get last year's plants out of there so that you can have the new plants you are going to learn about this year. I have a friend who says some of these things have more mileage on them than the car! But everybody does it, I discover. You remake the garden every year partly because it's an improvement but mostly because you've just acquired all these plants and you don't know what to do with them." Spoken like a true gardener!

Given Patty's predilection for scholarship, it isn't surprising that one of her plant enthusiasms is old roses—roses with a history. She has 'Ispahan' of the Persian caravan routes and 'Rosa Mundi,' named for the fair but unfortunate Rosamund who was forced to drink poison by Henry II's jealous queen. According to Patty, 'Rosa Mundi' is striped pink and white and is a sport of the emblematic red rose worn by supporters of the House of Lancaster in the fifteenth century. She is about to acquire 'Tuscany,' a relative newcomer from the nineteenth century which she describes as "a lovely Gallica with velvety dark purple petals and lots of yellow stamens." Other roses in her collection have seductive French names which roll musically off her tongue: 'Felicite Parmentier,' 'Therese Bugnet,' and 'Jacques Cartier.'

Most of Patty's roses are New Hampshire–grown on their own roots. "When I first started, I put in hybrid teas and a couple of grandifloras and floribundas—the sort of thing that Granny grew—but they all died. Then I read an article about Mike Lowe in *Yankee* magazine. He runs Lowe's Own-Root Rose Nursery in Nashua—about forty minutes from here. So I called him up and got this nice man on the phone. I told him what had happened to my roses and he wasn't a bit surprised. 'Ha!' he said. 'Of course those things won't live!' I thought, well at least he's frank and I like that. I went right over to his nursery and bought a couple of roses on their own roots. When I had no trouble with them, I organized my gardening ladies and we all went over. Now there are forty-five different old and hardy roses growing right here in town." Patty caught me smiling and added, "I know. I'm always organizing things. I can't help it, I'm a born organizer." It's just as well she is. Otherwise, I might not have graduated from eighth grade! And the garden of the Barrett House in New Ipswich might not have emerged from oblivion.

The Barrett House, an imposingly large, handsome, Federal-style mansion, was built in 1800 by Charles Barrett, Sr., as a wedding present for his son. It remained in the family until 1948, when a Barrett stepdaughter gave the property to the Society for the Preservation of New England Antiquities. Behind the house—which is open to the public—there was a derelict garden. It occurred to the custodian that there might be somebody who could muster a group of volunteers to tackle the garden. Being a canny young woman, she approached Patty, and before you could say "Jack Robinson," the garden ladies were hard at it. They removed the grass from the old beds, relaid the stone paths, and installed new beds around a sundial that someone unearthed elsewhere on the property. The present garden, Patty is quick to point out, is not a historic reconstruction, nor is it the official garden of the house. "The idea," she explains modestly, "was just to improve the backyard with some flowers. So we began by digging it out. Actually, that's how I found some of my garden ladies in the first place—they came to dig. Mary and Peggy dug; my friend Faith dug, and her sister, too. People kept turning up, that's how it all happened."

Patty, her mother, her grandmother—even her great-grandmother. They are part and parcel of my life. Together and separately, they appear in the pattern of the garden like a motif repeated in different shades of the same color. Now, having also met Patty's friend Mary, I feel connected by a thread of acquaintance to her and to the other garden ladies of New Ipswich, and so on—ad infinitum. Although we are all making different designs, we exchange the materials—the plants and the knowledge, the labor and the camaraderie—and work them into our own patchwork gardens.

Lillian

LILLIAN'S PATCH IN MY QUILT IS ASSOCIATED LESS with specific plants—though she has given me bulbs that I love— than with a color. Yellow is one of her favorite colors and mine, too. It's a happy, upbeat color that reminds me of Lillian and makes me smile. As a gardener and as a person, she's an original. The other day she told me that the way she got her orchid to flower was by leaving it outside in the cold. "You know, the way the Eskimos leave their old people out in the snow. Well, that's just what it needed," she said triumphantly. "That orchid hadn't bloomed in years and now it's got a big flower spike on it."

Small in stature but great in heart, she loves plants, pets, people, and wildlife. She has no patience with the compelling force of facts and events and regards the works of men with suspicion. A few years ago, unable to dissuade the town fathers from widening and paving the dirt road on which she lives, she threw herself in front of the bulldozers and steadfastly refused to move until they withdrew. Foiled by this startling maneuver, the highway department accepted defeat and retreated with their equipment. To this day, the blacktop stops just short of Lillian's driveway.

This is a woman who never does anything by halves. When she has been to look at the garden, it seems more beautiful than it was before her visit. And her whole-souled appreciation fills the gardener with gratitude and delight. Less tangible than the gift of a plant but no less real, her sensitive, generous response is a gift beyond price. Nor does her generosity end with words. Not long after we met, I told her with excitement and trepidation about the impending visit of the estimable Hortus Club from New York. On the morning of their visit, there was Lillian at daybreak—dead-heading my daylilies. And ever since, whenever I have been desperate, she has turned up out of the

126

blue—as a result perhaps of telepathic communication.

Born, raised, and still profoundly attached to William Penn's "fine green Countrie Towne" of Philadelphia, Lillian has always gardened. In the gentler climate of the Delaware Valley, she grew prizewinning delphiniums, roses, and shasta daisies. "People used to stop their cars to look at them," she remembers wistfully. Her life then revolved around gardening. She belonged to the Pennsylvania Horticultural Society and to a local garden club about which she speaks with great warmth. "It was an exhilarating experience to be with so many knowledgeable, interesting people. And we used to take wonderful trips—to the Pine Barrens and to isolated places on the south Jersey shore. We went to Longwood Gardens and Winterthur and dozens of other places. Our club also was very involved in the Philadelphia Flower Show. We had a fabulous group of women. They were real growers and doers and they spurred you on. It wasn't just the competition, you did things for the challenge and because you wanted to see what you could do."

She had a small greenhouse in those days. "Bill asked if I'd like one and I said yes. It had everything you could want: hot and cold running water, its own gas heat, an automatic ventilating system. I loved that little greenhouse. It was fantastic for propagating plants. You could propagate any thing." She can still propagate anything. For years on end, she has kept my variegated ivy geranium going from cuttings. Her Newtown house has two big sunlit rooms with floor-to-ceiling windows that face south and east. In the winter, there are always pots of geraniums in bloom and long, graceful sprays of cymbidium orchids, hanging baskets with trailing stems of little blue bell-shaped flowers, and an offspring of Mrs. Knox's clivia that flowers in March. I once gave Lillian a tiny camellia plant that had come to me as a membership gift from the New York Botanical Garden. Recently she sent Bill over with a huge picture-perfect blossom and another round bud showing a frill of pink petals.

Her success with indoor plants is legendary. She literally resurrected a standard fuschia of mine. It was so near death's door from neglect that it looked like a desiccated bird's nest perched on a stick. There wasn't a single green shoot on it. Clucking her disapproval, Lillian seized this pathetic object from my unworthy arms, wrapped it in a clear plastic bag, put it in her intensive care unit, and murmured a few encouraging words over it. In a matter of weeks, the bird's nest had miraculously sprouted leaves. Even Lillian's nongardening husband was impressed. "I knew Lil was good with plants," he remarked, shaking his head in disbelief. "But I didn't know she could walk on water."

Leaving Philadelphia was a sad wrench for this lover of hearth and home. But because of Bill's work they have moved often, and wherever she has lived Lillian has gardened. Returning to visit Philadelphia, she drives by the house where she and Bill used to live. "I can see that some little whips I planted years ago have grown into beautiful big trees," she says, "and it makes me happy. I always plant trees because I feel that I am leaving something of myself behind." In Des Moines, Iowa, she left a handsome European beech, a rose garden, and a flourishing stand of marijuana. During the war, marijuana was raised out in the Midwest for the hemp fiber. The plant escaped from the fields and naturalized in the fencerows.

"There's good soil in the fencerows," Lillian hastened to explain, "and I had gone out to the country to get some for the rose beds. I guess I must have picked up marijuana seed because the next year I had this beautiful lacy thing growing among the roses. It has pretty little leaflets spread out like fingers and nice little yellow flowers. It's a lovely plant and I think it is pitiful the way its reputation has been ruined by what has happened to it." It is typical of Lillian to have a good word even for marijuana.

However, her views on gardening in Connecticut are less charitable. Deer are a constant menace and a freak snowstorm in October 1987 decimated the trees in her garden. "It's not difficult to garden here—it's impossible. If it isn't the deer, its a drought or a flood or a blizzard. I can't raise anything in this crazy place—except moles and snakes and bugs and weeds. It's unbelievable! Weeds—I could get first prize for the weeds!" Nevertheless, in a bed by the terrace she grows beautiful roses, hybrid lilies seven feet tall, peonies, daylilies, phlox, shasta daisies, and an unusually attractive form of ageratum which she raised from seed brought back from a trip to Japan. Built on a color scheme of pink, mauve, and blue-violet, the little perennial garden she has created is lovely.

Lillian handles color with skill and sensitivity. A few years ago, I gave her a pair of flame-orange Exbury azaleas that had been an impulse buy soon regretted. I tried to hide their light under a bushel, but no matter where I put them, they blazed forth—clashing with everything else in the garden. Finally I banished them to the woods—only to discover that they flowered at the same time as the native pink azaleas. In dismay, I called Lillian, who agreed to rescue them. With great care, she removed them to her own garden, gave them a place of honor beside her driveway, and surrounded them with a host of snow-white bearded irises. Now they reward her with a fire-and-ice display that would stop Philadelphia traffic dead in its tracks. Here, only a few cars creep warily along the unpaved section of Lillian's road. But you can't have it both ways.

She also salvaged my Japanese irises, which were dying of thirst. In her garden, they put on a show in late June that arouses envy in my breast. Last year after a month of heat and drought, I made the grumpy observation in my composition book that "Lillian's garden is just as dry as mine, but full of flowers—many, many Japanese irises (the ones I gave her!) and masses of a particularly dwarf, flowery shasta daisy, some roses, and pink veronica." I had the grace to add that the garden "really looked lovely."

In the mid-seventies with a new garden to fill, Lillian was pleased to accept divisions of my more prolific perennials. Now they give pleasure in both places. It is fascinating to see plants that I use in one way being used in quite another in her garden. In my border, daylilies are planted in groups of yellow, terra-cotta, red, and orange and repeated throughout the garden. Lillian has threaded a single color—I had an excess of a cultivar called 'Morocco'—like a red ribbon among native cedar trees, clumps of sunflowers, and other perennials along her driveway.

As mine is the older garden, the heavier flow of plants has been in the direction of Lillian's, but she has given me bulbs for the woodland garden and handmade terra-cotta flower pots shaped like chickens for the terrace. She has also brought me bags of manure and helped me spruce up the garden for visitors. And with her truck she has rendered innumerable services. Her truck is a very large pickup which she drives at hair-raising speeds. When I'm feeling adventurous, I enjoy collecting mulch hay from a neighboring farm. The three-mile trip with Lillian at the wheel is a real cliff-hanger—will we get there in one piece or won't we? Based on my experience as a passenger, I have come to believe in an inverse ratio: The size of a vehicle and the speed at which it is driven increase as the stature of the driver decreases.

Lillian claims to be five-feet-two, appears to be five feet, and admits that the only thing she has ever lied about is her height. On her driver's license, she is described as five-feet-one. All I know is that she needs a running start to mount the high step into the cab. Once inside the truck and behind the wheel—which she looks through rather than over—she drives with a kind of abandon that sends my right foot in frantic search of the brake pedal. At the helm of her venerable Cadillac, she is even less restrained. We once got to a garden in Westchester County in three quarters of an hour instead of the usual hour and fifteen minutes.

Lillian's assertiveness manifests itself only at the wheel of motor vehicles and in the presence of perceived threats to animals, the environment, or her friends—probably in that order. The very deer who mangle her yews and demolish her hostas are still welcome in her backyard, where foxes—gray and red—raccoons, opposums, and a skunk share the food she puts out for them. At night, a peaceable kingdom cavorts in the broad beam of a floodlight mounted on the barn roof. Cynic that I am, I witness these scenes in the sure knowledge that the skunk will tear up her lawn when it has eaten the food she has provided, the deer will crop off her rose buds for dessert, and the raccoons will heartlessly dump over her garbage can. Lillian knows this, too. But as she says, we may be the last generation to see wildlife like this in Connecticut. As the recipient of her many kindnesses myself, who am I to argue?

Mary: The Ties that Bind

WHEN MARY LEY'S HUSBAND DIED THERE WAS A MEMO-
rial gathering. I can't bring myself to call a memorial service a
celebration. But this occasion was so heartwarming and so overflowing with regard and affirmation that I found myself more moved than sad.
Harold's own children—five of them—and his four stepchildren spoke about
him with deep affection. A teenage grandson sporting an alarming Mohawk
hairdo wept openly. Harold's oldest son, who died much too young in an
accident, was represented by his two children and wife, now remarried. Wid-
owed for the first time in her early forties, Mary had remained close to her
former sister-in-law, who was there from Cincinnati along with childhood
friends from that city. Only Harold's first wife was absent—due to illness.
Friends swelled the throng. And as I watched Mary moving calmly and graciously among them all, I marveled afresh at her stamina, fortitude, and warmth.

Standing at the center of this ramified web of connections—familial and social—is a remarkable woman and a remarkable gardener. Characteris-
tically, her garden is like a sampler worked by each succeeding generation of
family and friends. There are snowdrops, winter aconites *(Eranthis hyemalis),*
and daffodils that came from her grandfather's country home in southern Ohio
and hostas that found their way to her garden from an old family friend via her
mother and her grandfather. "Of course, people garden in different ways," she
says, "but I find one of the greatest pleasures is to look out and see all my
friends. Mother sent me loads of hosta seeds that she got from my grandfather
but he got them from Mrs. Hutton originally. It means so much to have things
in your garden from other people. It's a continuation of life. It keeps the life
of the person who gave it to you going. So I have Mrs. Hutton and my
grandfather and different people in my garden and it's very rewarding."

Ten years ago, Mary took a shovel and uprooted an enormous clump of snowdrops just after they had bloomed—which, by the way, is the best time to move or divide them. She gave them to me, saying, "These came from my grandfather's garden. I think he started with a little clump that he dug up in some old graveyard. Of course, there were just zillions of them by the time I was growing up. The woods were full of them." Now, our woods are full of them, too. They have already formed a solid carpet and in March, I can look out of our upstairs windows and see a sheet of white beneath the trees.

The woods of Mary's childhood were part of a farm belonging to the doctor who looked after her grandfather one summer. As a boy, Carl Krippendorf had been sent to the country to recuperate from an illness. During the course of the summer, he not only regained full health and strength, he fell in love with the countryside and vowed one day to return. In the intervening years, the fragile lad grew into an oak of a man who was never sick another day in his life. In 1900, true to his word, he rescued the doctor's 175-acre property from developers and built a shingled home there for himself and his new bride.

Carl Krippendorf's love affair with the landscape of southern Ohio began that long-ago summer. How he came by his passion for plants, particularly for bulbs, remains a mystery. But for fifty years he poured his energies into a woodland garden that still lights up acres of the countryside with the colors of spring. "If you don't like yellow, you won't like the woods now," he wrote to his friend Elizabeth Lawrence. "There are tens of thousands of winter aconite in bloom, so thick that one can see them a hundred yards away. I love to see the patches of color repeat themselves in the distance." Ms. Lawrence visited the Krippendorfs later in the season and afterward wrote, "There, as if a door had opened into another world, was spring spread out before me—a carpet of daffodils as far as I could see."

Thanks to a group of public-spirited citizens, the Krippendorf garden has been preserved as the Cincinnati Nature Center. And the thousands upon thousands of snowdrops, winter aconites, and daffodils that Mary's grandfather planted—and divided and re-planted—keep on blooming to the delight of visitors. He once told Elizabeth Lawrence in a letter that he had just collected and sowed 60,000 winter aconite seeds. Mary remembers the pleasure he took in counting things. "He was always counting seeds and would use my grandmother's little gold thimble as a measure. He knew just how many seeds it took to fill the thimble, and he used to measure out thimblesful for everyone who came to see the garden."

Mr. Krippendorf named his sylvan world Lob's Wood for the enchanted forest in J. M. Barrie's play *Dear Brutus*. Mary, growing up in that magical world, came under its spell. All during her childhood, she would accompany her grandfather on his appointed rounds—gathering and sowing seed and planting the drifts of bulbs that make Lob's Wood a vernal paradise. Later, her own small daughter would do the same. As a little girl, Jerry Nelson wrote an essay about her great-grandfather. It begins, "I have a very unusual great-grandfather. He lives in the middle of the woods. He has two prunes and a glass of water for breakfast. And then goes out to inspect his flowers. His woods are filled with daffodils of all kinds. He has more than anyone else in this part of the country. He has hillsides of Virginia Bluebells. He sent seeds of these to a friend in England. This man planted them in Windsor Park for Queen Elizabeth to admire.

"My great-grandfather likes to grow plants. Every once in a while he pots a couple of thousand to keep himself busy. He gives most of them away, and he probably has flowers growing in all parts of the United States."

Like Jerry's very unusual great-grandfather, Mary has carried on the family tradition of giving away plants—not just plants of which she has a great many but her treasures as well. There is a hierarchy of garden givers. Most gardeners are reasonably generous and will gladly part with a little of this and a bit of that; all are happy to get rid of species that increase too rapidly; and a few are base enough to unload a real dog. A very, very few will share—with a twinge of reluctance—a wisp of something really precious. But it is the rare gardener with a heart big enough to lavishly spread around his or her best plants.

"My grandfather," says Mary, "gave things away by the bushel load every month of the year and he never held anything back. Some people have an unusual plant and they don't want to share it because they want to be the only ones who have it. He wasn't at all like that. He believed in spreading things around and so do I. It's so important, if you are going to be a gardener, to be as generous as you can." Many of the plants that I prize most have been given to me by Mary—hellebores *(Helleborus orientalis)* that have passed through the unselfish hands of three generations and traveled from Ohio to Connecticut, with a stopover in Greenwich, where Mary lived before moving to Newtown.

By the same circuitous route, a unique fritillary *(Fritillaria verticillata)* found its way to my garden. It was one of Mr. Krippendorf's treasures—an early-blooming bulb with enchanting cream-colored bells tinted green on the outside and faintly checkered with green on the inside. One of the most appealing features of this unusual bulb is the very pale green foliage which encircles the stem in whorls. The uppermost leaves end in curious tendrils that are very attractive. Other prizes from Mary include a tremendously tall Solomon's seal with arching stems that soar to six feet; a tiny primose with minute pink flowers borne in clusters the size of a quarter; and a miniature bearded iris with flowers of an indescribably delicate blue and an exquisite daffodil called 'J. T. Bennett-Poe.' Mr. Krippendorf sent a clump to Elizabeth Lawrence, who wrote, "I have never seen J. T. Bennett-Poe listed, nor met it elsewhere, although Mr. Krippendorf has kept it for fifty years. A cross between *Narcissus triandrus albus* and Emperor, it is a small milk-white trumpet in appearance, as sheer as Angel's Tears but not so tiny." Now this gem flowers in my garden, too.

Just as visitors to Lob's Wood went away loaded with plants, so today visitors to Mary's garden never leave empty-handed. But the random giving away of plants is not her only form of garden generosity. She charmed the town fathers into letting her plant bulbs at the main intersections and along our village streets. Occasionally thoughtless passersby pick the daffodils beside the road. When this happens, Mary promptly erects a courteous but firmly worded sign requesting that the flowers be left for *everyone* to admire. She involves friends and acquaintances in town beautification projects and has recently hatched a scheme whereby individuals and/or groups will look after tubs of flowers placed at strategic locations around town. Nor does she confine herself to beautifying Newtown. If you happen to see an attractive blond woman broadcasting seed along an interstate highway, it will be Mary planting wild-flowers.

Part of her own garden is a wildflower meadow. Contrary to popular belief, establishing a meadow is not easy. The site had to be plowed, the sods removed, and the soil raked free of rocks. Mary marked off her hillside in sections and tackled them one at a time. The labor involved was enormous. Seed planted over the open soil washed out the first time. A second attempt failed due to drought. A third try met with greater success but it has taken years of patience and persistence to establish the more desirable flowers and grasses. Less stalwart grasses, like Job's tears, were soon choked out.

Mary's interest in ornamental grasses predated the current fad for these graceful plants by many years. It began with the gift of a book from her mother. Her appetite already whetted by the book, she took a trip to England. "I went to Wisley [the Royal Horticultural Society's display and experimental garden in Surrey] and there was a trial garden there of every ornamental grass you ever heard of. It was the most wonderful display! And I can remember—oh, this was so long ago—but I remember writing down all the names, then, when I got home, trying to find sources. I grew some from seed ordered from J. L. Hudson, Seedsman. Later, I was introduced to Kurt Bluemel, Incorporated, where I first ordered *Miscanthus sinensis* 'Zebrinus' and some of the other more glamorous ones.

"This winter, I've really enjoyed the grasses. They're as good in winter as in summer because they get all bleached out and silvery. Then, when it rains, you think, 'This is the end.' The flower heads get all water-soaked and look like skinny rat-tails, and the stems bend to the ground. But as soon as the sun comes out, they stand right back up again; their hair dries out and they're just heavenly. They have a whole new permanent wave. One of the best things about the grasses is that they respond to every little change in the weather."

In Mary's garden, there is something to admire all year: in the spring, a replica of her grandfather's woodland—in miniature—with carpets of yellow aconites; by June, the rock garden ablaze with pinks and poppies and daisies; and all season long, the rich green brocade she has woven under and around the trees with hostas, ferns, and other shade lovers. But nothing is more spectacular than the autumn display of grasses. On her hilltop, the tall grasses not only look lovely swaying in the wind, they make swishing, whispering sounds as the air currents pass through their sheaves of fine foliage. One of the most effective for its music and its lithesome form is maiden grass (*Miscanthus sinensis* 'Gracillimus'). The six-foot stems and thin, arching leaves—each embellished with a white stripe down the middle—make an open, elegant clump

with fruiting stems that bear terminal clusters of fluffy white tassels. In order
to fully appreciate the special charm of the flowers, you have to take them
indoors and let them dry. Once they've dried, the leaves resemble the delicate
curling tendrils of a vine and the tassels turn into insubstantial puffs of silvery
brown. As soon as I expressed admiration for the maiden grass, a chunk was
hacked off the mother plant and deposited in my car.

Mary's contribution to my garden cannot be measured in a catalog
of the wonderful plants she has given me—extensive as it is. Far more important, she introduced me to new ideas and new ways of gardening. She urged
me to join the American Rock Garden Society. I dragged my heels: "I'm not
a joiner." "But this is such an interesting group of people," she insisted, "and
they're superb gardeners—the best in the country. Come to a meeting." "I hate
meetings." "Look, if you were interested in science, it would be like having a
chance to rub shoulders with people of Einstein's stature." I joined the society
and went with Mary to one of their winter study weekends, from which I
returned exhausted but exhilarated. That was ten years ago, and I haven't
looked back. Mary also showed me how easy, fulfilling, exciting, and economical
it is to grow hardy plants from seed. Again, I made excuses: "I can't, I'm too
busy. I have nowhere to do stuff like that." "Come and do it here," she said,
by now knowing my defenses were weak. "We'll work up in the potting
shed—I've got everything you'll need."

At first I did menial chores like washing pots in a weak solution
of Chlorox. But as my level of interest and competence rose, I moved on to
mixing the soil, tamping it down in the prepared pots, and sowing the seed. As
I don't have a rock garden and was chiefly interested in woodland plants, we
planted a great many primroses which now grace my woods. After the potting
sessions—which were happy, convivial occasions—I left the rest to Mary until
it came time to prick out the seedlings. This was difficult at first; I seemed to
have additional and very clumsy fingers when it came to handling the minute
plants. But seedlings are much tougher than they look. I was stunned by the
extensive root systems of tiny plants no more than half an inch high. I was
equally surprised when—despite my inexpert handling—the pricked-out seedlings put on a tremendous burst of growth. The next time I looked under the
lath house, they had become crisp little rosettes of leaves. It was a great thrill.
By early summer, I brought home boxes and boxes of small primrose plants
and put them in the woods, where to my great delight they flowered the
following spring.

I now do seeds on my own. But I doubt that I would have tried
had it not been for Mary. Nor can I leave Jim out of this. It was through Jim
that I met Mary in the first place, and together they persuaded me to join the
Rock Garden Society—an association that has contributed a rich, highly colored
assortment of patches to my quilt.

Wider Horizons

THE DEVELOPMENT OF OUR GARDEN FALLS INTO three ten-year segments. The early period was devoted to stripping away the rank vegetation and groping toward, not a plan, which would have been beyond my limited vision at the time, but toward a *way* of making our rocky, overgrown farmyard into a garden. During those years, the only suitable way seemed to be clearing and planting, clearing and planting. Meanwhile, I kept searching for the theme of this particular garden and discovered, finally, that it lay in cooperation with the land, not in contention and competition.

The same collaborative spirit directed the evolution of the perennial border. Through trial and error, I found out which plants took kindly to the site and which did not. Gradually, I accumulated a repertory of trustworthy perennials that proved they could stay the course and prosper with the kind and amount of care I was able to give them. So far, so good. As I began working along our east-facing slope, creating connections and paths, I sensed that something about what I was doing was right. But it was meeting the Gills and, shortly thereafter, Jim and Mary that opened my eyes to the immense possibilities in the world of gardening.

What I had been practicing so far had precious little to do with garden design and not much more to do with horticulture. I rarely knew the botanical name of any of the plants I grew, which in any case were all cultivars of very common species—daylily, iris, peony, and so forth. As for the specific Latin names employed by Helen and Mary, they were a whole new experience. When I was finally able to say *Kirengeshoma palmata* without hesitation, I felt I had arrived. It was a great step forward to learn that the names based on words from Greek and Latin actually meant something—and were often helpful.

Divining their meaning became a fascinating and instructive game. It gave me enormous pleasure to be able to say to myself—and, I fear, to my patient spouse—"Ah, yes, *Caltha palustris—palustris* means of the swamp, you see." Pride in this achievement was short-lived. After one study weekend in the company of the erudite rock gardeners, I felt that I was right back to square one. I doubt even now that I will ever feel really comfortable with *Thymus quinquecostatus ibukiensis* 'Alba.'

At heart, I am one of those gardeners that alpine enthusiasts refer to, a little condescendingly, as "border people." I am an unregenerate border person. I like big easygoing plants that show up from a distance; I love color but I am equally enamored of the subtle effects that can be wrought with evergreens—that aren't necessarily green but may be shades of blue or gray or gold; I even like plants with variegated foliage, though admittedly they have to be handled with care. I am interested in garden pictures and in design or form or whatever it is that makes for order and harmony. Over the years, I have become more and more intrigued by the plants themselves—by their origins and the environments they call home, by their forebears and their relations, by their personal quirks, habits, and requirements.

My expanding interests were fed, fostered, and encouraged by my new garden friends. They opened up a whole world to me. Helen broadened my view of perennial gardening—she knew and grew so many wonderful plants that were unfamiliar to me or that I had never grown. She combined the perennials with slews of bulbs—a ploy I was quick to copy—and introduced me to shrubs like pearlbush (*Exochorda x macrantha* 'The Bride'). Pearlbush is rarely seen even in today's more sophisticated gardens, and on behalf of Helen and myself I am making it my mission to drum up interest in this lovely, neglected plant. There should be one in every garden. It is an absolutely foolproof deciduous shrub growing to four and a half feet in fifteen years and its habit is graceful, with arching stems clad in willowy, blue-green leaves. In May, every twig ends in a raceme of perfectly round white buds that open into five-petaled flowers with dark, recessed throats.

Although I would have been hard put to analyze why the Gills' garden was so immensely satisfying, I was subliminally influenced by the design. Not that I could or would want to try to reproduce it in my garden but because I found the orderly relationships between its various spaces and enclosures so restful. All the pieces of their garden seemed to make sense. I still wouldn't know how to fit a round garden into a rectangular space and have it seem absolutely right. However, I realize that the uniform green background had something to do with the feeling of unity. Part of the background was provided by a boxwood hedge, part by the sentinel yews, and there were a few broadleaf evergreens against which the border of gray lamb's ears stood out in sharp relief. Jim's preoccupation with his "visual" wasn't lost on me either, though it was infinitely harder to share the vision he was pursuing. However, once he had finished a section of the garden, I would belatedly see what he had been driving at.

All during the seventies, there was a lively exchange of visits among our four gardens—the Gills', Jim's, Mary's, and ours. By the end of the decade, a great many of the same plants appeared in all four gardens—but the gardens themselves couldn't have been less alike. There was Helen and Johnny's Connecticut Sissinghurst—country formal, for want of a better description of its subtle blend of refinement with the rustic simplicity of uncut native stone in the walls and steps; Jim's work-in-progress toward a highly individual, controlled landscape; Mary's extensive garden—informal in spirit but complex in execution, with a staggering variety of species furnishing her woodlands, rock gardens, and the many containers surrounding formal terraces and a swimming pool; and our own rambling Anglo-American country garden-in-the-making. To me, having spent the first ten years gardening in virtual isolation, the influx of new ideas was enormously stimulating. And the gradual infusion of new plants transformed our garden.

The Perennial Border: Phase II

OVER THE TEN-YEAR PERIOD FROM 1970 TO 1980, THE perennial border grew by increments to its present length of a little less than a hundred feet and a width of fifteen. In basic form, it has changed very little since then. My earliest and clumsiest wall-building efforts are still being redone a little at a time and I continue to fool with the lines whenever I work on a section of the wall. But I have resisted the temptation to extend the bed. As for the plants, some are refugees from the original perennial border on the lawn: the rose-red peonies left behind by Mrs. Knox, *Lythrum* 'Dropmore Purple,' and the lemon yellow daylily 'Hyperion.' Other daylilies from the sixties include 'Pinafore,' 'Marionette,' and 'Norwegian Lass.'

The first "new" peonies I ever planted are still there—all doubles with the huge flowers of which I was so enamored then. Now I infinitely prefer the single types, but how can you cast out 'Nick Shaylor' and dear old 'Mrs. F. D. Roosevelt' when they have been faithful for all these years? Both have flowers the size of soccer balls—'Nick' blushing white sometimes flecked with red and 'Mrs. FDR' clear pink ones. In mid-June, we always have what I've come to think of as the "peony rain." Predictably, it finishes off the beauty of these two cultivars. Even propped up individually, the wet blossoms are so heavy that their stems break. Peony rings seem to offer no better support; the weight of the flowers bends their stalks across the hoop of steel and they snap.

Not having the strength of character to discard old plants in favor of new creates a problem in an aging perennial border. I'm stuck with some of my first and least suitable choices—which would be all right if I had the self-discipline to refrain from acquiring new plants. But I don't. As a result, the design of the border suffers. During the period of expansion, the problem didn't arise. The new could be incorporated and the old retained by adding another

142

ten feet to the garden and shuffling things around. It was during the expansion years that the border often looked its best.

One of the most valuable lessons I learned from studying the Gills' spring garden was that by combining bulbs with even a few early-flowering perennials you can have a wonderful display without sacrificing too much precious space. Their use of tulips was particularly striking. Planting them in masses of one color had tremendous impact. The tulips bloomed at the same time as a wealth of herbaceous plants: amsonia, early bearded irises, *Iris tectorum, Iris lactea,* trollius, nepeta, and the many geraniums that Helen grew. Later, their ripening foliage—which really is very messy and unattractive—was hidden by their perennial partners and by the emerging foliage of later-blooming perennials.

In the Gills' enormous borders, there was room for a great variety of herbaceous plants. As I didn't have that much space, I adopted the idea of pairing bulbs and perennials with a different and much more limited selection of plants. I began planting tall Darwin and Cottage tulips—cream to white only—in the middle and at the back of the border, always behind or in association with a clump of daylilies or a peony, to provide cover later for the bulbs' dying foliage. In addition to hiding the ripening tulip leaves, the foliage of the perennials provides an attractive filler among the flowering bulbs. The daylily leaves are fresh and green and the immature peony foliage is dark green to deep red.

As a color scheme, I've always loved the combination of white, yellow, and blue, so I added a band of deep lavender-blue grape hyacinths *(Muscari armeniacum)* all along the front of the border, and in front of that—at the top of the low retaining wall—mats of yellow *Draba sibirica.* I am often asked about the draba, which is a member of the mustard family. This species has thin trailing stems set with tiny pale green leaves, and the flowers—which are produced in great quantities—stand above the mats of foliage on wiry four- to six-inch stems. Although *D. sibirica* is the only perennial in bloom and no more than two kinds of bulbs are employed, the effect is very pleasing—with the yellow accenting a ribbon of blue that binds together the groups of pale tulips.

The maturing peony and daylily foliage takes care of the old tulip leaves, and the hyacinth foliage soon disappears and is inconspicuous anyway. The little hyacinth bulbs are a bit of a nuisance. They seed everywhere—coming up through the clumps of daylilies, in the middle of the Siberian irises, and even in the lawn. A double hybrid form called 'Blue Spike' has sterile flowers and therefore doesn't produce seed but the blossoms aren't nearly as dainty and charming as those of the single variety. Anyway, the self-sown bulbs don't seem to do any real harm among the perennials. But every time I divide something, I disturb masses of the little things. Fortunately, grape hyacinths have the odd habit of sending up foliage in the fall, so wherever I see a great hole in the edging, I stick in some more bulbs.

I learned the hard way that a reliable method has to be found for identifying groups of tulip and daffodil bulbs in a perennial border. At first I blithely stuck in wooden or plastic plant labels. These were removed whole-sale—and consumed in their entirety—by Abby when she was a puppy. There is more than a grain of truth in the saying that a bored Jack Russell Terrier is a bad Jack Russell Terrier! I eventually found dog-proof labels but often couldn't remember whether the bulbs were planted behind or in front of the label. Either way, it is important to be consistent. Another problem arose when—as often happened—the tulips were eaten by rodents. If I forgot to remove the label at the time of making the discovery, fall would come and, seeing the label, I would assume that it marked a group of bulbs. The following spring, there would be a gap. Now when I find that bulbs are missing, I put a piece of plastic tape around the label marking the spot and plant new ones in the fall.

My bulb losses have been considerably reduced by planting tulips in miniature plastic laundry baskets available from hardware stores. I cut out the solid plastic bottoms and replace them with rectangles of half-inch mesh hardware cloth. Then I make a planting hole in the border, install the prepared basket, add a thin layer of earth over the wire mesh, and put in the bulbs. Their roots grow right through the hardware cloth and through the plastic mesh sides of the basket. It is worth the additional trouble. I rarely lose a protected tulip to the mice, voles, shrews, and other small, greedy creatures that ply the mole runs during the winter.

It took quite a few years to master the art of combining the spring flowering bulbs with the perennials but it was eminently worthwhile. Now the season begins in April with groups of white and cream-colored daffodils. In order of appearance: 'Mount Hood,' a creamy long trumpet early bloomer; 'Ice Follies' next with a large shallow cup of primrose yellow that fades to white; the very similar but later-blooming 'Spring Fever; 'Iceland,' a spectacular giant version of the former with a frilly primrose cup and white perianth—a less vigorous bulb, however, that multiplies slowly; pure white 'Cantrice'; and fi-nally, my favorite of all, 'Stainless.' Some of the daffodils are still in flower when the grape hyacinths and draba begin to bloom and the early 'White Emperor' tulips take up the paler theme. 'Stainless'—which is still in bloom with the Darwin tulips—is a treasure. The flower is medium-sized with a small, shallow, perfectly made cup, and perianth petals that look as if they had been cut with great precision from a sheet of heavy white paper. The long-lasting flowers are proudly displayed on tall stems.

The tulips, too, have been chosen for extended bloom, starting with 'White Emperor,' a Fosteriana hybrid which overlaps with 'Ivory Flora-dale,' a variety developed by crossing Fosterianas with Darwins. 'Cream Jewel,' a Darwin, and 'Maureen,' classed as a Cottage tulip, are both late bloomers. And another Darwin, 'The Duke of Wellington,' is the latest of all. It is a source of relief to me that the names of the hybrid tulips manage to be so dignified compared to those of the daylilies. I am passionate about tulips—every kind of tulip, from the exquisite little peppermint stick *Tulipa clusiana*—which blooms early and has narrow pointed petals, white within and striped deep pink on the outside—to the last late-blooming Darwin with large, perfect oval flow-ers elegantly balanced at the top of tall stems. If I could have only one tulip in the perennial border, it would be 'Cream Jewel.' The acme in terms of shape, its mouth-watering cream-colored blossom has a fine thread of red at the edge of each cupped petal.

Another Gill-inspired—and Gill-augmented—period of bloom occurs around Memorial Day. This is the pink, blue, and red stage. The hybrid peonies which bloom at this time are a relatively recent addition to the garden—as recent as six or seven years ago. And what a pleasure they are! I have two cultivars—the radiant 'Burma Ruby' that Lori gave me and 'Scarlet O'Hara,' a much taller plant, also with single flowers but not of quite such a glowing red. These peonies don't produce side buds, confining their efforts to one lovely flower per stem. No heroic measures are necessary to support them, though I do use peony rings to give 'Scarlet' a helping hand because it is such a tall, vigorous plant. The crimson peonies bloom with Helen's Memorial daisies and Siberian irises. I already had a pansy-purple cultivar called 'Caesar's Brother' and a white whose name I forget. Helen gave me a great clump of the heavenly, pale blue 'Gatineau'—still my very favorite, which I've spread throughout the border.

Siberian irises in new and beautiful shades of blue with hints of turquoise have recently been developed. And there are sumptuous new flower forms with wide falls and flaring falls. Naturally I crave them, but have no room—because I can't part with the old-timers. In my garden, all the shades of blue and purple—and, of course, the whites—seem to go well with 'Burma Ruby' and 'Scarlet O'Hara.' There are four big red peonies spaced at intervals along the front of the border with adjacent patches of the Memorial daisy, and throughout, clumps of Siberian irises: 'Gatineau' and 'Perry's Blue'—a deeper, medium blue; 'Navy Brass,' a rich, deep blue from Jane Conningham; and 'Ego,' a blend of truly royal blue with a suggestion of turquoise. 'Allegiance,' the sole survivor from my fling with bearded irises, and *Iris pallida* bloom at the same time.

Last but far from least, Gill-given lamb's ears edge the entire perennial border. Typically, Helen pressed me to take a large flat of them. Also typically, I had nowhere to put them. There wasn't room in the bed above the retaining wall. So on the spur of the moment, I cut away a narrow strip of lawn at the foot of the wall and stuck them in there. As the length of the border increased, so did the edging of lamb's ears. The mats of furry silver leaves spread rapidly by means of horizontal stems which send down roots as they go along. I was thrilled by the unifying effect of the scalloped edging of silver foliage and eventually widened the band. Quite simply, Helen's lamb's ears *(Stachys byzantina)* are the making of the perennial border. No single plant does more for the garden than this humble native of the Mediterranean.

Somewhere along the line, I got it into my head that the flower spikes of lamb's ears were ugly. Maybe Helen thought so, maybe I read it somewhere. Anyway, the blossoms certainly don't amount to much. They appear at the top of stalks eighteen inches tall—tiny magenta things tucked into gray woolly heads that resemble mullein. Convinced as I was that these were not decorative, I used to cut them off as soon as they appeared. Then one year

I didn't get around to it. To my surprise, the effect of a two-foot-wide band of these tall, furry candles was even more appealing than the flat band of silver foliage. Moreover, the combination of the felted silver stalks coming up through the Japanese maple's lacy red leaves was a knockout. Henceforth, the flowers were allowed to remain. The stalks arise during the last part of May and add considerably to one of the garden's most effective moments.

What really makes the two-week period around Memorial Day a high point in the garden year is the simultaneous flowering of the red, blue, purple, and white border with the pink rhododendrons on the hillside. The rhododendrons that bloom at this period include vivid pink R. 'Scintillation,' R. 'Roseum Elegans,' with slightly bluer-pink blossoms, and pale pink 'Janet Blair.' The massive rhododendrons—planted in the late sixties and early seventies— covered with great trusses of pink flowers are a sight to behold against the green hillside. The scale is right for a big, rambling country garden, and with the perennials in the foreground, the colors—if I do say so myself—are gorgeous. For this one shining moment—if we don't get a heavy thunderstorm or a drought or a breach in the deer fence or a plague of caterpillars and if the winter hasn't been bitter enough to damage the rhododendron buds—I look outside and feel a sense of accomplishment.

By mid-June, my border goes into a slump. Helen's garden, on the other hand, was a paradise at this time of year. Flowering trees and shrubs dominated the scene, with the *Cornus Kousas* producing their landslides of flat, creamy bracts; Kolkwitzias sending up huge fountains of dainty pink flowers at the back of the great curving borders full of shrubby deutzias in white and pink; and in front of them, blue and pink geraniums, pale yellow achillea, and white dianthus. Naturally, there were a great many other plants in bloom which I don't remember, but suffice it to say that the entire month of June was a period of peak bloom in the Gills' garden. There are many lovely perennials that flower at this time of year but I have very few of them in my garden—not that Helen didn't urge upon me anything in which I expressed the slightest interest. It was a matter of choices.

The misconception has arisen recently that "you can have it all." But you can't—at least, not in a garden. Time, energy, space, money, skill, and experience are all limiting factors. Take even the Gills and their enormous garden. The space was more than generous. They were retired and had unlimited time. When we first knew them, both Helen and Johnny were still able to garden. However, they were also seventy years old and had diminishing— though in Helen's case phenomenal—energy. Moreover, they were without regular outside help, except for a man who cut the lawn and came in a few times a year to mow the orchard. When it came to pruning—which was very difficult for two small elderly people—they nabbed whomever they could, when they could. After Johnny's death, a young man who ran a landscape business used to come in once in a while just because he admired Helen. These are very real limitations. Of course, strength in one area goes a long way toward compensating for deficiencies in another. Helen's gifts as a gardener and her long experience in combining plants resulted in a feast for the eye from spring to fall. And even after the perennial borders had gotten out of hand, the garden retained its beauty and dignity, thanks to Johnny's basic design.

In my perennial border, there are several limiting factors, among them a weakness for daylilies. If I had fewer daylilies, I would have enough room for some of the lovely June-blooming perennials that Helen used; or if I had unlimited energy I could make the border extensive enough to accommodate both; or if money were no object, I could enlarge the border even more and have a June display, a daylily extravaganza and an autumn show of later bloomers—and somebody to look after the whole works. But none of these are options. The only one that appeals to me anyway is the unlimited energy. I could make do very well with that. If I had the experience of the 1980s and the energy of the 1960s, I'd be in business. So would every other gardener I know! Failing this magic combination, gardeners are stuck with choices.

After I had been working on the border for some time, I realized that I couldn't have all the different kinds of plants that I would like and still have all these daylilies. But the daylilies were so well suited to the site, so willing to grow for such a modest outlay of time and energy, and so generous in terms of color and beauty of form that I eventually made a conscious decision. I would aim for a few high points: tulips and daffodils in the early spring; the red, pink, and blue period around Memorial Day; and the midsummer display of daylilies—with suitable companions. For the rest of the season, I would have to find a few things to hold the border together and give us something to look at.

If I were willing to sacrifice the space, the "something to look at" could be annuals that bloom all season and last well into the fall. But there isn't enough room. Once in a while I've tried to squeeze in a few as young plants—before the perennials have gobbled up all the space—but in the end the annuals have always been shaded or crowded out. I would like *very* much to have an autumn garden but the only answer seems to be to have it somewhere else. And it's a moot point whether I would be able to look after another flower bed, even if I made one. Every perennial gardener has to resolve this same dilemma—whether to aim for a garden that always has something in bloom or to shoot for one knock-your-socks-off seasonal display. Gertrude Jekyll and Vita Sackville-West solved the problem by having different garden "rooms" for different seasons. I can see that this scheme could be adapted to a smaller scale—but not here, not now. It's too late for creating enclosures and garden rooms on our property.

The upshot is that I sided with the daylilies, surrounding them with a congenial group of strong, floriferous perennials that bloom at the same time. Together, they paint the hillside red, gold, and yellow, and bronze, buff, and apricot for six glorious weeks in midsummer. False sunflowers *(Heliopsis scabra)* intermingle their semi-double yellow daisies with the predominantly trumpet-shaped daylilies. Purple coneflowers (*Echinacea purpurea* 'Bright Star') add a surprisingly effective accent with their richly colored purple-pink rays and electric-orange centers. It was this daring color combination in a single flower that reassured me about including exclamation marks of purple-pink lythrum in the red-yellow-gold scheme. A solid mass of this strong hue might be disastrous but the spires of lythrum are narrow and restrained in form. Dotted around among the daylilies, they add a piquant note.

Silver-blue globe thistle *(Echinops ritro)* provides a refreshing change from the blaze of warm colors. A single plant grows into a bold clump of leafy stalks with interesting dissected foliage topped by prickly heads made up of crowded bracts that appear frosty green, then blue as the minute flowers open. Orange and yellow daylilies surround the four large globe thistles planted at intervals toward the middle and back of the border. In the foreground, flat yellow heads of achillea and little sky-blue discs of flax *(Linum perenne)* turn up here and there among the lower-growing daylilies, while at the back of the border I've shoehorned in lilium lilies 'Golden Splendor' and 'Copper King.' These Aurelian hybrids take up very little room and give enormous value, rising up among the tallest of the sunflowers on five- to six-foot stems that carry clusters of large, outward-facing trumpets. On a warm July evening, their heavy perfume seems to roll down the hillside and gather in pools at the foot of the slope.

Meanwhile, the spring flowering bulbs have become a memory. Having long since gone tactfully dormant, their space has been usurped by the burgeoning herbaceous plants. The peonies and irises, however, are still very much in evidence and those perennials that have not yet flowered are a green presence in the garden—which is why foliage that looks presentable all season is a vital consideration in choosing plants for the border. *Sedum* 'Autumn Joy' is a hands-down winner in the foliage department. This wonderful plant is on every perennial gardener's list of the top ten performers. There is not a single day in the year when its foliage is not an asset—even in the dead of winter. If there isn't any snow, I can go out and find a cluster of tight rosettes waiting for the first warm day to shed their purple hue and start lengthening out into leafy blue-green stalks. The eventual height of the stalk is about two and a half feet, and in August each one develops a broccoli head of frost-white buds that are attractive from the minute they form until they open a month later into fuzzy, flat-topped pink flower clusters. Gradually turning from pink to dark red to rust, the flowers are almost as durable as the foliage.

Choosing a percussive crescendo of midsummer bloom in preference to a season-long melody meant sacrificing many of the June-blooming perennials as well as an autumn display. But the border doesn't stop flowering suddenly with a clash of symbols. After the pink-blue-red period in early June, a few things either begin to bloom or go on blooming: the Memorial daisies are very persistent and clumps of a pale yellow achillea from Helen come into flower at this time. This yarrow has greener foliage and a sturdier constitution than the very similar cultivar 'Moonshine.' Last year, biennial mullein that I grew from seed delighted me with six-foot candelabras of light yellow flowers in June, and these lasted well into July. In addition, there are always the lamb's ears keeping it all together.

Appropriately, the fireworks begin the first week in July and reach a climax the third week in the month. There follows a long, gradual diminuendo.

In August, the reds begin to give way to more yellows: the sunflower *Helianthus mollis,* black-eyed Susans (*Rudbeckia fulgida* 'Goldsturm'), Helen's flower (*Helenium* 'Butter Pat'), and the double sunflower *Helianthus x multiflorus* 'Flore Pleno'). A tall, not so common mugwort *(Artemisia lactiflora)* blooms with the sunflowers. Slender, arching stems carry sprays of cream-colored flowers so small that you can't tell the buds from the flowers—or the fresh flowers from the faded, which is why the airy clusters are effective for such a long time. A few alliums bloom at about this time along the front of the border, along with *Sedum spectabile* 'Star Dust'—an off-white 'Autumn Joy' but not nearly such a strong, reliable plant. In fact, it sometimes throws a weird magenta-pink flower head or two. Soon, however, 'Autumn Joy' will swell the ranks of later flowering perennials.

Last fall, I halved an enormous clump of peony 'Mrs. FDR' and moved some daylilies in order to make room for two shrubby blue-flowered *Caryopteris x clandonensis* to break up the monotonously yellow and white August border. These little woody plants are often killed to the ground in the winter and are never supposed to grow out of scale with the perennials—or so I've read. It would certainly be a pleasure to see their small tufts of blue among the yellow sunflowers. Another shrub that I want to try in the border is the blue form of August-blooming Rose of Sharon (*Hibiscus syriacus* 'Blue Bird'), which allegedly can be kept a reasonable size by severe pruning in the spring.

For September bloom, there is the faithful 'Autumn Joy,' which is just beginning to turn from pink to red as masses of little white asterlike flowers open on a fabulous, relatively little-grown perennial—*Boltonia asteroides* 'Snow Bank.' Boltonia is a sturdy, attractive American native and 'Snowbank,' an eminently desirable cultivar that develops into a bushy, indestructible shrublike plant with beautiful linear blue-green leaves that cover the four-and-a-half-foot stems from top to bottom. 'Snowbank' is the only tall plant in my garden that never needs staking. In full bloom, it has held its own against hurricane winds and rain that leveled every other perennial in the garden. That's what I call a stalwart plant! Moreover, it flowers when very little else is in bloom. Enough clumps of 'Snowbank' paired with clumps of *Sedum* 'Autumn Joy' would make show enough for September, and I'm working on it—gradually spreading the boltonia around.

Which brings me to the pairs theory. A perennial border can be effective for a very long time if two well-matched plants—repeated throughout the garden—are in bloom at every season. In the spring, for instance, one could pair bulbs and an edging plant such as the draba or perennial candytuft—or another plant that blooms at the same time and has attractive foliage for the rest of the season. At the front of the border, good foliage is absolutely critical. A ratty-looking edge can ruin an otherwise beautiful bedding scheme. *Draba sibirica* isn't ideal because the mats of tiny leaves suffer in the heat and actually turn brown in a drought but they are so low and the leaves so small that they escape notice. For early June, the peonies and irises are a classic combination; for later, one might try a back-of-the-border combination of tall, lupinelike yellow *Thermopsis caroliniana* with blue *Baptisia australis,* another lupinesque plant. Helen's geraniums, pinks, and achillea were a lovely pastel combination. Ideally, three compatible plants would give an added richness to a long-blooming border, but two would still do the trick.

In the Northeast, the September-October perennial garden is the hardest to handle. The array of frost-tolerant plants from which to choose is limited. Individually they may be fine, handsome plants, but as a group they do not necessarily a garden make. There's the boltonia, which begins blooming in mid-September in my garden, goes on for about three weeks, and just overlaps with a smashing sunflower, *Helianthus salicifolius.* If they overlapped for longer, these two would be dynamite—but they are more apt to meet in passing. Even by themselves, I enjoy the dark-eyed bright yellow sunflowers which cover the top third of many-branched six-foot stems. The narrow, shiny, dark green leaves are a plus, too. I think I would like to see the sunflowers with some of the ornamental grasses—but that's for another time, another garden— and maybe some shrub roses, which carry on until very cold weather. Anyway, I have by no means solved the autumn garden but I enjoy thinking about the challenge. And who knows? I may be tempted yet.

Oh, Deer!

NOWADAYS, IT WOULD BE IMPOSSIBLE TO WRITE ABOUT gardening in Connecticut without mentioning deer. From the chic suburbs of Greenwich to the rural northern corners of the state, these large, beautiful animals are a menace to orchards and vineyards, food crops and nursery stock, vegetable gardens and perennial borders. They eat anything and everything from corn, apples, and grapes to evergreens, hardwood seedlings, and herbaceous plants. Naturally, they have their preferences—like everybody else. And healthy, well-fertilized garden plants are at the top of their list. Deer favor cultivated plants for the simple reason that they taste better than lean, hungry plants competing in the wild for water, nutrients, and sunlight, and for the complex reason that well-grown plants have a higher protein content and therefore more nutritional value. Somehow the animals know it.

Deer have been around for some fifteen million to twenty million years and have taken more kindly to the advent of civilization than many other forms of wildlife. Adaptable, gregarious creatures, they have changed their life-style and come to terms with suburbia. More and more of their habitat is taken away every passing year, and with it their natural food supply. But not to worry; they have very sensibly adjusted their diet. Instead of eating wild strawberries, pokeweed, goldenrod, poison ivy, witch hazel, sumac, and red cedar, they've substituted tulips, hostas, hybrid lilies, hemerocallis, yews, azaleas, and euonymous. As a result, the deer population in Connecticut is thriving. In fact, they are more numerous now than ever before and their numbers are increasing at an annual rate of from 3 to 5 percent.

If we had not erected a deer fence in 1982, I would not be gardening today and this book would be a nostalgic reminiscence of the predeer 1960s and early 1970s. At the time we bought the property, there were four other houses on our road, all farmhouses built before the turn of the century. Cows still grazed in some of the pastures. The rest were overgrown, like ours. More than a thousand acres of woodland surrounded this rural enclave, and the combination of forest and field was ideal deer habitat. White-tailed deer are not forest dwellers. They take cover in the woods to sleep and to rest between food-gathering excursions but their food requirements are better met in more open countryside. Abandoned pastures provide an abundance of the weeds and shrubs that they enjoy most. In those days, there must have been numerous deer quietly getting on with their lives but we rarely saw them. They had an adequate food supply and enough room and they never bothered us.

It seems unbelievable now that there ever was such a time. But for a long period, the deer were no trouble at all. Then came the building boom. The old farms along our road were subdivided into two-acre building lots. New homes began springing up in the fields like mushrooms. Soon there were more houses than cows. Development continued throughout the seventies, drastically reducing deer habitat and driving them into a cervine ghetto in the eight-hundred-acre state forest surrounding our property. At dawn and again at dusk, our garden looked like a deer park. Having heretofore kept to themselves, they began coming in droves—as many as nine at a time. We had lived happily side by side for years—together but apart. Now we were all one big unhappy family.

I suppose we got what we asked for. In the early days—just after we had the field cleared—we saw deer for the first time. For a minute, forget what your taxus hedge looks like now and try to recall your first sight of a doe with fawns. The doe stands alert, watchful—motionless as only a wild animal can be motionless—great oval ears tuned to the slightest sound of danger, the elegant column of her neck taut with vigilance, while the two youngsters pick their way between the tufts of little bluestem grass, pulling at a weed here and there and swishing away flies with the white frills of their tails. We had never seen anything like it and we were grateful to be allowed this glimpse of domestic bliss. Indeed, we felt privileged and were flattered whenever they returned—which was not often enough to suit us. So as an added inducement, we provided them with a block of salt. The doe and her two offspring graciously accepted this gesture of goodwill and became more frequent visitors.

Their timing was impeccable. They arrived in the morning with their slender legs wreathed in ground fog just as we were having breakfast and returned in time to enhance the dinner hour with their stately grace. At first we spoke in hushed voices and crept about in order not to alarm them but these precautions became unnecessary. The deer weren't in the least frightened. If I opened a window, the doe would raise her head and stare straight at me, then calmly resume her meal. At that time we had a small, elderly dog who took no notice of the deer and they ignored her. They were used to us. What I didn't realize but discovered later—to my cost—is that deer can get used to anything, including a feisty, furiously barking Jack Russell Terrier, loud country and western music, nightlong murder and mayhem on CBS, and a flashing disco light.

For the time being, however, we were pleased to watch and be watched. The deer came in the spring, remained in evidence for a few weeks, and then disappeared. We never saw them in the summer. But around Thanksgiving, they reappeared before going into hiding for the winter. Lulled into a false sense of security, we eagerly awaited their return in March. Those were the good old days! I don't know how long this went on—two or three years perhaps. The older doe undoubtedly produced a fawn each year. It is customary for a family to stay together in a loosely knit association. But during that time, we never saw more than three animals at once. They kept to their side of the stone wall and we kept to ours—except to mow the field a few times a year.

The first time the deer came into the garden and cropped the emerging tulip foliage, I was shocked—and hurt! When it happened again, I became angry and removed the block of salt. As the assaults became routine, I took to bellowing and waving my arms at the ungrateful brutes. Unperturbed and knowing I was harmless, they would peer at me, twitch their white tails insolently, and saunter away. Gradually their numbers increased and the garden became a battleground. In the spring, the perennial border looked like the east coast of England during World War II. There were barricades of chicken wire everywhere and yards of plastic-coated netting draped across forked sticks. At night I made deer-scares out of old sheets—tying them loosely around shrubs and trees so that any breeze would rustle the cloth and make it flap. The sheets were one of the more effective home remedies—as long as they were moved every night.

Spring and fall had become ordeals. But for a while, we still had the garden to ourselves during the summer. As the field turned green, woody plants put forth tender new growth, lush weeds shot up in the warm sun, and life returned to normal. The does retired to raise their young and I could enjoy the peonies and irises and the summer-blooming perennials. Perhaps my enjoyment of them was sharpened by my struggles to protect them. In any case, summers were still sweet—until 1980. By that time, imposing pseudocolonial houses dotted the fields where there had recently been cows. And we no longer even knew our neighbors, who came and went with corporate speed. The deer may have felt just as disoriented by the changes as we did but they took them in their stride. The new development provided them with a delicious array of food, and their numbers increased in geometric progression. Soon they were wreaking havoc in the garden for twelve months of the year.

At this stage, the alternatives were grim: give up the garden or put up a fence. We had tried everything else. Thiram-based repellents plugged the sprayer, left a residue, and did very little to discourage the deer. A cat's cradle of strings soaked in creosote seemed to be effective around individual shrubs—for a while. The *son et lumiere* we devised with a portable radio and the disco light were a complete waste of time. And human hair in bags may have put off one or two of the more fastidious but the majority weren't so squeamish. So it came to pass that we hired a local company to install an eight-foot-high fence.

At this time, there was not a lot of literature available on deer fencing and ours is an improvisation. We were able to employ the trees growing along the stone walls to replace some of the twelve-foot cedar posts we needed. The wire we used was two-by-four-inch mesh turkey netting. We stapled the turkey wire to the trees and posts so that the top was eight feet from the ground. It was safe to leave a gap at the bottom because the stone walls created an adequate barrier. The total cost of the fence, installed—with difficulty in rocky terrain—came to a bit less than $5.50 per foot. Once a solitary deer breached our defenses. After that, I got a roll of baling wire and added two strands to the top of the fence. For seven years the fence was 100 percent effective—but not 100 percent trouble-free. Twice, sections have been badly damaged by falling tree limbs. Repairs would be costly and we have done nothing yet about the sagging wire and broken posts. Other posts have shifted. The gates no longer close properly and have to be chained shut. I dread the day we have to repair the damage. However, I consider myself lucky—I was able to continue gardening. But this year the deer have been crawling under our fence!

Helen Gill had no deer fence and for years no problem. Then, in the early eighties, they came—destroying the sentinel yews and eating her tulips. With so few more springs in which to enjoy her bulbs, it was a bitter blow. Mary Ley gave up acres of her garden because of the deer and had to erect a fence around her rock garden. Jim's shrubs have been mauled and mangled. No garden in our area has been spared. Lillian's has been ravaged time and again but she holds out against a fence. "I can't garden in an armed camp," she says.

In 1975, aerial surveys put Connecticut's estimated deer population at nineteen thousand. By 1988, the number had risen to thirty-one thousand. The greatest yearly increase regularly occurs in Fairfield County. State wildlife biologists and researchers at the Agricultural Experiment Station offer gardeners little hope of an immediate solution to the problem. The wildlife biologists shrug. They talk euphemistically about inadequate "herd regulation." In Fairfield County, most of the property is in private hands and antihunting sentiment is strong. Small undeveloped holdings such as our own provide good habitat and there are no predators, except domestic dogs and their masters. Potential wild predators, coyotes, are returning but find themselves no more welcome than the deer.

The deer issue is not a simple one. Having carelessly upset the balance of nature, we are paying for it—and whining about the cost. We don't want wild predators to return but we don't want deer in our gardens. And we don't want hunters either because they dump the ashtrays of their pickup trucks and throw out beer cans. I find myself torn by conflicting emotions. I have wept over plants on which I've lavished years of tender loving care—destroyed in an instant. I have felt rage enough to kill on the spot but I do not rejoice in seeing a doe ignominiously lashed by her hocks to a makeshift yoke, her proud neck dangling limply between two burly men in orange jackets. She destroyed the beauty of my plant by chance; they destroyed hers deliberately.

Nature isn't pretty. Sometimes at night in the spring, I'll hear a most frightful, rending little scream of terror as an owl seizes a baby rabbit. It is quite horrible. Even city dwellers see enough TV specials of carnivores preying on herbivores to know that death in the wild can be as agonizing and ugly as anywhere else. But there's an order to it all that escapes us. If the deer population is excessive—as it assuredly is—is it best to "cull" the herd or let large numbers starve? Or should we just let nature take its course? That's the problem. It is no longer possible for nature to take its course. We've seen to that. Meanwhile, I go on gardening uneasily behind my tall, unattractive fence.

So far, a properly installed, slanted, seven-strand high, tensile wire deer fence is the only deterrent purported to be completely successful. Repellent sprays have been developed that offer a modicum of protection. According to tests conducted by the Agricultural Experiment Station in New Haven, BGR (Big Game Repellent) has proved the most effective in tests on nursery stock with a 50 to 60 percent success rate. But it is expensive and cannot be used on edible crops. Hinder and Miller's Hot Sauce are registered as safe for food crops and have been found to reduce damage to treated crops—somewhat. Everyone with whom I have talked agrees that a repellent works well when the animal has alternative foods available and best when the alternative foods are more palatable than the crop that is being damaged.

I found a glimmer of hope in talking to a young man involved in research at the Agricultural Experiment Station. "For many species of mammals, the answer to what repels them has already been provided by native plants which produce defensive compounds that are a real turn-off." Warming to his subject with engaging zeal, he went on to describe the findings of researchers in Alaska. Apparently, the birch tree—historically the chosen food of the snowshoe hare—has over a period of evolutionary time developed a compound called papyriferic acid. "Papyriferic acid can make up as much as thirty percent of the dry weight of a juvenile birch twig, and snowshoe hares won't touch the stuff. The key for the future lies in trying to synthesize chemical compounds like papyriferic acid into a repellent. Sprayed on the foliage of plants needing protection, it would convince the animal that this plant is now toxic, unfriendly, and unpalatable. That's a possibility we'll be exploring in the future."

Millstream

H. LINCOLN FOSTER AND HIS WIFE, LAURA LOUISE, BET-
ter known as Timmy, were as central to the third decade of my
gardening life as the Gills were to the second. I met them through
Mary Ley, but long before that Marie Luise drove me past Millstream on the
way to visit Mrs. Crane's Summer Hill Nursery in Dalton, Massachusetts.
"That's the Fosters' garden," she said in reverential tones. I looked. There was
an old gray colonial house backed up against the mountainside with a wonderful
brook leaping down the slope over and between slabs of rock. It was high
summer. The landscape was green and lush but I didn't see a garden. I did,
however, think that the back road we had taken was the most beautiful I had
ever been on in a singularly beautiful part of Connecticut. The road hugs the
western face of Canaan Mountain, overlooking a valley as peaceful and pastoral
as anything in the Swiss alps. Across the valley, other mountains rise with an
abruptness that makes them appear higher and bolder than they really are.
Blueberry-colored in the winter, deep green in the summer, Mt. Prospect
reaches a height of a little over 1,400 feet, Bald Peak just over 2,000 feet, and
in the northernmost corner of the state, Mt. Riga attains 2,380 feet, making it
the highest point in Connecticut.

After that trip to Massachusetts, I tried once or twice to find the
Fosters' road and failed. It's easy to miss. But I recognized it at once when
Mary took me to Millstream for the first time. I have always thought it a
measure of her generosity that she could bring herself to share the Fosters.
I feel that if they had been my discovery, I would have guarded them jealously
and tried to keep them a secret—which would have been difficult. They were
already a household word to rock gardeners throughout the United States and
in many European countries. Millstream, their secret garden, was a secret

158

everybody knew. But as Mary once said, "It becomes your own secret the minute you see it."

Although the Fosters' name and reputation had been familiar to her for years, Mary didn't really get to know them until we began going there together. She had met them years ago when she was living in Greenwich. As a member of the program committee for the Greenwich Garden Center, she called and arranged to have them come and speak about ferns. At the time, Timmy had recently completed the illustrations for Broughton Cobb's *A Field Guide to the Ferns,* the tenth volume in the Roger Tory Peterson Field Guide Series, and Linc had contributed a section to the book on the use of ferns in the garden. After this introduction, Mary didn't see the Fosters again until she became a member of the American Rock Garden Society and began to attend the meetings and plant sales.

Rock Garden Society plant sales require some explanation. They are remarkable events. If you have never been to one, you haven't lived. I have the most vivid recollections of the first plant sale I ever attended with Mary. It took place at the home of a member—in the driveway. By the time we arrived, a large number of people of all ages, sizes, shapes, vocations, and preoccupations had already gathered. On a low retaining wall all along the drive were hundreds and hundreds of little pots containing grassy wisps, little rosettes of leaves, and other small, unpromising-looking shoots and sprouts. It was hard to see the plants for the people and only the most determined managed to get anywhere near the wall. An atmosphere of anticipation vibrated through the crowd as members, in good democratic fashion, drew lots. Each participant—in the order determined by a draw—selected a plant of his or her choice. That done, a signal was given. And suddenly, all hell broke loose. The crowd charged at the wall like the Light Brigade, little old ladies diving under the outstretched arms of taller competitors, well-dressed matrons shouldering aside elderly gentlemen. In the free-for-all, the plants vanished—all except for a few little pots of some species that everybody seemed to have.

It was at one of the plant sales that Mary really got to know the Fosters. "I remember it so well," she says, "because I had just picked out some plant that I wanted when I realized that Linc had been studying it, too. It was something unusual, I forget just what, but I could tell that he *really* wanted it. I knew he'd be able to raise it and that I'd probably kill it, so I gave it to him. He was terribly pleased and we struck up a friendship then and there." But Mary had only been to Millstream once before when we made our memorable excursion together. She was as spellbound as I was. "That garden was perfection," she remembers. "One of the things that I loved so much was that rock—way up on top—just studded with lewisias *(Lewisia tweedyi)*. And every time you turned into a little nook or cranny, there was a planting of primroses. It was just a fairyland—a treasure hunt. Then all those wonderful Jacks that he had—and that thing with huge leaves—the petasites—down by the bridge. The drinking cup by the spring, remember? And that chicken coop where he raised all those incredible saxifrages—and the cellar with the boxes he made where he raised his seedlings. It was a whole Lincoln Foster world."

How could anyone forget a visit to Millstream! We had brought lunch to have with the Fosters and the four of us sat at a picnic table on their terrace. Above the terrace, the phlox in the alpine meadow was in full bloom, and afterward we walked through the flowery coverlet of pink, white, and lavender. To the right, the stream shot off the mountain and rushed down between the walls of the old mill race and among the huge boulders. We joined the grass path on our left. It led to a wooden footbridge that crossed the stream. Nearby, under a tall sugar maple, a carpet of little blue and white wildflowers *(Collinsia verna)* covered the ground like a bolt of Liberty print spread out to dry.

Linc lead the way across the bridge with Mary close behind. Timmy and I brought up the rear. As this was before I became conversant with botanical nomenclature, I kept asking what everything was. And with inexhaustible patience, Timmy would repeat the unfamiliar names—over and over again. There were so many things in bloom, that I couldn't take it all in: a flood of lavender-blue *Phlox stolonifera* and primroses everywhere; pink *Primula kisoana* from Japan with beautiful fuzzy leaves that looked as if they should belong to a geranium; masses of a gorgeous rosy-purple Caucasian primrose *(Primula abschasica);* my mother's favorite moonlight-yellow primroses; and hundreds and hundreds of little English cowslips *(Primula veris)* in shades of yellow, orange, and red. In addition, there were the fabulous Japanese Jack-in-the-pulpits *(Arisaema sikokianum)*—big patches of them with sleek, upswept mahogany-colored hoods rising arrogantly above gleaming white interiors. The hoods terminate with a flourish in sharp peaks.

All along the paths we passed small areas of carefully prepared soil where tiny rhododendron plants were labeled and set out in rows. These were Linc's nursery beds, where his hybrids were being grown on for later evaluation. We stopped at a bed in which the rosettes of rhododendron foliage were no bigger than nosegays. I had never heard of a compact, handsome species named for the Japanese island of its origin, Yakushima. "These are some of my yakusimanum hybrids," Linc explained and knelt down to turn over one of the dark, shining oval leaves. The underside was covered with beautiful, fawn-colored indumentum, which he invited us to touch. It was as soft as the most expensive suede. Mary and I were speechless with pleasure when he potted up two rosettes and gave them to us. That was eight years ago. The plant in my garden is now thirty inches high, the same across, and covered with flower buds—for the first time.

The tour continued among mature rhododendrons and azaleas in full bloom. We passed a huge glacial boulder with rare ferns growing in every crevice and came finally to a high plateau and the lewisia rock. Returning along a different series of paths, we made our way along a tiny ravine where a trickle of water threaded its way down the mountainside. The banks were thick with clumps of Japanese candelabra primroses, ferns, grasses, and wildflowers. And at the bottom, just before the footbridge, there was a miniature snowstorm of mitrewort *(Mitella diphylla)*. We stopped for a drink from the clear mountain spring before collecting the picnic basket and taking our leave.

Millstream as we saw it that day is no more. Inseparable from their garden and from each other, the Fosters died within fifteen months of one another—Timmy in January 1988 and Linc in April 1989. It was their wish that nature be allowed to reclaim the mountainside. Only the strongest and best adapted of the plants they introduced will survive, which is as it should be. The Fosters' lives and the lives of their plants were so completely interwoven that the one could not possibly continue without the other. The property belongs to Timmy's children now and the gardening public will respect their privacy. But memories of a horticultural Camelot will glow in the hearts of a myriad of visitors for years to come.

Of all the gardens I have ever seen, before or since, I still find Millstream the most moving. It was the product of love, labor, knowledge, and shared joy. It was a garden that had everything. It was rich and wild and beautiful, and exciting. It was also surprising, and fun. It was an artist's garden and a gardener's garden. To make your way along its paths without entering into the spirit of the place would have been impossible. The garden's animating principle overtook you and made you emotionally conscious. It sharpened all your senses, and in this heightened state of receptivity, you were permitted a tantalizing glimpse of another world—the world of two down-to-earth poets. The garden invited you to see it through their eyes and to experience it with their sensibilities.

Linc and Timmy did everything in tandem. They won awards together. In 1978, they received the Arthur Hoyt Scott Garden and Horticultural Award, which had never in its then fifty-year history been presented to a couple. And together they won the Massachusetts Horticultural Society Silver Medal. They produced the rock gardener's bible, *Rock Gardening: A Guide to Growing Alpines and Other Wildflowers in the American Garden.* Timmy executed the exquisite line drawings; Linc was responsible for the text. In the forward, he wrote, "Together we have built Millstream, together we have made garden visits and field trips, and together we have written this book." And in a note to me after Timmy's death, he concluded with, "We really shared almost every moment."

It was an extraordinary partnership. Linc, whose birthday, I recently discovered, was on the same day as Abraham Lincoln's, was the most enchanting and forthcoming of men. Timmy was charming, witty, and reserved—and, I always felt, the spark that ignited and fanned the creative flames of Millstream. Although Linc was the plantsman and Timmy the self-appointed weeder, they were both reflected in a garden that made a single coherent statement. They had, after all, a great deal in common, including a shared gift for language and a passionate love of the natural world. After her death, Linc found a secret notebook in which Timmy wrote poems—one appeared in the *Quarterly of the American Primrose Society* in the fall of 1988. Entitled "Summer is Dying," her response to the approach of winter is expressed in language as powerful as it is elegant.

Linc's respect for and delight in words make reading the text of *Rock Gardening,* or any of his dozens of articles for American Rock Garden

Society bulletins, a treat for lovers of good writing. And anyone lucky enough to have letters from Linc saved and savors them. I had a note from him at the time he was preparing an article on arisaemas. He wrote, "In trying to find a word to describe the special quality of the arisaema inflorescence, I ran into an archaic meaning for quaint: skillfully wrought, hence graceful. I like that." A former teacher of Latin and English, his anthology of American poetry and an edition of *Moby Dick,* both written during a sabbatical in 1962–1963, are still in use by high school students and have recently been reprinted.

The list of Linc's horticultural accomplishments is endless. Several different nurseries are currently working with his rhododendron crosses and the name 'Millstream' identifies superior alpine phlox hybrids of his making: clear, pink 'Millstream Daphne'; 'Millstream Jupiter,' with lavender flowers; and lovely soft pink 'Millstream Laura.' He worked with dozens of different species, from draba and primulas—I have a beautiful white primula with a golden eye called 'Millstream White'—to his beloved Kabschia saxifrages. When the saxifrages used to bloom in March, the chicken coop was transformed into a jewel case displaying delicate pink, yellow, white, and peach-colored flowers on tight little green cushions of linear foliage.

Not long before he died, Linc received an award for distinguished service to rock gardening. The citation—in addition to enumerating the achievements of this multitalented man—commended him for his generosity. Linc wrote the book on garden giving. My garden, Mary's garden, and hundreds of other gardens all over this country, in Europe, and in Japan are the richer for plants from Millstream. "Visitors without number," the citation reads, "have received gifts of plants or cuttings, and Linc has donated equally countless numbers to ARGS plant sales and auctions."

An entire bed in our garden is devoted to dwarf rhododendrons that came from Linc—either directly or through ARGS plant sales. Most were planted in 1980 and 1981 as single rosettes of leaves. It has been a source of intense pleasure to watch these little plants mature into beautiful shrubs, and this should be a banner year for bloom: The winter has been mild and the flower buds are encouragingly plump. Several of these rhododendrons will flower this year for the first time. *Rhododendron Degronianum,* now a bushy thirty by thirty inches with extremely long narrow leaves that clothe the branches right to the ground, is covered with buds; a natural hybrid of *R. yakusimanum* with lighter green leaves and no indumentum is about the same size now and also heavily budded. Little *R. racemosum* has been blooming for several years. The leaves of this species are only about an inch long and the small rose-pink flowers occur in tufts at the tips of the stems.

Millstream covered a six-acre mountainside. Our woodland garden occupies a scrap of low ground about eighty feet wide and a couple of hundred feet long. You could walk two abreast across the Fosters' substantial wooden footbridge. Our brook is an evanescent freshet crossed by two bridges—each made from a single long narrow fieldstone. Water pours off Canaan Mountain. Once the stream overflowed its banks and raced down through the Fosters' woodland with such force that a great portion of the garden was washed away.

Our most dramatic waterfall plunges over a rock and drops eighteen inches into a pool no bigger than a dishpan. For the rest of its length, our stream dawdles along until it collects in a shallow pond that dries up by mid-June.

Despite the obvious differences, our woodland garden is the spiritual child of Millstream. It wasn't just the great infusion of Foster plants that established the familial relationship. Working in the woods, I have unconsciously shared the Fosters' experience. I have known their joy in discovering the first purple flower of the Caucasian primrose and felt their impotent rage at the deer. Timmy and Linc are as much a part of our woodland garden as their plants. I sometimes wonder, in fact, whether those hoofprints were made, not by deer or by the Arcadian god that wandered Mount Cyllene, but by a spirit that still inhabits Millstream and many other woodland gardens.

Woodland

EVERY MARCH, NO MATTER HOW FOUL THE WEATHER has been for thirty of the thirty-one days, there is one day—at least one—so inexpressibly beautiful that you suddenly think you know what it's all about. If you had lived only for this one day, it would be enough. The feel and smell of the air are intoxicating. If you are very young, you want to throw away your jacket or sweater and roll on the damp ground. Your mother will have a fit and say, "You'll catch your death of cold!" But of course you won't. You are never going to die of anything—you're immortal. If you are old enough to know better, you forget it for the moment. This day in March is instantly recognizable. The sky is a special shade of blue so pale and translucent that it doesn't really seem to be there at all. And looking up, you understand the meaning of infinity. There are no clouds to set limits in the vastness. The sunlight has no color and seemingly no source or direction. It is just an immense radiance in the even more immense sky.

In swamps, the peepers are heard for the first time on this day, and green frogs start uttering the loud, insistent "Grak-Grak-Grak" that apparently identifies the males and draws an audience of silent, admiring females. The very first spotted turtle ventures forth to sit on a tussock in the sun. Mallard ducks with an eye to the future begin looking around for nesting sites. For years, a pair has returned annually to our temporary pond. On that first spring day, we'll hear a loud splash and the self-important quacking that makes ducks both ludicrous and charming. How anything as sartorially splendid as a mallard drake could possibly quack, eat upside down, and waddle like an obese human being beats all. This is also the day that phoebes start to repeat their strangled two-tone call over and over again. For the first time, there are enough insects in the air to keep them darting into action.

166

It was on just such a day ten years ago that I began making the woodland garden: "Today, I started a wild 'Brook Garden.' Truly, I've never enjoyed myself more—making a little wall along the trickle that goes into the Knoxes' old pond behind the barn. I kept all the while thinking of Hugh [my younger brother] and the fun we used to have playing in the brook at home. Even in the summer after it had dried up, it made an interesting tunnel through the undergrowth." This is what a woodland garden with a stream has to offer—childhood revisited and pleasures as acute as any I have ever experienced.

What is it about water that is so universally appealing? Perhaps its fascination has to do with our watery, primordial beginnings. Everyone is susceptible to its charms. I remember years ago being left to babysit my eighteen-month-old nephew. His mother was in the hospital producing his sister and he was behaving very badly—in anticipation of the day when he would be presented with this unwanted rival. I had no children of my own and didn't know what to do with a screaming toddler, so I filled the kitchen sink with water and sat him in it. Miraculously, the shrieks stopped, and for the rest of the afternoon he was quite content to splash around in the water with a set of plastic measuring cups.

It was the tiny stream that first drew me to the site of the woodland garden. It had been a wet spring and you could actually hear the sound of running water from the house. It was irresistible. Apparently the Knoxes had found it so, too, because they had attempted to make a pond behind the barn in an odd little enclosure surrounded by stone walls. The blurred outlines of a lozenge-shaped basin were still visible but trees and brush had grown up in the pond. At one end, a rusty culvert intended to handle the overflow had become home to a family of raccoons. The water has never yet reached the level of the culvert. Nevertheless, that spring, the trees, and saplings at the deep end of the pond stood in as much as four or five feet of water.

The brook itself has very special charms—one of which is its mysterious source. From a swamp somewhere high up in the state forest, the thread of water finds its way through underground channels and emerges on our property from beneath the stone wall. There isn't a drop of water anywhere in sight until the stream suddenly issues with a throaty gurgle from a little underground cavern. It continues on the seventy-five-foot journey to the pond making a variety of melodious sounds at different stages along the way: an almost imperceptible whisper as it slides along a flat sandy stretch; a high-pitched trill where it falls over a boulder; a low, mellow tone where it descends into a deep pocket. When the rest of the brook has long since dried up, this pocket holds a basinful of water where small birds come to bathe. There are always birds. Flycatchers like the phoebe are attracted to the insect life that hovers over the surface of the pond, and as the water recedes, little brown creepers run along the newly exposed mud searching for food.

The woodland garden began to take shape along the banks of the stream. At first the project involved more engineering than gardening. The stream didn't have very well-defined banks. Instead, it wandered at will among the rocks, taking several different routes to the pond. So I began by channeling the water into a canal, lining both sides of the canal with large rocks, and steering the water between them. Then I back-filled behind the rocks with soil scraped together from along the stone walls. An accumulation of leaves and debris had collected at the base of the walls and decomposed, adding much-needed humus to the otherwise meager rocky topsoil.

The soil in a southern New England hardwood forest has nothing in common with the moist, humus-rich soil found in northern hardwood forests or in the forests of the Catskill Mountains, where Patty and Carl had their fishing camp and where I collected so many of my wildflowers. In the mountains and in the hardwood forests of the north, a variety of shrubs and wildflowers grow vigorously in the shade of maples, birches, beeches, and oaks. Here, in southwestern Connecticut, the woodland floor is virtually bare—except for dead leaves, spindly saplings, and tough Christmas ferns *(Polystichum acrostichoides)*. The difference between conditions in the north and in the south lies in the amount of moisture available to the understory plants. The summers here are longer and hotter, and our major forest tree is the notoriously thirsty, greedy, shallow-rooted maple. I have read that a single large sugar maple transpires hundreds of gallons of water through its porous leaves in a single day. That water has to come from somewhere—the soil. Tulip trees *(Liriodendron tulipifera)*, which abound along the northern bank of the pond, aren't much better. They have masses of sinewy roots that lie just below the surface and drain the surrounding soil. There are two kinds of soil in the woodland garden: dry, depleted, humus-poor woodland soil on the high ground; sticky, close-grained, water-retentive clay on the bottom of the pond and around the edges. Throughout, of course, there are rocks.

The water is here today, gone tomorrow. In March, the brook flows briskly along its narrow course and gathers in the pond. Two months later, the level begins to recede gradually, and by the end of June the pond is dry. In another month, a thriving crop of tickseed, jewel weed, and knotweed takes over the bottom and the banks become as dry as a bone. Autumn rains begin to fill the pond in November. Then runoff from the melting snow augments the accumulation, spring precipitation does the rest, and the cycle begins again.

Another major atmospheric change accompanies the gradual departure of the water. The light diminishes as the trees leaf out. One very large maple stands within the garden on the southern edge. On the opposite side, tulip trees line the shore of the pond. Maples, a multistemmed ash, and several black birches *(Betula lenta)* grow at intervals around the perimeter, and trees in the state forest close ranks on the garden's northern border. In March, sunshine easily finds its way through the network of bare branches. The garden and the state forest beyond are flooded with light. By May, however, the picture is quite different. The state forest has been plunged into darkness, while in the woodland garden, the big maple produces a shifting patch of dense shade and the tulip trees throw heavy shadows behind them. As the sun crosses the sky from east to west, the trees on the other three sides blotch and stripe the woodland floor—shade alternating with bright sunlight. Before Martin came to my rescue with the chain saw, the contrast between March and May was even more dramatic.

It isn't easy to accurately describe the quality of the shade in the woodland garden because it doesn't fit into the accepted categories—dense, moderate, and light or "dappled shade." Dappled shade is a phenomenon produced by trees with small leaves that move with every current of air and admit sunlight but break the force of its direct rays. It is a lovely kind of shade found in birch groves or in manicured woodlands where trees have been removed. The crowns of those remaining do not meet overhead, which allows light to reach the ground between them. Both situations are highly desirable. Delicate foliage and controlled spaces between trees permit understory plants to enjoy the benefits of adequate light and rainfall. But these conditions are not easy to simulate in a crowded forest of maples and other trees that have large, overlapping leaves. The compromise at which we arrived might be described as "patchy shade."

In the beginning, there wasn't nearly enough light once the trees had leafed out. So I prevailed upon Martin to fire up the chain saw and told him to be ruthless. He cut down all the maple saplings under three inches in diameter and a few bigger ones along the wall. Sunlight streamed in. I was delighted but unprepared for the side effects of this Godlike interference with nature. Across the wall, in the state forest, weeds are few and far between. Only a handful of herbaceous plants cling to life in the Stygian gloom. But in our woodland garden-in-the-making, long-dormant seeds suddenly germinated, and almost overnight the clearing was inundated with weeds. It took at least three years to get the situation under control. In the process, I learned the first lesson in making a woodland garden: proceed slowly and replace the undesirable plants with more desirable ones as you go along.

The primroses I had planted in April appeared to welcome the sunlight—temporarily. But as the season wore on and the sun's rays grew stronger and hotter, increasing amounts of water evaporated from the lush rosettes of foliage and from the surrounding soil. The primroses, a species native to the damp meadows of England and Europe, reacted to the stress of drought by losing many of their leaves. By August, they were a sorry sight. Ideally, primroses and other moisture-loving woodland plants should be watered during the summer if rainfall is inadequate. Unfortunately, we are in no position to supplement nature's efforts. Our water supply for the house comes from a drilled well that produces four gallons a minute. To water the woodland garden would put too great a drain on this vital resource. A nineteenth century hand-dug well equipped with an electric pump provides additional water—for as long as the supply holds out. But it usually dries up by August.

Two years after I started the woodland garden, Linc and Timmy came to see it early in July. There was no water in the pond, which at that time was still full of saplings. And the primroses along the dry stream bed were beginning to look shabby. In fact, it took great imagination to see even the possibility of a garden. But the Fosters were full of encouragement, enthusiasm, and advice. Afterward, Linc wrote:

> I'm thinking about your wet area. What a truly challenging spot. Just look at the weeds that take the flooding, then burgeon with summer dry. There are some gorgeous plants that are born to that kind of environment. Think Himalayan wet meadows—primroses, irises, et al. Do take out the trees, kill the roots—and experiment. Can you see a sweep of Japanese iris— interplayed with tall candelabra primroses—That's their world.

I could indeed see the tall pink, rose, and deep red primroses with their lovely tiered flower heads swaying among swords of iris foliage—and later, the great flat blossoms of the Japanese irises hovering just over the tips of their own leaves like huge purple and blue and white moths. Timmy made other suggestions and even provided me with a list of potential candidates: yellow flag *(Iris pseudacorus),* an immigrant from Europe that has naturalized here in the northeast; our native blue flag *(I. versicolor);* marsh marigolds *(Caltha palustris);* violets; bottle gentian *(Gentiana Andrewsii);* turtlehead *(Chelone glabra);* blue lobelia *(Lobelia siphilitica);* cardinal flower *(L. cardinalis);* and many others—all of which I eventually grew with varying degrees of success. And I have been experimenting with plants ever since. I also took to heart Linc's admonition about the trees. In the beginning, however, I had other priorities.

The woodland garden needed a path—for access and for fun. One of my very first memories has to do with paths. I must have been four—my younger brother was not yet born—when my parents took my older brother and me to Jamestown, Rhode Island. At the place where we stayed, there were winding grass paths leading through the scrubby seaside vegetation down to the shore. I remember them clearly—mysterious highways of grass cut through a tangle of bushes and vines overhung with rugosa roses and other tall shrubs. I've been a pushover for paths ever since. In the woodland garden, there was no way to get from the opening in the stone wall to the stream— except by plowing through the undergrowth. So the first and most important path led from the entrance down to the brook and along its length—away from the pond—to its point of entry. With the loppers and my little Swedish hand saw, I took down the saplings and grubbed out the intervening barberry bushes, then, with a rake, drew the curve of the path in the dead leaves.

I soon discovered that there is more to path-making than meets the eye. In addition to creating a pleasing line, several things should be taken into consideration, including the comfort and safety of strollers. There are rules of thumb about the width being adequate for people to walk two abreast, but in a small, secret garden, a major thoroughfare doesn't seem appropriate. However, the surface of the path should at least be free of booby traps and relatively smooth. As mine traverses tree roots, some sections had to be built up and others excavated a couple of inches. Hoping that a thick layer of wood chips would cover a multitude of sins, I edged the path with sections of log held in place with stakes, spread the wood chips, and pronounced it fit for a visit from Helen Gill. She arrived with her sister-in-law Becky, another keen gardener. Becky and I were deep in conversation when suddenly we heard a soft thud and turned to see that Helen—then in her late eighties—had toppled over into the primroses. She had tripped on one of the stakes holding the log edging. Fortunately she was unhurt and the little archaic smile never left her face. As we righted her, the corners of her mouth drew up in the shape of a U. "I didn't even run my stockings," she announced cheerfully.

I made other mistakes with the path. The first year, I neglected to lay a light-blocking material before applying the wood chips. Consequently, weeds became a nuisance. Their seeds need light to germinate and plenty reached them through the wood chips. The following year, I scraped up the chips, put down black plastic, and added more chips. Old, rotted chips are a wonderful source of humus, and every year I recycle part of the path, adding it to the primrose beds and topping up the path with more chips. Time and foot traffic have compacted the layers and made the surface of the path springy and pleasant to walk on. The log edging is not an unqualified success because eventually the logs rot and have to be replaced but they keep the chips where they belong and fit into their surroundings.

Once this major path was usable, I turned my attention to plants and planting. Again, there was more to preparing a suitable home for primroses and native plants than I had anticipated. Woodland wildflowers need six inches of soil rich in the dark, crumbly, moisture-retentive material called humus—the end product of decayed organic matter. The Catch-22 is that in order to have humus, you first have to have an abundance of herbaceous plants that will die at the end of the growing season and contribute their remains to the ongoing cycle of decay and regeneration. Our woodland floor is shy of vegetation. The shade is too dense and the tree roots too numerous and too near the surface. The layer of topsoil is thin—a scant two inches deep—and the rocks are many. If you dig up a fern in a southwestern Connecticut forest, the spade inevitably meets loose rock or bedrock with a jarring clang. And by the time you wrest the clump out of the ground, the amount of soil clinging to the roots is negligible.

Something had to be done about the soil in the woodland garden. In many places, digging was next to impossible. The alternative was to build up rather than dig down—which is basically what I did. Where possible, I would dig first and remove the loose stones, then add organic matter. The log edging of the path served as a six-inch-high retaining wall for the additional soil—which really is homemade. It has been manufactured out of whatever I have been able to buy, beg, borrow, or steal. Mulch hay which breaks down into soft black gold has been heavily used as a bottom layer, and on top of that, soil scraped from other parts of the property combined with compost, peat moss, decayed wood chips, and rotted tree stumps. It takes time to make a bed this way and some beds are much better than others. If there are a couple of inches of workable topsoil, I just add the amendments and call it a day. Once a bed is planted, it receives a mulch of chopped leaves the first year, and thereafter the natural accumulation of fallen leaves from the woodland trees serves the purpose. Ideally, the leaves should be raked up in the fall, chopped with the lawn mower, and returned to the beds, but I just don't have time. So in the spring, I have to push aside some of the natural mulch to free the plants as they begin to grow.

In the course of constructing the planting beds, I learned the exact dimensions of the opening in the stone wall that leads from the civilized garden into the wild garden. The gap is precisely twenty-four inches wide—no more, no less; the wheelbarrow is twenty-five inches wide. On making this discovery, I was unperturbed. There was always the small yard cart. To be on the safe side, I measured the bed of the cart first and was gratified to find that it was twenty-three inches wide. Perfect. I filled it with compost and trundled it to the entrance of the woodland garden. Oops, forgot the wheels. The two large bicycle-type wheels added another four inches to the overall width. Nothing except the hand truck fits through the opening in the stone wall. So every bit of mulch hay, compost, peat moss, or top soil has to be carried into the garden by hand, by armfuls, or in a bucket. For this reason, the soil in the primrose beds is very precious. And much as I love to give away plants, giving away the homemade soil is like parting with a little piece of my life.

I love our whole garden. The perennial border has given me a great deal of pleasure; the success of the evergreen garden surprises and delights me. I am devoted to the rhododendrons and pleased with the paths among the shade plantings. The field is a constant source of fascination. It not only gives us a little open space and a modest view, it affords us glimpses into another world. We once watched a red fox attacking a woodchuck. The aggressor circled his intended victim and launched quick hit-and-run attacks from all sides. But the clumsy rodent stood his ground, keeping his assailant at bay the way a boxer feints with an opponent. Another time, a pair of coyotes materialized on the crest of the hill. For ten minutes, they lay side by side without moving a muscle, their doglike heads raised above the long grass in a listening attitude. Then, as we watched, they rose in unison and performed a vanishing act that would have confounded Houdini. We have seen wild turkeys and their chicks. The adult birds are enormous and quite hideous—like little old men with shrunken heads dressed in ill-fitting black suits covered with mildew. There are bluebirds—thanks to Mary Ley's gift of cedar posts and nesting boxes. And yet, none of these exquisite pleasures measures up to the experience of making the woodland garden.

Nothing, of course, is quite so much like child's play—dabbling in the water, building little dams and bridges. But the feelings aroused by these activities can't be explained just as a form of retrogression. On the contrary, all the odd pieces of my life have been gradually coming together during the last ten years and this part of the garden has been a focal point. It seems to gather in my mother, her primroses, and a bit of England; my own upbringing and close ties with the Connecticut landscape—rocks and all; Rob Clark and a lifelong affection for wildflowers; Martin's and my life here on this piece of land; and the connection with our predecessors—Mr. and Mrs. Knox—and with the past. I feel a bond with every farmer who ever laid a stone on one of these walls. The woodland garden is about connections. But that's not all. It is also a garden for spring—that moment in the year before "dawn goes down to day." And primroses are the quintessence of spring—fragile, ephemeral, and perfect.

My interest in the genus *Primula* received an enormous boost from joining the American Rock Garden Society. Heretofore, I had known only two primroses: the common primrose and the cowslip. It was a thrill to discover that there are more than five hundred species of these lovely things. And that a dozen are content to grow in the slightly raised beds along my woodland path. Mother's flower, *Primula vulgaris,* with its single pale yellow blossoms, continues to hold a very special place in my heart, but there is room for a minute woodlander from Japan, *P. modesta,* which has a four-inch stalk crowned with golden-eyed white flowers in a cluster no bigger than a coat button; another all-time favorite from Linc, rosey-purple *P. abschasica,* which blooms for two months without flagging; and *P. sibthorpii,* with blossoms like the common primrose—only in a delicate shade of pink. Towers of *P. japonica* are now a reality among the irises at the edge of the pond—just as Linc envisioned them—but he forgot to mention the hummingbirds which zero in on the red-flowered form. I am very partial to another Japanese native, *P. sieboldii,* a beautiful cluster-producing primrose with flower patterns as varied as snow-flakes—which some resemble. Called "Sakurasoh" at home (*Sakura* means cherry blossom and *soh,* herb), there are so many permutations of flower form that a complex system of classification exists to keep them straight. *P. sieboldii* is the last primrose to flower in my woodland before rising temperatures signal the arrival of summer.

If primroses and nostalgia account for part of the woodland garden's hold over me, its secluded location explains the rest. It really is a secret garden. Lying at the bottom of a hollow and enclosed by stone walls, it is completely hidden from view. You have to stand right at the gate before you know it's there. Even the extreme narrowness of the opening in the stone wall adds to the feeling of exclusivity. So when the primroses are enduring their leaden hour, no one bears witness to their miseries. Many of the European species will put forth new growth in the early fall. And I have faith that enough will survive the rigors of summer and the ordeal of winter to make spring a joy. In the meantime, I take comfort in their concealment. In no other part of the garden is it as easy to revel in the beauties, ignore the blemishes, and accept the reality that these plants and I are intruders here—tolerated but temporary.

Rock Gardeners:
A Breed Apart

DURING THE LATE NINETEENTH CENTURY, BRITISH travelers seem to have taken to the mountainous regions of Europe in droves. Born gardeners that they were, they fell in love with the diminutive flora of the high country and, upon returning home, sought means of replicating alpine conditions in order to grow dwarf plants from above the treeline. Alpines are a law unto themselves. Delicate as they appear, they have adapted to conditions that would make even the toughest daylily shudder: a nine-month winter of blizzards and gale-force winds, intense summer sun but frosty nights, and during the brief growing season, scant rainfall. The strategies that enable alpines to cope with this harsh environment are part of their particular charm.

Given a total growing season of only three months, alpines have to be quick about producing flowers, luring pollinators, and setting seed. By reducing the size and surface area of their foliage, they buy extra energy to spend on their blossoms. Among the most prized alpines are those with small, tightly packed leaves and proportionally large flowers that literally cover the tiny tuffets and "buns" of foliage. Their small stature serves another purpose. Lush, leafy plants would soon be torn from their moorings by the winds that lash mountain peaks. The reduction of leaf area also prevents the loss of too much moisture by transpiration during the often dry summer. Alpines are exacting little plants to grow at lower elevations. They require a cool, moist root run but a bone-dry surface on which to rest their leaves; warm days but cool nights; and above all, low humidity. Fulfilling their somewhat contradictory demands gave rise to a highly specialized branch of horticulture—rock gardening.

The late Reginald Farrer, a British plant collector and writer, is generally credited with being the father of rock gardening and his book *My Rock Garden,* published in 1907, helped popularize the cultivation of alpine plants. In wet-weather climates, he found that the secret of their culture lay in providing good drainage. Mountain soils are largely made up of pieces of broken rock of different sizes. Even the loam of upland pastures is open and rocky. At higher altitudes, the proportion of soil to rock decreases until there is virtually no soil—only particles of crumbled rock that accumulate in pockets and cracks in the bedrock. Water runs through the gravelly soil very quickly, leaving the foliage of alpine plants high and dry—conditions essential for their continued good health. Farrer maintained that "more alpine plants are annually lost by defective drainage than by all other fatalities of the garden put together." In due course, this message and his contagious enthusiasm for alpines spread to susceptible gardeners on both sides of the Atlantic. On the first day of spring in 1934, a group met in New York to found the American Rock Garden Society—an organization that now has over four thousand members—including eight hundred in foreign countries.

The roster of the society reads like a horticultural Who's Who, with institutional members—the directors of botanical gardens and arboreta—here and abroad, and any number of nurseries and growers, plant professionals, and hybridizers. But the great majority are gifted amateurs. Even the rank and file members garden with a degree of expertise and an obsessive dedication that sets them apart from ordinary gardeners, while the elite tend their tufts and "buns" in a state bordering on religious ecstasy. The fervor increases as the size of the plant diminishes: The smaller, rarer, and more difficult it is to grow, the more exhilarating the challenge; the higher and more inaccessible its aerie on some remote mountaintop, the more desirable the plant. Nor are rock gardeners content with trying to understand their temperamental little charges out of context. Nothing will do but firsthand observation of these plants in their natural surroundings. No distance is too far to travel, no mountain path too steep to climb.

To study alpines in their native habitats, modern American rock gardeners range far and wide—from the western mountains of the United States to the Pyrenees to the Himalayas. And I don't mean just the youngest and ablest among them. Men and women no longer in the first flush of youth—people who should know better—spend considerable sums of money for the privilege of courting disaster and enduring discomfort. These wonderful—if misguided—gardeners willingly risk their necks scrambling up vertical slopes and teetering along knife-edged ridges thousands of feet above sea level. Just seeing slides of their adventures makes me reach for a seat belt.

You may well wonder what a timid, earth-bound border person like me is doing in this rarefied company. I have often wondered myself. I don't like heights; the only time I've ever been in the mountains was by mistake when a wrong turn on the Italian border took me over a pass in the French Alps—instead of along the riviera; there isn't a single alpine plant in my garden; I'm devoted to large, amiable perennials—which rock gardeners shun; and I plead guilty to enjoying plants that you can see with the naked eye just as much as those for which you need a magnifying glass. Then there is the problem of my dark past. If any of my colleagues knew how hard I had tried to get rid of the rocks in our garden, my standing in the Rock Garden Society—such as it is—would plummet. Nevertheless, I have been a member for ten years and on the strength of the pleasure it has given me, have also joined the American Primrose Society, the New England Wild Flower Society, the Hardy Plant Society, and the American Hemerocallis Society.

No other affiliation has been as rewarding as my unlikely association with the alpine enthusiasts. There is something so inspiring and endearing about rock gardeners that you can't help throwing in your lot with them. Committed to the principle of service to their plants, they are among the best gardeners in the country. They know a lot, care a lot, and have the highest standards of excellence—qualities any gardener would do well to emulate. In addition, they have wide-ranging interests that include plants found lower down on the mountain slopes. En route to Shangri-la, rock gardeners are obliged to travel first through moist woodlands where firs and larches overhang the streams and primroses nestle along the damp banks. As avid plant-lovers, they embrace these denizens of the shady woods and all the other wildflowers encountered in their pilgrimage to the heights. This diversity gives the Rock Garden Society a broader base than other plant societies.

The members are as diverse as their multiple interests and as quirky and individualistic as the plants they most admire. In fact, I sometimes wonder what a stranger would make of an annual meeting where as many as three hundred rock gardeners gather. What could such a heterogeneous group of people possibly have in common? Among the members I know personally, there are bankers, lawyers, schoolteachers, business people, writers, dentists, housewives, and landscape designers. But you would never know it. If two or three rock gardeners are gathered together, there is only one subject of conversation—plants. These horticultural Walter Mittys put their everyday lives far behind them when they attend annual meetings and winter study weekends. Annual meetings take place in different locations each year with a local chapter of the society playing host. Winter study weekends are held on both east and west coasts. During these events, all thought of school, office, or place of business is banished in a world of words and pictures pertaining only to alpine, saxatile, bog, and woodland plants. There will be slide lectures by experts; workshops on how to grow difficult species from seed or propagate woody plants from cuttings; eagerly awaited plant sales; and a plant show with classes for different genera. Tours of members' gardens or field trips are a popular feature of the annual meetings, which usually take place during the spring or summer. Finally, there is the informal talk about plants at communal meals and the Saturday night banquet. Sometimes at these affairs I try to find out what my table companions do in real life. But they look at me vaguely, like patients coming out of an anesthetic. Gardening is far more real to them than the jobs they hold in order to support their families—and their habit.

My daylily friend, Jane Conningham, and I were once comparing notes on the plant society phenomenon. "I'm not a joiner," she admitted, "but

I used to go occasionally to meetings of the Iris Society, the Hemerocallis Society and the Orchid Society. The groups are amazing! Talk about a totally mixed bag. What's so remarkable is the way a disparate collection of people can operate in concert—as an enthusiastic group." Which is not to say that plant people aren't competitive! Rock gardeners are certainly not above a little friendly rivalry. They're only human. But they are the best of the best and I've learned more about gardening since I joined the American Rock Garden Society than in the twenty preceding years.

Viki

JIM YORK SAID, "YOU'VE GOT TO HEAR THIS ENGLISH girl. She's fantastic! I mean, the mouth on her! It's nonstop, the knowledge, and it just keeps coming. . . ." Words failed him. That was ten years ago when I still needed prodding to attend meetings of the American Rock Garden Society. Jim was insistent about this one. "She's talking about wildflowers. You'll love it and her pictures are to die for." Thus persuaded, I went to Viki Ferreniea's lecture on American woodland plants of the Northeast and was as impressed as Jim had been.

Afterward, I heard her speak as often as I could. Her superb photographs were sensitively orchestrated into evocations of spring in New England and an effortless flow of information accompanied the shifting patterns of color on the screen. At last, somebody was speaking my language—hepaticas, bloodroot, trailing arbutus, marsh marigolds, trilliums. This was more like it. Having struggled at the previous meetings to memorize the generic and specific names of numerous unfamiliar alpines, it was a treat to see old friends and to learn the correct botanical nomenclature. Most of all, the response of this young Englishwoman to the beauties of American wildflowers touched me. She had fallen in love with *my* wildflowers—the very plants my fond mama had rejected, perhaps because they were yet another reminder that she was far from home.

In due course, Viki and I became friends. Having English forebears gave us an immediate bond but we also discovered many common interests. We're both country bred and fond of animals, we share a great enjoyment in hiking and the out-of-doors, and of course, we're both passionate gardeners. Viki, however, made horticulture her profession and in an informal way has been my tutor, giving me advice, ideas, and encouragement. She also introduced me to many native species which were new to me but which soon found a place in the woodland garden: Bowman's-Root *(Gillenia trifoliata),* quite a tall plant with three-part leaves and dainty sprays of flowers having five white to pink scraps for petals—lovely en masse; goldseal *(Hydrastis canadensis),* a handsome eighteen-inch-tall foliage plant with palmate leaves, single insignificant little gold-tipped white flowers, and attractive fruit like miniature red pineapples; creeping phlox *(Phlox stolonifera),* which became a great favorite and is a wonderful carpeter with snowdrops; foamflower *(Tiarella cordifolia),* a charming small woodlander with spikes of fuzzy white flowers; and many other plants.

For years, Viki didn't have a garden, but her interest in mine was generous and genuine. Her beautiful photographs, taken over a period of several years, have allowed me to look at the garden through rose-colored glasses. An expert photographer, she has recorded more than the outward manifestations of a twenty-eight-year-old love affair with a piece of property. Her camera's kindly eye has perceived the dream, brought it prematurely to life, and told it, not the way it is, but as I would have it. Her photographs capture a moment that has never been—and which will, indeed, never be because it has passed already. Often, the angles of the shots are unexpected—views that would not have occurred to me. Sometimes looking at her slides of our garden is like visiting a place that is hauntingly familiar and yet strange and exciting. Everything always looks better in the photographs than in the flesh. At the same time, the images are true to the pictures in my mind's eye, which are less about reality than about creation.

Finally, Viki has a garden of her own. It is brand-new and the South Carolina clay is hard to work. There are no mature shade trees—only a few pines—and a scruffy bit of lawn. It is impossible to get help, so she is doing everything herself. By her own admission, the prospect is daunting. There are not even the bare bones of a garden here. "I mean, I've got nothing. But every day I come home from work, change my clothes, and go straight out to wander around and look at everything. I only planted the stuff yesterday and of course it hasn't grown, but I look at it anyway. Even in a new garden there are a few things. . . . I've got azaleas and they're in full bloom. The flowers are basically white with a pink overlay. In front of them I have *Prunus subhirtella* 'Autumnalis,' which is all of four feet tall with scattered blossoms on it. And in front of that there is a pink tree peony, 'Hana Kisoi,' with one blossom on it that makes the whole garden smell lovely." Where does a love of gardening come from? Many of my gardening friends have been hard put to account for their spontaneous urge to dig and plant. But Viki attributes hers to a country upbringing, a gardening father, and her own interest in wildflowers.

"I used to spend hours as a child riding horseback over my uncle's farm in Sussex," she says. "I became totally enamored of the wildflowers there and used to pick bunches of primroses and bluebells for my mother. As I was a great animal-watcher, I also spent a lot of time looking at birds and in the process became very aware of trees. I loved the woods. But basically, I get my love of gardening from my father and from exposure. We had an old Elizabethan house with grass terraces down to a lake surrounded by daffodils; then, we had espaliered pear trees leading down pathways—and topiaries. It was just one of those lovely old English gardens. In those days, we had two full-time gardeners. My mother gardened too, but it was my father who was really keen. He was crazy about gardening."

As a child, the only time Viki was ever permitted to miss school was when he took her to the Chelsea Flower Show every other year. A reserved, formal Englishman studying the latest rose introductions in the company of his small daughter conjures up a nice picture. But her father's interest in gardening by no means prepared him to accept his daughter's decision a few years later to become a professional horticulturist. While Viki was a postwar child, it must be remembered that she had a prewar father who did not welcome displays of independence in his only offspring. If she insisted upon having a career, it must be a suitable one. And by the time she was fifteen, he had decided that she should become a doctor.

It can't have pleased Mr. Ferreniea, therefore, to discover that Viki was being urged in another direction by one of his best friends. Gus Bellchambers worked for a large British seed company. Quite apart from his professional association with horticulture, he loved plants and was a fine gardener. It was this mutual interest that had drawn the two men together in the first place and Gus had become a close family friend. By this time, it was clear that Viki and her father did not see eye to eye about her future. And having known Viki all her life, Gus felt compelled to intervene on her behalf. Apparently he saw in her something neither she nor her parents had seen, because he kept nudging her toward a career in horticulture. He did more than that. He actively facilitated her entry into the field.

"At that time, in order to get accepted at the horticultural colleges in England, you had to have a year of practical experience. It wasn't easy, but he got me into a nursery, and then recommended Swanley Horticultural College in Kent. Gus was right. At Swanley, for the first time in my life, I felt that what I was doing was right. I'd always struggled at school. I hated it and felt out of my depth. But I knew within the first ten days that Swanley was right for me. It was incredible. All of a sudden, my life just fell into place." Which is not to say that it was all smooth sailing from then on. At the end of the first year, her father summoned her to his office and said, "Now, you will be sensible and study medicine." But her mind was made up. She had found her niche. Returning to Swanley, she completed her training and shortly thereafter was offered her first job.

After graduation, Viki had been toying with spending a year in Holland or Germany before settling down in England. But in the meantime, her parents had moved to the United States. At about the same time, Longwood Gardens in Kennett Square, Pennsylvania, made her an offer that she couldn't refuse. So she arrived in 1967 with the intention of staying for a year and has been in the United States ever since. Her decision to remain was in no small part influenced by a love of American native plants. "We grew quite a few when I was in college—things like trillium and bloodroot. Then I got over here and started going down to the Blue Ridge on long weekends. I used to spend all my free time in the woods, and eventually word got around that I was very interested in American native plants. At the end of the year, I was just putting together my plans to return to England when the opportunity of developing the new wildflower garden at Longwood arose. I jumped at it. Two years after that, I was offered the job at Garden in the Woods and that clinched it. I'd always been crazy about wildflowers but this was love of an indescribable kind. That garden made an imprint on me that is just incredible. It was so beautiful. And the charm of those plants—they look so delicate, and yet they're so sturdy and tough."

If the years at Swanley showed Viki her direction, the experience at Garden in the Woods gave form to everything that had happened previously. A small botanical garden specializing in native American plants and their Asiatic counterparts, Garden in the Woods in Framingham, Massachusetts, became the property and headquarters of the New England Wild Flower Society in 1965. Viki still speaks of the woodland garden there with deep affection. "I lost my heart to Garden in the Woods and never got it back. It is still there." Although her career in horticulture has finally taken her to South Carolina, where she is the assistant director of horticulture for Wayside Gardens, a part of her remains in New England—and in my woodland garden.

Spinoff

ONE SUREFIRE WAY TO HAVE AN INSTANT PATCHWORK garden is to join the American Rock Garden Society. Before long your garden will be full of plants, memories, and mementos. For instance, I have a lovely pulmonaria (*Pulmonaria angustifolia* 'Azure'), with intensely blue flowers and leaves of solid green, that was a souvenir of my first visit to the garden of Dick and Herb Redfield. At the time I joined the society, Dick was chairman of the Connecticut chapter and the speaker at one of the first meetings I attended. His topic was "Easy Plants for the Woodland Garden." I still have notes from that meeting. Incidentally, if you do join a plant society, be sure to stock up on composition books. I began to go through them at an accelerated rate of one every six months, instead of one every ten years!

Once again, it was Mary Ley who organized the trip to the Redfields' garden. After leaving Hartford and the interstate, we drove through the farmland and unspoiled villages that still survive in northeastern Connecticut. The Redfields' garden lies a few miles outside the town of Scotland on high land that spreads out like a skirt and slopes down to a spring-fed stream. The property had been in the family for years. But work on the garden didn't begin until the mid-seventies when most of the plants were transported from New Jersey to the Redfield homestead. Richard and Herbert Redfield had been employed in the Garden State for most of their working lives. When the brothers retired, they dug up their New Jersey garden and moved it—lock, stock, and barrel—back home. The labor involved must have been backbreaking. Indeed, it is hard to imagine how these two frail-looking gentlemen could have contemplated such a task, let alone carry it through unaided. It is easier to imagine them behind desks in their city suits than in work clothes struggling with heavy root balls.

In an extensive note written the day after our May visit, I describe their remarkable achievement:

> The garden was fascinating—from the driveway, we walked toward the stream with a relatively new-looking rock garden on one side where there were cacti and shrubs set in gravel. But to me the most lovely part was the natural stream running at the base of a west-sloping bank and, beyond the stream, pines and light woods. On the garden side of the stream, paths switched back and forth among masses of primroses: pale yellow *Primula vulgaris* and two spectacular hybrids of *P. pruhoniciana*—'Wanda,' a deep magenta with a yellow eye and 'J. J.,' a solid, very, very deep purple-red. These next to great clumps of little yellow hose-in-hose primroses. Dick Redfield says that primula naturalize readily and that the candelabra type are easy from seed—if they're happily located. For the candelabras, he says constant moisture is an absolute must. His must be gorgeous! You could see them all in the grass along the stream with foliage the size of lettuce heads—not unlike the light green crinkled leaves of Black Seeded Simpson.

There were many other beautiful and at that time unfamiliar woodland plants in bloom in drifts and sweeps all along the paths: *Jeffersonia dubia,* an exquisite lilac-colored Japanese relation of our own white-flowered twinleaf *(J. diphylla); Ranunculus ficaria cuprea,* with lacquered, deep yellow-orange flowers like a cross between buttercups and marsh marigolds; a white form of plumy bleeding heart *(Dicentra eximia* 'Snowdrift'); barren strawberry *(Waldsteinia ternata),* a very low growing plant with shiny, leathery leaves and small yellow flowers like strawberry blossoms; a lovely Japanese woodlander called *Hylomecon japonicum,* with two-inch bright yellow flowers made up of four round petals and a bunch of deeper yellow stamens; and the real show stopper, a breathtaking patch of double bloodroot *(Sanguinaria canadensis* 'Multiplex'), covered with intensely white, many-petaled flowers like small, incredibly fragile chrysanthemums.

At the time I met Judy Glattstein, she was an up-and-coming younger member of the American Rock Garden Society. A single plait of hair a yard long, as thick as my arm, and as black and glossy as a crow's wing hung down her back. She has since cut it off and wears it short and stylish. But she once told me that after delivering a lecture, she heard a member of the audience remark to her companion, "That girl has the most beautiful hair but did you notice her fingernails?" Those fingernails can be blamed on a chance encounter with a proselytizing rock gardener. At the time, Judy had been married to her husband, Paul, for a few years and had two children, two dogs, four cats, six chickens, and a goldfish but no consuming desire to grow things. The Glattsteins had recently moved from Pittsburgh to Norwalk, Connecticut, where they bought their first house. And Judy had started working part time at a food and grain store as an outlet for her prodigious energies.

As she recalls the incident that launched her career in horticulture, "One fall day, a man came in and ordered a hundred *Scilla sibirica.* I was counting them out and, like a damn fool, started a conversation. I said, 'You know, I often think these small bulbs are more charming than the big ones.' 'Ah,' he says, 'then you will like the American Rock Garden Society.' And who had I hit on? Larry Hocheimer, who was then the national chairman. He sent me a membership form. Well, he'd gone to such a lot of trouble, what could I do? I had to join. That was the beginning and it took off from there. It's worse than crack or cocaine—its consuming." However, at this point Judy couldn't get into much trouble because she didn't drive a car. She commuted to work on a bicycle and every now and then her tolerant, nongardening husband would take her to a Rock Garden Society meeting. To no one's surprise except Judy's, he didn't always have the patience to stay to the bitter end and usually she had to leave before the meeting was over. But she still didn't quite have the incentive to get a driver's license. Then a friend called her and said, "I have a wonderful job for you—taking care of a private greenhouse. The trouble is that it's in Westport and you are in Norwalk." That did it. Judy hung up the phone, looked up a driving school in the Yellow Pages, and called her friend back. "Don't laugh," she said, "but I've signed up for driving lessons."

From here, it has been onward and upward all the way. A former chairman of the Connecticut chapter of the American Rock Garden Society and now a sought-after teacher, lecturer, and garden writer, Judy has parlayed an addiction into a full-time career. When she tells me what she has done in the hours between dawn and dusk, I feel like a wimp. She may have planted a few hundred bulbs by breakfast time; written a magazine article before lunch; taught courses all afternoon at the New York Botanical Garden; and returned home in time to squeeze in another hour in the garden before dark. The garden is eleven years old and occupies a wooded hillside and a small valley furnished with hardwoods. So far, Judy hasn't run out of space or things to do. "We moved from Norwalk," she says, "because I had to have a bigger garden. I said to Paul, 'Either we move or I will plow up your driveway and turn it into a rock garden.'" Unshaken by this threat, Paul, a calm, humorous man, expressed his willingness to cooperate, on one condition: The new house must have a second bathroom. Their present property in Wilton fulfills the requirements of both Glattsteins and provides a lovely setting for Judy's fascinating collection of native and exotic plants which border woodland paths.

As early as the first week in April, there are dozens of things in bloom in her garden: eight or nine genera of bulbs; four species of hellebores; a couple of kinds of pulmonaria; *Trillium nivale,* a difficult-to-grow native from the Southeast with snow-white flowers; and *Primula abschasica,* the early bloomer with rosey-purple flowers. Plants that bloom early and late, extending the season at either end, are one of Judy's many enthusiasms. Jack-in-the-pulpits are another. One of the most unusual is a sinister-looking Japanese species *(Ariseama Thunbergii)* with a very dark hood that overhangs an equally dark interior, from which the spadix emerges like a long whip. Many of her "jacks" have been grown from seed procured through exchanges with American Rock Garden Society members in Japan. Apparently, one reason that Japanese plants from the northern islands do so well in southern New England is similarity of climate. At the time Japan was part of the Asian continent, a continuous band of temperate-zone vegetation encircled the globe. When long ago volcanic disturbances interrupted the vegetative chain, once identical species evolved along comparable but different lines. Consequently, many species of Japanese wildflower—such as the Jack-in-the-pulpits—have American analogs.

In one way or another, I have learned a lot from Judy and many lovely Japanese species have found their way from her woodland into mine: a pale pink form of *Primula kisoana,* a whole flat of *Hylomecon japonicum,* and a seedling of *Paeonia obovata,* which will one day have beautiful single white flowers and even now has attractive foliage—purple in the spring, later turning deep green. Once when I was relieving Judy of an embarrassingly large number of plants, both Japanese and native, Paul—whom I had never met—came home from work. He peered into the back of my car. "Taking away plants, I see?" And then, after a rather nerve-wracking pause, he added with a smile of obvious satisfaction, "Good!"

How does a graphic designer with a masters degree in American civilization become—at a relatively tender age—national secretary of the American Rock Garden Society? Through Judy Glattstein and the long arm of coincidence. During the early sixties when Buffy Parker was studying at the Parsons School of Design in New York City, she became friendly with Judy's sister-in-law, Susan. After graduation, Susan moved to Connecticut while Buffy remained in the city. But the two young women kept in touch. "What happened," Buffy said, "was that when my mother died, I gave up my apartment and came home to Connecticut to keep house for my father. I'd never gardened before but I started puttering around outside, not knowing what I was doing—just figuring that it was time to do something because the place was a mess. Then one day I was with Susan, and she said, 'Well, if you're into gardening, you should probably meet my sister-in-law, Judy. She's a real nut on the subject.' " Before Buffy knew what had happened, she was being hustled off to meetings of the American Rock Garden Society. And in less time than it takes to say "Connecticut chapter," she found herself on the board.

"Linc was president of the chapter when I first joined the society and he latched onto me pretty quickly. He must have asked me to make coffee or something. Then I got involved with Timmy and the bulletin. I was her layout designer. We actually did the dummy of the first issue together, cutting and pasting, and I designed the cover. They're still using the typeface we used. And the Connecticut chapter is still using the layout I did for their newsletter." I can well imagine the delight with which the Fosters greeted this newcomer. If Peter Pan had been a girl—he is traditionally played by lithe, agile young women—and if she had been permitted to mature and reach a willowy five-feet-nine-inches in height, she would now be computerizing the American Rock Garden Society mailing lists and dealing with the thousand and one details of record keeping and memberships. Linc and Timmy knew a good thing when they saw it! The feeling was mutual. Buffy lost her heart to the Fosters and to Millstream and a wonderful friendship ensued. Not everyone has a rhododendron named after them but a hybrid of Linc's breeding with trusses of peach-colored flowers—which he described as "long and leggy"—rejoices in the name 'Buffy Parker.'

When Buffy wasn't working for the Rock Garden Society or as art director of a local advertising agency, she was busy making a woodland garden for her father. She and Judy used to go off into the woods to collect plentiful native species—trilliums, bloodroot, and wild ginger. She added *Phlox stolonifera, Iris cristata,* and primroses from Millstream, and whatever else she managed to pick up from the seedling sales. Some of the same plants accompanied her to the house she bought in Darien eleven years ago. Although I haven't seen her garden yet, she is very much a part of mine. She has lavished appreciation on it and said the words that are most musical to my ears: "It works in the total landscape—it flows."

She has brought me seeds of *Primula bulleyana,* which will bloom this year for the first time. Once, when I couldn't make it to the major Rock Garden Society seedling sale, she stopped by on her way home with a whole flat full of treasures—among them a tiny rosette of pale green leaves silvered over with the powdery bloom called "meal." The label identified the seedling as *Primula modesta,* a woodlander from Japan which bears a cluster of enchanting gold-eyed white flowers. It bloomed the following year and Judy took a photograph of it for me. For the next three years, I brooded over this one plant before working up the courage to tease apart the little cluster of rosettes that had formed. To my infinite relief, the divisions survived the dreadful heat of last summer and this year's open winter. I now have five little rosettes—each with a minute cluster of buds at its heart—waiting for warmer weather to draw up the flower stem to its full height of four or five inches.

Every year when the primroses are in full bloom, Buffy makes a pilgrimage to our garden with another garden friend. We look forward to their visit all during the unsettled month of April. The weather warms and *Primula abschasica* opens its rich, red-purple flowers, then wet snow batters the blossoms and they turn blue with cold—literally—and the sun returns, warmer than before, and the drumstick primroses *(Primula denticulata)* blossom. Meanwhile, the other primroses are still small green rosettes. We have another cold snap, and I think there won't be anything in bloom when they come. But miraculously, there always is. Buffy's visit and the primroses are sure signs that spring has not only come but is finally here to stay.

Shortly after I joined the American Rock Garden Society, a mysterious letter addressed to me and sent by air from Czechoslovakia appeared in our post office box. "Dear Madame," it began:

> I found out from the Bulletin of the American Rock Garden Society that you are a new member and that is why I am writing a letter to you. It would be a great pleasure for me to exchange plants or seeds with you, if you want, of course. In case you are interested, be so kind, please and let me know. We can exchange them in the fall or next spring. If my proposal is of no interest to you, accept my apologies for bothering you.

It was signed with a name that, of course, meant nothing to me, but I was charmed by the diffident style of the writer—clearly, a man—and by his generous idea.

In my reply, I explained that I really didn't have a rock garden—just a perennial border and a woodland garden—and that I had never raised anything from seed, except annuals and vegetables. But I would like to accept his kind offer if he did not object to my sharing the seed with my friend, Mary, who was an experienced grower and had a beautiful rock garden. He answered at once—by all means share with my friend. Seeds were on the way and he looked forward to hearing from us. A manila envelope duly arrived containing two dozen small packets of seed. There were different kinds of primula and dianthus and many unfamiliar species suitable for a rock garden. That March, Mary and I planted sixty three-inch pots with the seed from Czechoslovakia. By May we were pricking out seedlings, and in August we put the small plants in our respective gardens—I took the primulas, she planted the rest in her rock garden.

For several years, a delightfully bizarre verbal exchange skimmed back and forth across the Atlantic—accompanied sometimes by seeds, plants, and literature. I sent Linc and Timmy Foster's book after receiving a particularly generous gift of dwarf evergreens. In the course of our correspondence, some confusion had arisen about my name and gender and the letters I received were sometimes headed "Dear John," other times "Dear Mr. Eddison," and occasionally "Dear Friend." In order to clear up the mystery as tactfully as possible, I sent a photograph of our garden, one of Mary's, and one of Mary and myself in her rock garden. Our Czech friend reciprocated. I had somehow imagined my correspondent to be an elderly gentleman of the old school with a beard. Instead, a handsome, heavyset young man brooded darkly out of the two-by-three-inch color print. It was accompanied by a note: "Many thanks for your nice letter and the lovely pictures. You and Mary are really very nice ladies. My best regards to your friend Mary." Henceforth, there were always tender inquiries for my friend Mary. And when it appeared that she might actually visit Czechoslovakia, the news was greeted with great joy. Mary must visit him. In the same letter, he expressed doubt that he would ever be able to come to America. In the days before Glasnost, traveling to a nonsocialist country was "rather complicated and highly expensive."

Although Mary's trip never materialized, the lively flow of correspondence continued uninterrupted—until 1984. Then, all of a sudden, silence. I went ahead and sent seed of some American wildflowers that he wanted but there was no reply. Almost two years later, out of the blue, I received a very brief communication saying that he had not been living at home for ten months. He would write again when his problems were solved. Another two years went by. To my utter astonishment, I received a Christmas card from Canada which read, "You might find it interesting that I live in Canada since October." I have had Christmas cards ever since—but no more letters. Unfortunately, the story has been fleshed out for me from other sources and it is the sad, all too familiar tale of a broken marriage. I much preferred the mystery.

More Help

WHILE A GREAT MANY PEOPLE HAVE CONTRIBUTED patches of different sizes, shapes, colors, and designs to the all-over pattern of our garden, only a few have had a hand in assembling and cobbling together the quilt. For many years, the garden which I find myself referring to—erroneously—as "my" garden was entirely a two-person operation. You will find that behind every rabid gardener there stands a patient spouse or companion. And believe me, they also serve who only stand and wait—and wait and wait. The spouse or companion waits for meals (and then does the dishes because the gardener is too exhausted to move another muscle), and waits for the return of the gardener from meetings, flower shows, courses, or from gardens in far-off places (and in the meantime does the grocery shopping, walks the dog, and feeds the cat).

In addition to waiting, my spouse mows the lawn and shreds the leaves. He is the mechanic who services, repairs, and refuels the tractor, the small lawn mower, the gasoline-powered string trimmer, the leaf blower, and the chain saw. As resident hydrologist, this nongardener is in charge of the pump and the garden well—snakes notwithstanding. In his hat as resident electrician, he installs outlets in convenient places for my electric string trimmer and the hedge clippers. And as chief carpenter, he puts up shelves and assembles storage units for garden-related paraphernalia. In short, making and maintaining this garden would have been impossible without Martin's total participation. Until the last dozen years, we managed very well without any outside help. But when the sides of the swimming pool cracked and collapsed in 1978, we were plunged into a cleanup operation that was beyond our capabilities.

There was some good news: The pool was beyond repair. And

some bad news: We would need to buy fill and hire a backhoe to bury the evidence. So we bit the bullet and summoned a cheerful young man with the required equipment. A couple of days later, the deed was done. But even then, we were left with about three thousand square feet of dirt and rubble. Faced with the task of repairing the lawn, I began thinking about help. Earlier sources of cheap labor had long since dried up: The doughty Vincent from the F. W. French Company had left town years ago; Patty was married and had a garden of her own; and my cousin had returned to London to pursue a career in publishing. I didn't know where to turn for a stalwart helper. Then a kind friend told me that her hired man had a young nephew staying with him and that the boy was looking for work. The only snag was that he had no transportation. I said that I would gladly pick him up and arrangements were made. The next day, I collected John from the center of town, where his uncle had deposited him.

It is difficult to say how old the boy was—between sixteen and eighteen, going on forty. He was wearing blue jeans and what remained of a short-sleeved T-shirt. A pack of cigarettes was ingeniously twisted up in the sleeve of the shirt. John and his clothes were filthy beyond description and they both smelled. But under the layers of grime, he was extraordinarily handsome in a decadent way. He had almond-shaped blue eyes with heavy lids that made him look as if he had just woken up from a nap. His chin was as full and soft as a girl's with the suggestion of, nothing as macho as a cleft, but a dimple—and when he smiled, the dimple became more pronounced. He smiled very effectively and kept calling me "ma'am" in a sinuous Georgia drawl. As we drove home, I asked him about himself. The only thing I remember now was that he claimed to have just come north from Florida, where he was an extra in a movie. I believed him about the movie. Otherwise, he was a complete stranger to the truth.

It transpired that he was also a stranger to physical labor. For a while he pushed topsoil around with a rake, then resorted to leveling it by running back and forth over it with the tractor. But at least he had carted away a good many loads of loose stones by lunchtime. Part of the deal was that I would feed him before returning him to his uncle. He came in looking even filthier than before and I handed him a towel and steered him toward the bathroom. En route, he spied a half-finished portrait in oils. For fun, I had been taking an evening class in portraiture. John studied the painting with interest and said in honeyed tones, "It's mah mama's birthday next week, ma'am. Would yo'all paint mah picture for her?" Like a fool, I said that I would spend four hours on a portrait in return for the same number of hours in the garden.

The next day when I went to meet John, I almost didn't recognize him in his Australian bush hat with a red bandanna wrapped around the crown. He also had on a dark green plaid lumber shirt over a spotless blue T-shirt and a clean pair of jeans. Scrubbed and freshly shaven, he was nothing short of beautiful. His golden skin and fair hair were artfully set off by the theatrical costume. Naturally he couldn't work in this get-up, so I painted his portrait. He cannily insisted on wearing his hat, which was an inspired choice. I have to admit that working very quickly and without mucking about the result, I got a good likeness. He was well pleased. After lunch, he took the picture with him—holding it gingerly in order not to smear it or get paint on his good clothes. We agreed that he would come the next day and I drove him back to town. That was the last we ever saw of John.

I don't remember how Allan came to us. He was as honest and reliable as John was sly and shiftless. He came for three hours a week during his summer vacation from school and returned for three consecutive years. He was charming, amiable, and as strong as an ox. At school, he won prizes for wrestling. And together, we moved some of the biggest rocks on the property. After Martin began to find chain-sawing too laborious, Allan and I managed to cut down all the saplings in the woodland pond with hand saws. We finished putting in the lawn over the erstwhile pool and cleaned up the dump in the northwest corner of the garden. Allan was intrigued by the contents of the dump and kept salvaging "antique" bottles—probably from the thirties. I still have one of his finds—a clear glass bottle tinted blue-green with CASTORIA plainly printed in raised letters on one side, but it is quite a pretty color and the shape is just right for a sprig of witch hazel. Martin and I became fond of Allan and were touched to be invited to his high school graduation party. After that, he went on to bigger and better things and now runs a health club.

Allan's successors were a motley crew. A wiry eleven-year-old helped me build two large cement block compost bins before getting a better job mowing lawns for an outrageous hourly wage. Two smooth-talking high school juniors with a "gardening service" relieved me of a few dollars before I discovered that their business acumen exceeded their energy level. And a sixteen-year-old Adonis with curly blond locks came twice before deciding that the work was too hard, and anyway, he could get more money as a bagger at the supermarket. In the end, I gave up trying to find youthful help. The kids were amusing but, with the exception of Allan, more trouble than they were worth. However, for the past six years I have been more than lucky—I've been blessed—first with Lou and now with Ann.

Lou

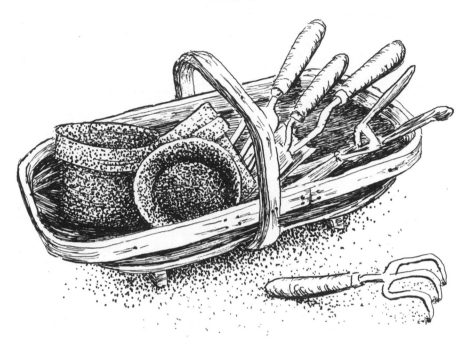

THE GILLS AND THE FOSTERS SHOWED ME WHAT AMER-
ican gardens could be and immeasurably broadened my gardening
horizons. Mary Ley introduced me to the pleasures of growing
primulas and other hardy plants from seed, and Viki expanded my vocabulary
of native plants. I have learned something of value from everyone who has
come to my garden or been kind enough to invite me to theirs. But no one has
influenced the way I garden more than Lou. Like so many other things in our
garden, she came through the good offices of Helen Gill. And during the three
years that Lou helped me, she not only transformed much of the thin, lifeless
soil in the perennial border into active, fertile loam, she changed my approach
to gardening.

Even this modest tribute—however richly deserved—will embar-
rass Lou, provoking nervous laughter and self-effacing disclaimers. But because
her contribution to my garden has to do with its very foundation—the soil—it
is impossible to overestimate its importance. Before she came, my care of the
soil consisted of scratching in a little 10–10–10 chemical fertilizer—the formula
based on soil samples I sent to the University of Connecticut Soil Testing
Laboratory—keeping down the weeds during the growing season, and raking
the surface clear of debris in the fall. Individual planting holes I prepared with
some care—excavating to the depth of the shovel, removing the rocks, and
mixing the topsoil with compost and peat moss before returning it to the cavity
and installing the plant. But I was performing these activities more or less by
rote. Having once read that this was the way to plant perennials, I had been
doing it the same way ever since. I employed mulches on the border largely
for my own convenience—to reduce the weeds. Where the plants were close
enough together, I didn't bother too much about keeping the ground covered.

Their own leaves shaded out most of the weeds, and like Helen, I liked the look of open cultivation. The way the garden looked was very important to me and if it *looked* attractive, I was content. Lou roused me from this complacent torpor.

An early convert to Ruth Stout's theory of mulch gardening, she applied it to the first garden she ever made. Lou and her husband had recently settled into a rented cottage on what had once been an estate in southwestern Connecticut. "There was the large main house and this little carriage house which we ultimately bought," she says. "The whole place had been neglected and was terribly overgrown. It was such a jungle at our house that there was nowhere for a garden. But I was friendly with the people at the big house and they said, 'We're putting in a vegetable garden. Why don't you do one up here next to ours?' So I got a local farmer to come and plow up a fifty-by-fifty-foot plot. When it was done, it looked huge and I had to work like a dog to get it ready for planting. I'd never had a garden before but I'd been reading Ms. Stout's book and decided to try her method.

"I found an old man up the road who had a big stack of spoiled hay. He didn't want it and was surprised that anyone else would, but I came up and got a truckload of it. 'What are you going to do with all that?' he wanted to know. And when I told him, he just shook his head. Anyway, I got it home and mulched like crazy! I'm one of those people who thinks that if a little is a good thing, a lot is better, and after I used up the hay, I went down our hill to the woods. I brought back pine needles and leaf mold and all sorts of things and just ladled it onto the garden. I was raising collies then, and I used to take one of those big burlap sacks that the dry food came in and stuff it with half-rotted pine needles. I'd stagger back with it over my shoulder, like Santa Claus. Everybody thought I was insane, but boy, did things grow! I grew everything that year. I went crazy for oddities: pumpkins and all kinds of strange winter squashes, soybeans, chickpeas, even peanuts. There were enough soybeans to feed an army!"

After that year, the people next door moved away and Lou dug up part of the jungle at the side of the carriage house. "At first, I literally couldn't get a fork into the ground! It was all sumac and privet and poison ivy—dreadful things. I dug and pulled out what I could but when I didn't have the time or the strength to dig, I'd push the sumac down flat and mulch it very heavily with hay, hay, and more hay—I used hay by the hundred bales. I'd put down two or three 'books' of it and layer them with manure and peat moss. The next year, I'd be able to dig that in and I just kept doing it. It worked beautifully and not one scrap of poison ivy or sumac came up through the hay. So I did the same thing with my first perennial bed. I built up a berm of hay, peat moss, and manure, then I took some of the good soil from the vegetable garden and put that on close to a foot deep and planted in that. The perennials grew like weeds!"

A strange young man who involved himself in other people's affairs, pulling strings from behind the scenes, brought Helen Gill and Lou together. He was a figure as shadowy as any Robertson Davies character who controls the lives of others without appearing to do so and about whom there is an aura of mystery. Helen often mentioned David but we never met him. She became acquainted with him after Johnny's heart attack in 1981. Never a good driver, she had been casting around for someone to transport her to and from the hospital and to take her grocery shopping when, fortuitously, David materialized. And after Johnny came home, it was David who put Helen in touch with Lou.

Meanwhile, Lou's marriage of twenty years had broken up and she was suddenly on her own with no means of support. Although she had raised three children, taken care of a stroke victim—her husband's aunt—and bred collies, she had never worked outside of her home and scarcely knew how to begin. But through the omnipresent David, she learned that Helen was thinking of putting on an afternoon shift of home help for Johnny and she applied for the position.

"I went for an interview that February. I knew from David that Mrs. Gill was a great gardener, and even in the winter you could see that the place was beautiful. There weren't any plants to be seen—except the evergreens. But coming up the front path and just looking out of the windows, you could see that the garden was something special. I said to her, 'I know nothing's blooming right now but I can see that you have a special garden. If you ever think you need some help in the garden, I know a little bit about perennials.' " With this typical understatement, Lou inadvertently found her way straight to Helen's heart. Afterward, when David asked Helen if she was going to hire Lou to take care of Johnny, she replied, "Certainly not! I'm saving *her* for the garden."

While Helen lost no time in making up her own mind, she neglected to mention her decision to the person it concerned the most. Weeks went by and Lou didn't hear a word. She was sure that Helen must have found someone else or changed her mind. Then one day early in April, her future employer called. I can almost hear Helen's funny, flat New England voice saying, "Louise, can you come to work in the garden tomorrow?" At that point, Lou had no car but said she could arrange a ride on the weekend. In the end, she bought an ancient Chevy Impala and went to work in the Gills' still lovely but long-neglected garden.

During the preceding few years, Johnny's failing health had taken its toll on Helen's energies. Finding teenage helpers a lost cause, she had been unable to keep up with the weeding. In the interim, giant, taprooted thistles and other perennial weeds had taken hold among the shrubs at the back of the great curving borders and grass had invaded from the front, penetrating deep into the beds. "I could never get the grass out of the Siberian irises," Lou admitted long afterward. "It was all underneath and kept coming up right through the clumps." Nevertheless, slowly but surely, she began to get the front sections of the borders under control.

If genius is the capacity for taking infinite pains, Lou is most certainly a genius. With characteristic thoroughness and patience, she dug up the overgrown perennials, removed the invasive grasses—strand by strand—

and returned the plants to holes in which she had layered old hay with peat moss and manure. Helen, who liked the appearance of open-ground cultivation, resisted the idea of applying mulch. But Lou gently wore her down. It was the only possible way to revitalize the soil and to maintain her hard-won victories. By her third season with Helen, Lou had done the impossible—she had restored a semblance of order to the badly neglected garden. Although Johnny did not live to enjoy the fruits of her labors, they were Helen's lifeblood for the next three years.

At the same time, Lou was having her own problems. Her husband had put the carriage house they once shared—and in which she was still living—on the market. Her future was now uncertain as well as bleak. It was at this precarious moment that she entered our lives and garden. She needed more work and Helen suggested that we might have something for her. A note for March 24, 1983, in my composition book reads: "Louise came and looked at the garden. For now, our arrangement is that she will come for a few hours one day a week during the spring planting season. After that, we'll see." But long before the buds opened on the trees, Lou had become a valued friend and an indispensable sister of the spade.

That summer, I began to catch glimpses of her own garden because it was en route to the home of her married daughter. The carriage house had been sold and the garden traveled piecemeal in the trunk and on the backseat of Lou's old car. Her plants—temporarily homeless and dug in great haste—spent the remainder of the season and the next winter parked at her daughter's on sheets of plastic with their roots covered in a thin layer of earth and a heavy layer of hay. That they survived and were soon thriving in their new location is only part of the miracle. Many gardens are beautiful and a few are inspiring but Lou's is a triumph of the human spirit.

The first time I went there, she warned me about the driveway. "It's terribly steep," she said, "and there isn't really room to turn around at the top, so you might want to back up the hill." Even so, I was unprepared for a driveway so steep that a visitor might be better advised to park in the street below. The houses on the north side of this street cling to an immense wall of rock that rises directly behind them. Lou's daughter lives near the top, where a scant layer of topsoil partially covers the bedrock and trees venture down the precipitous slope. Lou's garden occupies a shelf at the side of her daughter's house. There is no lawn and nothing in the back, except the perpendicular hillside. In front, a three-story drop gives you a bird's-eye view of houses and yards across the street.

The strip of land supporting the house and garden couldn't be as much as fifty feet wide but Lou had already begun to extend her domain. Where the land fell away most abruptly, she had stacked bales of hay angled back against the grade. These she reinforced with rocks dragged down from the woods above. She used this bulwark as a miniature landfill on top of which she intended eventually to make a perennial bed. Where the incline was less acute, she had started building retaining walls. At the entrance to the garden, a huge, redolent pile of manure lay next to more bales of hay. Dirt paths worn between the areas under development were booby trapped with lengths of hose, tools, and buckets full of rocks and weeds. My first reaction to the chaotic scene was one of horror. How could anyone hope to transform this war-torn hillside into a garden? Especially a middle-aged woman with no help and no material resources.

But Lou was full of good cheer, and as we threaded our way through the obstacle course, she unfolded her master plan. I began to see a long narrow bed of yellow and white bearded iris interspersed with white columbine and *Geranium* 'Johnson's Blue' curving along the perimeter path on the east side of the garden. There was going to be a pink climbing rose and a purple clematis at the foot of an ailing dogwood so that when the tree finally succumbed, its bare branches would form an armature for a bower of roses and clematis. And beneath a healthy dogwood, there would one day be a shade garden full of bold-leaved hostas edged with a filigree of Japanese painted fern and silver-spotted pulmonaria.

Lou's belief in her vision was so compelling that I could picture the narrow paths trimmed with "blush-blue *Veronica repens*—like eyelet on a dress" and imagine the landfill as a perennial bed in a pastel medley of lavender, pink, and white. In June, there would be the bell-shaped flowers of campanula and soft mounds of nepeta, and tufts of spicy-smelling dianthus and shrub roses, which might mingle their flower clusters with the gray-green foliage of the nepeta at their feet. In August would come phlox and asters and a late flush of bloom from the roses that flower intermittently all season.

For the next five years, Lou labored to synchronize the dream and the reality. Meanwhile, Helen—by this time in her nineties—needed help more and more frequently. For nine months, Lou put aside her gardening tools altogether and moved into the Gills' house. The dream was deferred. But despite delays and interruptions, the garden progressed according to plan. The island bed on top of the landfill took shape. A dogwood stump now supported the rose 'Bonica,' and pale lilac-colored clematis 'Will Goodwin' had begun working its way up through the rose canes. Lou went overboard on interesting new perennials, alpine gems for her recently completed retaining walls, and hard-to-find rarities which she added to the expanding garden.

In the spring of 1988, she finished the system of paths, which she surfaced with a mixture of compacted sand and peat moss. But that June, Lou and the garden were dealt a bitter blow. Her daughter, son-in-law, and young grandson wanted an in-ground swimming pool and work was scheduled to begin at once. Although Lou's daughter begged the pool contractor to exercise the greatest care, her pleas fell on deaf ears. A month later, a third of the garden was buried beneath four feet of clay. Lou, for once, was utterly devastated.

For garden and gardeners, the weather was appalling that summer. The spring had been unusually dry and we received only two tenths of an inch of rain during the entire month of June. Drought accompanied by record high temperatures continued into July. By the middle of the month, there had already been more than thirty days when the mercury reached ninety or above.

Then the heat finally broke and we had three inches of rain in the space of a week. What hadn't shriveled up in the drought rotted in the humid aftermath of the monsoon. In our garden, even trouble-free hostas developed fungal disease. Local gardeners were sunk in gloom. But at some point during the worst of the heat and drought, Lou felt her courage returning. And at the end of August, she invited me to come over and see what she had been doing.

I was greeted by a shocking sight. The pool occupied the entire shelf of land on which the house sat. In a savagely executed cut-and-fill operation, part of the wooded hill to the north had been gouged out and used to bolster the raw bank of earth that propped up the pool's long southern side. The bank covered a great section of Lou's garden. It had also engulfed the last healthy dogwood, which now stood four feet deep in clay and rubble. But resigning herself to the tree's demise, Lou already envisioned its skeleton supporting another canopy of climbing roses. She talked enthusiastically about a new path at the foot of the retaining wall she planned to build against the bank—she had made drawings on graph paper. She had ideas for new beds and new plant combinations.

It was incredible. The sheer guts of the woman! In that moment, I learned what it means to really *love* gardening. Lou and Helen Gill had more in common than met the eye. Both were shy, diffident women who poured themselves into their gardens, giving everything and asking little in return, and their reward was a sustaining well of pleasure. No garden burnout for the likes of Lou and Helen. It was appropriate that the mysterious David had brought them together. I can't think of anyone except Lou—kind, discreet, fastidious, noninvasive Lou—who could have lived with Helen during the last year of her life. Independent people who live to be over ninety and are of sound mind have well-formed opinions, and hers were very definite. She also had a temper.

"It was usually very well controlled," Lou said later. "She set very high standards for herself and kept to them. But she wanted what she wanted and that's the way it had to be." Helen used to tell a story about herself as a child of five or six. Her distant, Victorian parents, who had little use for children and frequently left them with the servants, were going to Europe. They asked Helen what she would like them to bring back as a gift. A doll, she told them—one that walked and talked. On their return, they presented her with the doll. It walked but it did not talk. Helen, in a rage, seized the doll by the hair and flung it down the staircase, smashing its bisque head to smithereens.

The last time I saw Lou and Helen together was on a terribly hot day about a month before Helen died. My friend Lillian and I had come for a quick visit. Lou was bent over a spade in the border. Helen, who had recently been released from the hospital, stood at the edge of the garden with one hand resting on the back of a lawn chair. She watched intently as the spade sank into a clump of overgrown Siberian iris. The sun beat down mercilessly on the women's bare heads. As we approached, they both looked up. Lou was dripping with perspiration and Helen's face was scarlet. Lillian, who was very fond of Helen, hurried forward, saying, "Oh, Mrs. Gill, shouldn't you be wearing a hat?"

To which Helen replied with withering scorn, "I don't own a hat." Lou and I exchanged smiles.

Helen has been dead for three years now, but Lou still thinks of her constantly. "A while back, someone gave her a good, strong little wicker basket that she used to carry her tools in. When I left, I asked her nephew if I could take it with me. I keep my tools in it now and I think of her all the time."

Ann

WHEN I LOOK OUT OF THE WINDOW AND SEE ANN HOP-ping around among the emerging bulbs and perennials in the border, it gives me enormous pleasure. The same sight three years ago would have filled me with misgivings. When Ann came to us, she had only recently decided to make gardening her profession. The green business cards advising would-be clients that a "Notable Gardener" was available were hot off the press and we were her first takers. The circuitous route by which she came began with Mary Ley. By this time, the irreplaceable Lou was taking care of Helen and I was having a struggle with the garden. In order to get some pruning done, Mary very kindly lent me the young woman who had been helping her in the rock garden.

Pat had a cute baby-face, a degree in horticulture, and an earnest desire to get out of her chosen field. The work was seasonal, physically taxing, not well enough paid, and she was fed up with it. Nevertheless, she manfully pruned back our huge, overgrown euonymous and helped me for a couple of days before quitting altogether and escaping into a career in graphic design. On her last day here, she mentioned casually that she'd been in touch with a girl who might like to take her place. The girl in question had been working for a landscaper and was thinking of going out on her own. Would I be interested? I said that I would and that's how Ann came to work in our garden.

Pat is quite right about gardening as a profession. It can be gruel-ing—Ann works a twelve-hour day during the height of the season. And she works in all weather. When it rains, she turns up in a bright yellow so'wester and matching pants. In the winter, her layers of clothing begin with long johns, a T-shirt, and a series of sweatshirts topped off with a jacket and a down vest.

In this costume, she looks like a little Michelin figure. When it is hot and she works in a tank top, shorts, and running shoes, you realize that she can't weigh much over a hundred pounds. She may be as thin as lath but singlehandedly she swings an industrial capacity wheelbarrow on and off her little gray truck in one smooth motion.

My father would have loved Ann. She's the living, breathing embodiment of the work ethic. Just watching her move is a joy—she's quick and energetic but also efficient and economical. She never lifts what she can drag, such as bales of peat moss, bags of wood chips, or balled-and-burlapped shrubs; she always carries a bucket when she's weeding, instead of making dozens of little piles that have to be picked up later; she uses a woven polyethylene tarpaulin for things like moving heavy shrubs, and she piles soil on it when she's excavating a planting hole, instead of heaping it on the lawn and then having to rake it up afterward; she collects the tools for a job all at once in her capacious wheelbarrow and rarely has to make a second trip to the barn or the toolshed; and she does everything at a brisk but steady pace. In short, she gets through more work in four hours than many gardeners do in a day and I'm afraid I don't know what I'd do without her now.

When she first came, Ann knew very little about perennials. In fact, she had never really gardened before. Although she started out in horticulture at college, she soon changed her major to soil science and received a degree in agronomy. "When I went to the University of Connecticut," she says with a chuckle, "I didn't know a maple tree from a geranium! But I was twenty-one and into that back-to-nature movement and I'd always been fascinated by farms. I grew up in little towns in Nebraska and Illinois, and out there you can drive from one little town to another little town and there's always space and farms in between. My mother was raised on a farm, and as kids my brother and I used to go and visit my grandmother in South Dakota. We used to chase her chickens, so they wouldn't lay eggs for a week after we left!"

Ann laughs easily and a lot—it's one of her most endearing traits. She's cheerful and fun and funny. But her life hasn't always been a laughing matter. When her family moved east, she was thirteen and on the brink of an angry, rebellious adolescence, which caused her—and her parents—plenty of headaches during her high school years. Nor did she have any idea what to do with herself after graduation. On vocational aptitude tests she had scored high in agriculture but wound up instead typing legal documents in a law office. Still directionless, she discovered soon enough that a sedentary, indoor, nine-to-five job was not what she wanted. At the end of three years, she was ripe for a change—any change. And on impulse, she enrolled in the horticulture program at the University of Connecticut.

"Even after I switched to soil science, I sometimes wondered whether I was doing what I wanted to do," she says. But she completed the course and after college drifted into graduate study. However, she found being an out-of-state student at the University of Maryland expensive and draining. She had to work a forty-hour week in order to pay for her courses and it didn't seem worth it—so back to Connecticut and odd jobs: more secretarial work, a stint in a greenhouse propagating plants, and finally the landscaping job from which she came straight to us.

Although she had done very little actual gardening, her appetite for work and her willingness to learn more than made up for her lack of experience. Over the past three years, I have taught her what I know about perennials and woodland plants. And I have learned from her. Ann showed me how to take a hard line with hoses that have willful, rebellious lives of their own. She came by her expertise in the greenhouse, where she discovered that if you plant your foot firmly on each coil as you reel the hose toward you, it knows you mean business and comes obediently to heel. She also introduced me to new uses for the humble whisk broom. A lick and a promise with the whisk broom greatly improves the appearance of the retaining wall along the perennial border and spruces up the fieldstone path. It's a landscaper's trick, she says: "Go for the edges." Naturally, clean edges define and clarify the design. Ann has a good eye for design.

Quite apart from the invaluable help she gives me in the garden, I enjoy Ann's company and so does Martin. Every Tuesday before going on to her next client, she has lunch with us and we look forward to it. In fact, we sit, like a pair of couch potatoes in front of television, and watch her eat—marveling at the amount of food this wisp of a creature puts away. I'd never thought of meals as a spectator sport but we are fascinated by her capacity. She regularly works her way through two enormous onion rolls stacked with half a pound of ham and cheese; she doesn't blink an eye at polishing off a whole pizza; and she can demolish an entire barbecued chicken—leaving room for dessert. But she never gains an ounce.

Ann attributes her wiry build to genes. "I'm like my grand-mother," she says with justifiable pride. "She lived to be ninety-nine years old and only weighed eighty pounds but she'd homesteaded in South Dakota and raised eight kids. That was some tough woman!" Ann's grandfather was no quitter either. He also lived well into his nineties. Once, after a protracted bout in the hospital, he came home and announced to his astonished family that they weren't getting off that lightly. "If you want to get rid of me," he roared at them, "you'll have to cut my head off and bury it separate from my body!"

Coming from this rugged stock, it's not surprising that Ann has stamina and fortitude. Her work is strenuous, precarious, and in the winter a hand-to-mouth proposition. Although the garden boom has resulted in more people wanting gardens—and someone to look after them—getting and keeping reliable help is next to impossible. The work is there. Ann could easily double the number of her clients, and when she can get good help, she makes enough money to justify the long days and hard work. When she can't, it is a struggle to get through the year. I worry for her—and selfishly, for myself. I wonder how long she can keep at it.

In the meantime, I'm enjoying my good fortune. It has been fun for me to watch her learn and grow as a gardener. I like the way she eyes rotted logs and decaying wood chips as a potential source of organic matter for the garden and I love her appreciation of plants at all stages of their miraculous life cycle. A girl who falls on her knees to examine the tiny leaf rosettes of *Primula modesta* is a girl after my own heart. And when she looks up with shining eyes and says, "They're just like little Barbie Doll cabbages!" she can do no wrong.

Flower-lovers only see the color and shape of blossoms. They regard scapes and branches as structural support. Roots, rhizomes, bulbs, and corms are only of interest as anchorage and sustenance. But plant-lovers grow rhapsodic over a seedling's healthy root system and lyrical at the sight of a stem elbowing its way out of the frozen ground; they are thrilled by the ingenious packaging of buds and leaves and wonder at the curious adaptations that nature has wrought.

Once I discovered Ann in rapt contemplation of a tired-looking daylily stalk that had given rise to a proliferation—a new fan of leaves from a stem node. She gazed at it dreamily and said, "I love this sort of stuff, don't you? When a group of cells gets the message to produce roots and leaves instead of a flower bud or something. That's what is so great about gardening." And that's what is so great about Ann.

Postscript

BEING A VERY OLD LADY WHEN SHE DIED, HELEN GILL had few contemporaries to mourn her. But her friends of many years who were in their seventies and eighties took her death hard. For so long, she had seemed indestructible. There was no service for Helen. She and Johnny had married relatively late in life and were childless, and her few surviving relations were scattered around the United States. There was a brief obituary in our weekly paper but that was all. I had a garden full of her plants; Helen's sister-in-law, Becky Gill, had generously asked me if I wanted anything else; Lou had her little basket and plants from the garden. But on the whole, people felt let down and we all shared a sense of unfinished business.

Then one day I learned about a reading garden that was being constructed at the local library. The two area garden clubs were donating teak benches to be placed in the new garden, and it suddenly struck me that Helen's friends might like to band together and donate another bench in her memory. I tried the idea on a couple of people, who greeted it with great enthusiasm. One old friend of the Gills wrote, "I'm so glad about this. It makes a big difference to me—and my feeling of not having something specific to do. I'll call Marge and Merlin who loved Helen, too, so you'll probably be hearing from them." I did. And from a friend of theirs—a stranger to me—who sent a note with her contribution: "I was so pleased to hear from Marge that you are planning to have a memorial bench for Helen Gill. She was such a wonderful person. Her flowers are all over my garden." Another friend expressed the consensus when she wrote: "What a relief to know something will be done to commemorate Helen's life among us. I'm sure all her friends feel grateful that the deplorable silence has ended."

The bench has been in situ for two years now. The design is

absolutely simple and the construction sturdy. Its four legs are set in cement and it looks good and solid. The little garden is only twelve by eighteen feet, arranged around a maple tree under which are planted hostas from Helen's own garden. In between the hostas, there are daffodils. They were in bloom today. After two winters of exposure, the bench has weathered to a soft shade of gray and the small bronze plaque on the back has mellowed with age. It reads: "Given by Friends and Family of Helen Davis Gill." I know Helen would be pleased. It is sad that she would also be surprised.

Helen's ashes are part of her garden. In a note to his brother, Allen, Johnny Gill once allowed that he and Helen didn't hold with elaborate rituals and had made no funeral arrangements. "We're a couple of grasshoppers," he wrote. "All we want is to be cremated and our ashes scattered in this garden." After Helen's death, her sister-in-law—Allen Gill's widow Becky—and Helen's favorite nephew and his wife carried out this request. They read the 121st Psalm and distributed the ashes over the noble perennial borders flanking the entrance to the orchard.

Six months after Helen's death, Becky and a friend stayed in the Gills' house for a couple of weeks prior to putting it on the market. It was early spring and the garden was a shambles. Between deer damage, neglect, and old age, the shrubs were detracting from the appearance of the property and Becky put in an SOS to the young landscape contractor who used to come in occasionally to do some pruning. He was very fond of Helen and also used to bring her Christmas gifts. And to her great embarrassment, he insisted upon kissing her. Nothing embarrassed Helen more than a kiss! Anyway, Becky got in touch with this kind young man about the shrubs. "It was his busiest time," she told me later. "But he dropped everything and came with two other men for two days of work. At one point, he asked if he could trim a bush at the back of the house. Helen never used to let him touch it. It was the one she used in making her live arrangements for indoors. But I said by all means go ahead. And we both laughed because we knew full well that she was probably watching every move we made!"

I have always believed that a garden dies with its creator. But lately, I have come to a different view. The picture we associate with an individual garden and garden-maker may disappear. But in the best of all possible worlds, another will take its place, to be replaced in due course by yet another. I think about this a lot now when I look out at my own garden. I'm not yet ready to pass it on. But I know that underneath the garden that I see—the one that Martin and I have spun out of our lives here—there is another, an old-fashioned garden full of rose-red peonies and pale blue *Iris pallida*. And beneath that garden lies a farmyard where old lilac bushes and orange daylilies brightened up the foundations of the ice house. Sandfords lived here once and gave their name to the road at the bottom of our driveway. And before them, families whose names were lost when the town records burned in 1857—wives who grew medicinal herbs by the back door and farmers who planted crops and built the stone walls embracing what I think of as my garden.

The garden that Helen and Johnny made is gone. But that is not the end of their garden. This spring, the couple who bought the Gills' property tracked down Lou through their real estate agent. They asked her to come and see them and she went. "They're young," she told me afterward. "And she's sort of a novice gardener. We walked all around the garden and I tried to point out what should be where. It was a jungle, of course. And there's going to be a lot that's just gone—but there *are* things. . . . " I protested that there couldn't be. When I had been there in February, there hadn't been a single sign of life. "It was early yet," said the indomitable Lou. "Now things are starting to pop up. You'll be happy to hear that your little yellow primroses came through. And they weren't even full of weeds—they were just as neat and clean as can be." And, in a tone of gentle but undisguised triumph, "That's because I mulched them!"

If you had asked me twenty-eight years ago what it means to be a gardener, I wouldn't have understood the question, let alone attempted an answer. The allied subjects of plants and garden-making are enormous in scope. What I know—even now—is painfully limited but I do know what it means to be a gardener. It means caring as much as Lou and knowing as much as the Gills and the Fosters. It means working as hard as Ann and being as generous as Mary. It means being careful, optimistic, patient, and observant. It means learning what plants like, want, and need.

Being a gardener means being part scientist and part artist. It means being as strong as an ox and as tough as old boots. It means being impervious to insect bites, rain, sleet, snow, heat, sunburn, and sunstroke. It means reading and learning; lifting and digging. It means knowing what you want to achieve and why. It means being nimble-fingered enough to prick out seedlings and heavy-handed enough to break rocks with a sledgehammer. It means blood, sweat, and tears. And it means ecstasy.

Index

A

Acer palmatum 'Crimson Queen,' 111
Acer palmatum 'Senkaki,' 111
Achillea, in summer gardens, 148
Ajay, Betty, 60–63
Akebia quinata, 57–58
Alliums, in summer gardens, 149
Alpines, 176
  in native habitats, 177–178
American Rock Garden Society
  diversity in members of, 178
  plant sales by, 159
  rewarding affiliation with, 178
  roster of, 177
Amsonia tabernaemontana, 103
Anemonella thalictroides, 4
Ann, 208–211
Antennaria rosea, 114
Arbutus, trailing, 4
Arisaema sikokianum, 160
Ariseama Thunbergii, 190
Artemisia lactiflora, 149
Artemisia 'Powis Castle,' 119
Asters, in perennial border, 39
Autumn gardens, 150
'Autumn Joy,' 148
  in summer garden, 149
Azaleas, 50
  colorful, 128
  in rock garden, 160

B

Baptisia australis, 103, 150
Barren strawberry, 189
Barrett, Isabelle, 120
Barrett, Patty, 118–123
Barrett House, 122
Bearded iris, 38
Ben Franklin's tree, 116
Betula lenta, 168
BGR. *See* Big Game Repellent
Big Game Repellent, 156
Bird's-foot violet, 6
Black-eyed Susans, in summer gardens, 149
Bloodroot, 4
Bluets, 4
Boltonia, in autumn gardens, 150
Boltonia asteroides 'Snow Bank,' 149
Bottle gentian, in Woodland garden, 170
'Boule de Neige,' 50
Bowman's-Root, 183
Boxwoods, English, 118
'Bright Star,' in perennial border, 37
Bugs, 15
Bulbs
  combining perennials with, 143–144
  identification of, 143–144
  losses of, 144
  in spring gardens, 143
Burnett, Frances Hodgson, *The Secret Garden,* ix

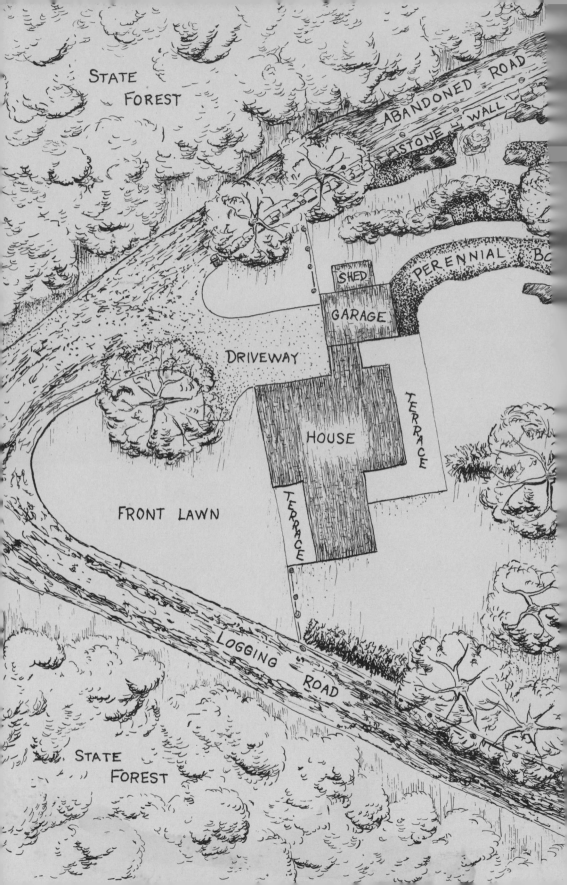